D0991400

Failing working-class girls

Failing working-class girls

Gillian Plummer

Trentham Books

First published in 2000 by Trentham Books Limited
Trentham Books Limited
Westview House
734 London Road
Oakhill
Stoke on Trent
Staffordshire
England ST4 5NP

British Cataloguing in Publication Data
A catalogue record for this book is available from the British Library
ISBN 1 85856 173 6 (hb ISBN 1 85856 174 4)

Designed and typeset by Trentham Print Design Ltd., Chester and printed in Great Britain by Bell & Bain Ltd., Glasgow.

Contents

Introduction • vii

PART 1

Chapter 1
An Historical Perspective – Defining and Reinforcing the Subordination of Working-Class Women through Education • 1

Part 1: Placing class and gender side by side • 1

Part 2: Education: why and how did the education system we fail come to be provided? • 6

Chapter 2
A Sociological Perspective – Educational failure of post-war working-class children • 19

Part 1: Education as an equaliser – a dangerous post-war concept • 21

Part 2: The on-going educational failure of working-class children • 24

Part 3: Access to higher education since the 1960s: differential class chances • 37

Chapter 3
A Psychological Perspective: Making the working classes invisible • 45

Part 1: The impact of class on working-class people's self-esteem • 46

Part 2: Socially-specific accounts which make up psychology's theoretical base • 49

Part 3: Fathers and daughters • 59

Chapter 4
Analytical Frameworks • 65

Chapter 5
Addressing an imbalance • 85

Part II

Chapter 6
Life in a Working-Class Family • 97

Chapter 7
Parental and Peer Support for Education • 135

Part 1: Parental Support •135

Part 2: Straddling Two Worlds • 149

Chapter 8
Schooling a Social Equaliser? Taking a Closer Look • 161

Chapter 9
Conclusion • 193

Notes • 203

Bibliography • 205

Index • 229

Introduction

Although some inequalities in educational attainment have changed quite radically over the last twenty years, those linked to social and economic inequalities persist. Social class continues to be *the* single most important influence on educational achievement in Britain. The majority of students from middle- and upper-class families persistently outperform the majority of students from working-class families.

Despite this situation, the greatest national concern at the present time is the underachievement of boys – class and race differences in performance are virtually ignored. The educational failure of working-class girls is hidden. First by interpreting statistics recording the substantial rise in achievements of middle-class girls to represent 'all girls'. Second by serious concerns about the deviant behaviour and particularly poor performance of many working-class boys. In ignoring the educational failure of working-class girls we ignore the many problems that underlie their failure and which manifest themselves in harmful behaviour patterns: self-exclusion, withdrawal, depression, anorexia, and early pregnancies (Plummer, 1997). Britain has one of the highest teenage pregnancy rates in the developed world. The vast majority of these mothers are working-class girls.

On one level this book attempts to establish 'how' and 'why' the education of working-class girls is and has always been such a low national priority. It looks at historical, social and psychological interpretations of working-class girls and women's relationships to education and achievement. On another level the book looks at the problematic nature of *educational success* for working-class girls. It takes as its subject the childhood of post-war, working-class girls who are now women and looks at the relationship between academic success and self worth. I am one of these women. The book also feeds into a much wider problem:

'How, in a capitalist society, are working-class girls today prepared at home and in school for subordinate positions as future working-class women? (Plummer, 1999)

What have educated working-class women said that could help girls today?

Valerie Walkerdine (1985) talked about education – after the 1944 Education Act – as being 'held out' to the working classes. It was argued that if you worked hard and had the ability you too could have the privileges academic achievement brought, via selective education. Some able working-class girls – proportionately a minority – took up the offer. As women, a small number have written autobiographically (See Steedman, 1986; Reay, 1996; Mahony and Zmroczek, 1997) about an unstated but 'prominent aspect' of the process, 'making the difficult transition to the middle-class' (Walkerdine, 1989, p.13). This transition involved rejecting their working-class lives. I draw on specific examples to illustrate key issues.

When talking about rejecting her working-class life Maureen Duffy says, it was 'nasty, brutish' (1983, p.viii) and offered those things she despised, 'houses, children, security, housework' (p.99), work in a factory or mill (p.ix).

It was a life about which one felt shame and uneasiness and it was to be concealed and kept at a distance. Educational success, it was believed, would enable bright working-class girls to escape this enslavement of domestic/maternal roles and low-paid work and escape the conditions of their parents' lives (Walkerdine and Lucey, 1989). As one woman said, 'I can't be a working-class wife, I watched my mother die of it' (Anon, 1987, p.6).

The fear of not escaping meant for some being 'a slummocking trollop, like Gladys living in one room screwing and scraping in filth and ignorance' for the rest of your life (Duffy, 1983, p.99). It also meant being perceived as 'stupid, shiftless, mindless, unambitious, ignorant, crude, rude, untrustworthy, dirty, violent, cruel' (Trevithick, 1988, p.73), or coarse, rough, simplistic, illiterate, thick, uncouth – all terms applied to working-class people.

Escaping meant being special, one of a select few. For this you had to get into grammar school which was part of what 'winning and being chosen meant' (Walkerdine, 1985, p.74). Failing to get access meant you were stupid. 'If I didn't pass I was stupid ... no different from everyone else ... I had to pass ... I had to' (Duffy, 1983, p.99). In practice this 'Desperate striving for an education and another way a life' (p.ix) meant being *educated out* of your class. Yet no one talked of 'the price exacted for working-class admittance into middle-class status' (Reay, 1998a, p.14).

Academic success brought home/school disharmony and conflict. For instance, the needs and aspirations developed in school distanced many successful working-class girls from their family: 'it increasingly set me apart ... even [from] my mother who had been the major instrument in winning this new life for me' (Duffy, 1983, p.viii). At the same time, family needs 'were a constant' threat. The pressure to conform, 'to leave school and go into the mill or factory, to get a chap was unremitting' (Duffy, 1983, p.ix-x). Irene Payne speaks of another fear, the 'constant terror of being exposed as a '*freak*'' amongst working-class peers. Assimilation in school constituted peer betrayal, she swore more and became louder to prove grammar school had not 'corrupted' her (1980, p.16).

School also raised fears of exposure, of being found out. Walkerdine and Lucey explain,

> There was supposed to be something terribly wrong with the way we were. We were not wealthy, we didn't talk properly, we didn't know anything. (1989, p.8)

Consequently, many working-class girls relinquished or concealed their working-class identity, for holding on to it marked out their unacceptability, their inherent inferiority.

> At school I felt ashamed of my background and attempted to conceal it. My dad was a manual worker and we were pretty poor and I didn't want my classmates to know this. Nor did I want them to know I lived in a 'rough' area, in a house that didn't have a bathroom. (Payne 1980, p.16)

It was assumed educationally successful working-class people would move easily and readily between social classes (Saunders, 1995), that their class 'identity is intended for disposal' (Zandy, 1995, p.1). Yet these girls reached adulthood with unresolved conflicts,

> I was straddling two very different worlds and felt considerably threatened by the fact that I didn't belong to either. I had a constant sense of being different, which I interpreted as inferior. (Payne, 1980, p.16)

> I felt split, fragmented, cut off ... I felt, in the old place, as in the new, that if I opened my mouth it would be to say the wrong thing. Yet, I desired so much ... to produce utterances which, if said in one context, would not lead to rejection in the other. (Walkerdine, 1985, p.64)

> The conjunction of my working-class history and a middle-class education could be seen to produce a fictive self; a multilayered, unresolved, fragmented subjectivity ... I have become more and more the chameleon, constantly evaluating and calculating to what extent, and with whom, I can reveal different aspects of self. (1998a, p.14)

When working-class women are seen to succeed, or to acquire middle-class traits, this level of our experience can be ignored.

The very possibility of success depended upon a physical, social and psychological split which left the women with 'the conviction that they don't fit' (Anon, 1987, p.6), don't belong, and some associated this with feelings of inferiority. Underlying this is a knowingness:

> I read a woman's book, meet such a woman at a party (a woman now, like me) and think quite deliberately as we talk: we are divided: a hundred years ago I'd have been cleaning your shoes. I know this and you don't. (Steedman, 1985, p.2)

There is, therefore, a pressure to be silent. In 'coming out' and speaking about her working-class past Valerie Walkerdine acknowledged that she had for years been frightened to reveal her past in academic circles and 'had engaged in a kind of masquerade' (1991, p.157).

Educated working-class academics in America 'speaking out' in the 1990s have raised similar issues. Several of the authors in *Voices of Academics From the Working Class* (1995) have argued that you can take the person out of the working class but not the working class out of the person. You change your material landscape not the internal landscape, states Peguerous. Ambiguity and discomfort in crossing 'the [class]-border' is a recurring theme. Law too argues, 'one can appear to be native in an adopted land [but] one is always haunted by voices from the other side of the border' (1995, pp.6-7). Tokarczyk and Fay's collection of articles in *Working-class Women in the Academy* (1993) shows how class continues to have a profound effect on educated working-class women, 'Passing is not the same as belonging', Saunders states (p.52). The women have few illusions about being accepted into their new class.

The hidden injuries of class are translated into an understanding of class oppression as these academic women try to come to grips with their position. They are in a double bind. The academy neither recognises nor respects their families and working-class culture no longer recognises 'them'. As educated working-class women 'what is immediately, overwhelmingly apparent' is our privilege (1998a, p.17). Given that proportionately few women from working-class backgrounds become academics, these are very specific experiences.

Taking a closer look: seduction and treachery

For working-class girls and women, the ideal of education as emancipatory, a means of escape from working-class life, is a seductive yet treacherous notion. A letter passed on to me in 1986 illustrates this point. It was written by two women who described themselves as, 'working-class, under-educated women ... women at the bottom of the pile'. They wrote on behalf of a small group of women, who were all in the process of acquiring formal qualifications.

> On leaving school at the age of 15 and 16 we neither had 'O' nor 'A' levels. Now at thirty years old we have gained within the last four years, between us, 8 'O' levels and 2 'A' levels.
>
> Some people have criticised us for taking the traditional 'O' and 'A' levels, but to working-class women who have had the self-confidence knocked out of us by the education system – it means a lot.
>
> That little 'O' level certificate which isn't much to somebody with a degree can instil confidence in you.
>
> If you want to go out in the world and compete on the same basis – you need the paper qualifications. Even though the exam system may be wrong – that's what they want.

There are three points of tension in this extract that I want to highlight.[1] The first is the way in which self-worth and academic performance become merged. Can educational success – defined in terms of examination results and paper qualifications – make working-class women more confident and able to compete 'on the same basis' as others? Or, is it simply the case that qualifications meet a need to be legitimised by the very system that both creates the aspirations – the desire to move up, to compete – and the sense of having the 'self-confidence knocked out of us'? That is, the 'need', 'want', 'desire', for academic success is not only to get on in the world but also to feel OK about one's self. This belief may be a fantasy rather than a reality but it has 'real consequences',

> Working-class women's hopes and desires for academic success ... inevitably include elements of rejection of self; a grasping at a conscious level that has always been known at an unconscious level – that to be what you are is 'not good-enough.' (Reay, 1998a, p.14)

A second tension is the relational link made between an 'exam system [which] may be wrong' and 'that's what they want'. This implies that examinations are perceived as a rite of passage, imposed by those who have the power to do so. It is *they* who are in control, 'they' being 'the gatekeepers of positions of success' (Walkerdine, 1991). Success, therefore, never feels 'owned', 'It feels if I am wearing someone else's clothes' (Anon, 1987, p.6).

The third tension is the existence of social interpretations that tend to demean the worth, values, purpose, of working-class women's aspirations to academic success. For instance, there is an implied arrogance from those who have ascended further rungs on the ladder of education and academic acceptance – projected or real – to whom 'that little 'O' level certificate ... isn't much', merely a 'flimsy paper qualification'. In *Schoolgirl Fictions*, Valerie Walkerdine illustrates this point when writing about doing her Ph.D:

> I had struggled and struggled against exclusion, and now they were telling me that what I had struggled for was worthless. But what is more, they said it from a position of success which I badly wanted and had never achieved. It is relatively easy, therefore, to apparently give up something you take for granted, but for those on the margins, it is excruciating. I remember feeling intense anger that people would give up a Ph.D, say it wasn't 'where they were at', when it had taken me years of battling to prove that I was good enough to do one, years of refusing to give up. How could I drop out of something I'd struggled so long to have? So it is a position which seems possible only if you are inside ... someone who has never been excluded. (1991, p.171)

The feeling of being *excluded* and having to struggle, implicit in the women's letter and explicit in Valerie Walkerdine's text manifested itself as a driving force. 'Exclusion produces a strong desire to be included, to belong', says Marion McMahon (1991), another educated working-class woman. The privileged academic rejecting the accomplishment of '0' levels, 'A' levels, a Ph.D as a significant act, is an affront to the women's internalised system of beliefs.

As an 'educated working-class woman', (Walkerdine, 1991, p.158) I too was trapped into this way of thinking. Like these women, I *needed* those semi-despised and ardently desired academic qualifications; as a means to another end. My self-esteem, like theirs, was bound up with academic achievement. Having got to the position of being asked, 'Why do you want to do a Ph.D.?, the answer lay, as with many other educated working-class women, in the need for validation and inclusion. 'I thought the B.A. and the M.A. and, please God, the Ph.D. would make me fit' (Anon, 1987, p.6).

For groups who cannot claim historical legitimacy to a position, individuals' work, in part, is motivated by the need to claim their 'right ' to be there (Jenkins, 1995, p.637). Yet such an act constitutes a failure to hold on to working-class values and attitudes (Reay, 1998, p.266).

Maintaining one's working-class identity while writing for the research community: a dilemma

While locked into writing a Ph.D. on 'the importance of educational success as self validation for working-class girls', and having an academic audience to consider, I found myself asking, 'How do I maintain my class identity and meet the requirements?' This dilemma is a marker of class difference. Academic texts are always middle-class.

Most research is conceived, and written, in the manner of academics conversing with one another. Academic conventions, it is argued, are 'a form of regulation and exploitation' which excludes others (Batsleer et al., 1985, p.9). Take for example, the imposition of a formal style of writing that renders ideas unavailable to many working-class people. Also, the refusal or reluctance to accept other styles as legitimate formats, particularly those that might address more directly the interest of non-dominant groups (Plummer et al., 1993). These constraints serve a purpose: they ensure existing knowledge and power relationships are legitimated and reproduced (Kramer-Dahl, 1995). If working-class people cannot understand the academic language we cannot challenge existing theories about working-class inferiority. That these constraints exist is demonstrated by questions such as: 'Why are theories of working-class life written in a language that most working-class people have difficulty in accessing?', 'Why are people not encouraged to speak in their own (non-academic) discourses?' (Pummer, 1999).

Formal academic writing as an analytical tool – its style, tone, vocabulary, the withdrawal from personal involvement, the separating of abstraction from concrete detail (Winter, 1994) – has been inappropriate for describing and analysing working-class lives. Not least because it has, of itself, been used to reinforce the myth of class superiority. Writing is not even a conventional working-class form of narration. 'When a working-class person begins to tell their own story in the written form, they are engaging in a middle-class activity, acquired through the education system'. In writing about my own and other working-class girls' experiences in the form of a Ph.D. I was confronted with excluding as an audience – implicity rather than explicitly – the very group I was writing about. 'Ph.D.s. are not generally read in working-class communities' where academic literature is often perceived as 'incomprehensible, irrelevant and alienating, not least because of its mystifying language' (Plummer, 1999). Yet denying access to the people one is writing about is a clear example of class oppression.

The structure of the book

It is only now that I realise that the *divided worlds* which educated working-class girls and women straddle are distinctly reflected in the structure of my research, and the book mirrors this. Part I is written in the formal style of the middle-class academic though it reflects an educated working-class woman's perspective. It critically reviews existing research and establishes 'inferiority' as a learnt position. Part II also reflects the educated working-class woman's perspective but is written in a very informal style, in keeping with its subject, memories of the working-class girl of the past. These two identities: 'middle-class women' and 'working-class girl' are not integrated, externally or internally. They remain separate and contrasting.

I take a multi-disciplinary approach in Part I, drawing on the disciplines of history and sociology – the two main traditions of work focusing on the working classes – and developmental psychology to set the experiences of educated working-class girls in context. These disciplines are analysed in terms of what they can contribute to our understanding of the problematic relationship between education and self-worth, for white, working-class girls – the subjects of this book. Key organising questions are 'who has a voice and who has not?', 'what is said?', 'what is left unsaid?' Wanting to place my research within an established theoretical context, I also analyse existing frameworks and research approaches which set out to explain class and gender differences in education. Would any lend itself to exploring 'structural relations and emotional relations' (Phoenix, 1987, p.61) allowing me an insight into the psychic developments of, in this instance, white, working-class girls? These concerns are important, for they contribute to the history in which I set my own and other educated working-class women's voices (Plummer, 1999).

In reviewing existing research, I discovered that mainstream accounts – whether historical, sociological or psychological – have ignored and erased individual, working-class lives, producing overarching theories which are the 'official versions' of truth. Similarly, in conventional methodologies and formulated theories of class and gender, working-class girls and women are marginalised or absent.

In Part II, I use autobiography and biography to demonstrate the experience of classism from a white working-class female perspective[2] and to make visible 'what it means to be working-class, a woman, and educated'. As a methodology it enables educated working-class women whose lives theory claims to describe and explain to take part in the construction and validation of their version of the theory. Without this, 'any possible dissonance or lack of fit between women's original class and their current social positioning remains invisible' (Reay, 1998a, p.11). Through autobiography, conflictual class relationship between working-class girls and education are identified.

This approach strained and challenged the conventional rules and associated notions of what counts as legitimate research. An approach where 'we' the respondents construct and validate the theory is an affront to the dominant discourses and structures of academic knowledge. Rejecting the expert authority of scientists and academics in interpreting the lives of educated working-class women, therefore, is a risky act. It 'involved challenging voices that were already validated and which had the power to decide both what is valid research and what can count as truth' (Plummer 1999).

The data consists of my own experiences and the experiences of a small number of women I knew as *friends* so the work is by implication anecdotal. The aim was to write analytically of class without abandoning my informal style. These features are downgraded in traditional research terms. The self as 'I' entails the learning of class and gender so conventional distancing mechanisms are abandoned and pronouns used, *I, me, my, our, we*. These indicated that *we* – the respondents – had information and knowledge to which others may not have access and to signal that, 'such knowledge is contextual, situational, and specific' as well as gendered, raced, classed (Stanley, 1993, p.49). Allocating knowledge, that is memory, as my/our knowledge, as I/we understand it, takes into account the often ignored fact that knowledge differs systematically according to social position (p.45). (Harrison and Lyons, 1993; Aldridge, 1993) However, it is in 'excising the 'I' from accounts' of personal experience that one is seen to be doing science (Aldridge, 1993, p.60; Plummer, 1999).

The women in this study aspired to obtain a formal education during the 1950s, 60s and 70s and were educated out of their class. The emerging stories illustrate the experiential existence of class as it is lived every day for working-class girls. I use them to explore a number of specific but closely related themes. How do girls, at home and at school come to recognise themselves as working-class girls? How is it that 'working class' and 'academic success' are contradictory terms? What is the relationship between class identity, educational success and self-worth in the early stages of girl's social repositioning? Is education really a way *out* of an undesired class and a way in to a desired class? What is the relationship between academic success and the 'erosion of workingclassness' for educated working-class girls? (Reay, 1996, p.453) The responses highlight very clearly the mismatch between how working-class life is theorised and how it is experienced.

PART I

Chapter 1

An Historical Perspective – Defining and Reinforcing the Subordination of Working-class Women through Education

This chapter outlines a history which I, and the other women in this study inherited. It is important to establish how this history has been theorised and how it has been experienced. Both aspects strongly affect the development of working-class women's attitudes and sense of self-worth today – as will be apparent in Part II of this book.

Part 1 of the chapter considers the positioning of working-class women within a domestic ideology and the process of learning *one's place* at home, school and work. Part 2 deals with the development of education, particularly for working-class girls, since the 1870 Education Act. Hence the development of working-class girls' education is traced in the context of prevailing ideas of 'femininity' and the class-based provision of education by the state.

Part 1 – Placing class and gender side by side

Traditional and socialist histories of education have marginalised female and working-class histories. Where do I look to find out what kind of education was on offer to the mothers, grandmothers and great- grand-mothers of the women in this study? How do I get a glimpse of *their* perceptions of, for example, the purpose of education and its availability? Where do I find the messages we – daughters, granddaughters and great-granddaughters – inherited from the generations of women in our families about our right to education and the benefits it can bring?[3]

Clive Griggs, 1989, writing about the history of education over the past century, argued that although gender has played a part in working-class women's oppression, it is subordinate to class difference. Carol Dyhouse, 1981, using Hannah Mitchell's story of a working-class life, has argued that girls felt a sense of deprivation in comparison with their brothers. Evidence of such deprivation, usually relating to domestic responsibilities and the devaluing of education for girls, is to be found in many school log books.

Prioritising one form of oppression over another is controversial both in the history of education and in other disciplines (Gomesall, 1988; Horn 1988). Griggs' argument, however, was that although women as a group have faced discrimination in terms of education, careers and legal rights, the education of both working-class boys and girls has been – and still is – limited and inadequate. For instance, most Board Schools, largely attended by working-class children, were mixed, and boys and girls had the same basic lessons. Interestingly, Griggs did note one difference, almost as an afterthought: sewing and cookery were for girls only. This seemingly insignificant difference is at the heart of feminist theorising which places gender before class. Whilst socialist historians emphasised the *collective* lived experience of the working classes and educationalists stressed the *male* class differentiation within state schooling, feminists talked of a *domestic ideology*.

The theoretical positioning of working-class women within a domestic ideology

Domestic ideology was a part of the middle-class family ideology and the regulatory apparatuses of nineteenth century society. Embedded within it were three major assumptions. First, separate spheres between the sexes were 'natural'. Second, women should be located within the home as wives and mothers and defined in relation to men. And third, women were inferior to men. It was, therefore, a form of oppression common to all women 'through the category of their common sex' (Purvis, 1987, pp.253-5). In reality the domestic ideology operated to divide women. The ideals of femininity contained within it were class specific.

> What was considered appropriate, relevant and attainable for middle-class women [who were to be 'perfect wives and mothers'] was inappropriate, irrelevant and unattainable for working-class women [who were to be 'good wives and mothers']. (Purvis, 1987, p.255)

The two ideals of femininity, the middle-class 'perfect wife' and the working-class 'good mother', were to form part of the context within which educational institutions were founded and reformed (p.257).

Working-class girls and women like my great grandmother and the great-grandmothers of the women in this study, were not to be educated to manage servants, to do unpaid philanthropic work, to learn complex rituals of etiquette – the characteristics of the 'perfect wives' described by Purvis. Instead, their education was to take the form of training that would enable them to be *servants* to 'perfect wives' and all men. The harsh conditions of working-class women's lives were used to justify these differences in educational provision (Sharpe, 1976).

However, the ideology of femininity, of family and domesticity, has tended to play down or displace female class division within education, perpetuating the myth of female classlessness (Arnot, 1983, p.71). Whilst it is true that both working-class and middle-class girls were being prepared for their future roles as economically-dependent mothers and domestics (p.71), and to fit into family life with its sexual hierarchy (p.78), girls of different social classes were prepared in different ways, in both *form* and *content*. Different types of school, with differentiated curricula were provided for girls of different social classes (Hunt, 1984). This was to have a huge impact on working-class girls' educational and, consequently, life choices.

A domestic ideology determining the role of 'good wives' related to a concern by establishment males about the inadequate training and socialising of working-class girls, in particular, their incompetence in domestic skills (Engels, 1845). James Booth, for instance, when arguing that working-class daughters should be 'brought up to fit them for their lot in life ... wives and mothers of men in their own station', suggested they should be taught 'to light a fire ... to wash crockery and glass without breaking half of them'; to wear clothes that were 'economical – [not] cheap, showy, tawdry rags' (1885, pp.12-15). Lord Shaftesbury also argued that working-class women should have knowledge of cookery, pronouncing that 'they are ten times less provident and more wasteful than the wealthiest in the land' (Adams, 1982, p.44).

Not only were working-class women thought of as incompetent and wasteful, they were also to be blamed for the poor health of the nation. It was the belief that our great-grandmothers – once trained in domestic skills would

> ... service the capitalist economy by supporting and nurturing a healthy work-force through their care of menfolk within the family and through the rearing of strong children. (Purvis, 1987, p.258)

In this way, social stability and social order would be maintained and social problems associated with working-class families (alcoholism, crime, disease, high infant mortality rates) would be alleviated. A powerful argument of the opponents of waged labour for women was that working-class wives were ignorant of domesticity. All this conflicted strongly with the demands of a capitalist economy that exploited working-class families – adults and children – as a cheap source of labour. For many working-class women the dual demands of home and family responsibilities alongside waged labour, produced 'lives of toil' (Purvis, 1987, p.148).

Learning subordination: at home, at school, in the work place

> Never again will I ever be on my knees with my nose to the ground. (Joyce Storey, 1987)

In her study of life in domestic service between the First and Second World War – the time of my mother's childhood – Pam Taylor identified a thriving dependence relationship between working-class females in desperate need of work and the demand from certain classes for cheap domestic labour (1979, p.121). Her interviews with working-class women who had been in domestic service led her to conclude that, even as late as the 1940s, 'the servant-mistress relationship', was 'between radically unequal individuals', in which 'power and subordination were continually reproduced' (p.133). The cultural and ideological support for such a system, Taylor argued, was 'so strong and taken for granted that it seemed *natural*' (p.121). Yet in practice, rules and rituals ensured the reproduction of the social subordination and reinforced a 'sense of social inferiority' (p.132): the wearing of a uniform, being summoned by a bell, having to wait on Madam's convenience, having to be given permission to sit, being ordered to stand, living in segregated spaces. It is of significance that all these characteristics have been mirrored (and prepared for) in the schooling system.

Taylor observed that working-class parents – meaning mothers – produced very 'good' servants. 'Parents, who had to be strict to manage at all, inculcated qualities in a girl relevant to domestic service' (p.127). Working-class girls had to comply: parents' words were law '... especially ... between mother and daughters' (p.126). They were disciplined to expect very little for themselves, to do more than their share of housework, and be resourceful in taking care of younger children (Powell, 1968; Foley, 1973; Scannell, 1974). The training of working-class girls in the *home* contributed to their skills, willingness and obedience in service and to their acceptance of long hours and small financial reward (p.129).

Taylor boldly argued that, 'there was a sense in which mothers contributed to the exploitation of their daughters' (p.139). For instance, it was mothers who pushed their daughters into domestic service. Flora Thompson's autobiography reinforces this view: 'About time you was earnin' your own livin', me gal ... From that time onward the child was made to feel herself one too many in the overcrowded home' (1973, p.155). Childhood, recalled Thompson, ended early, 'There was no girl over twelve or thirteen living permanently at home' (p.155). The reason was economic: working daughters were a mouth less to feed and a source of additional income (p.129). This early loss of childhood and the harsh consequences of domestic service emerge in other working-class women's stories: 'My childhood was dead: now I was the skivvy' (Foley, 1974, p.160). Interestingly, Thompson related that 'parents did not want the boys to leave home' (1973, p.155).

Taylor noted that it was mothers who attended domestic interviews and in some instances answered the questions, 'duly promising all such qualities relevant to her [daughter's] servantdom'. The girls 'were, in a sense, vassals, being handed over by the family to the employer for a small sum of money, plus lodging' (p.132). The relative absence of working-class women's voices leaves us guessing how they were affected by these oppressive positions.

Pam Taylor asked: 'What did a working-class girl feel when experiencing 'the deference of her mother', the fount of authority so far, to women of another class?' (p.132). What I wanted to know was, 'What does it feel like to be the mother (the giver) and to be the daughter (the given) in a transaction where you are both seen as inferiors and so are potentially exploitable?

Part 2 – Education: why and how did the education system we fail come to be provided?

> The provision of education for working-class children was thought of by and large instrumentally, rather than as likely to contribute to the life possibilities of the children themselves. (Miller, 1992, p.2)

Attitudes to the education of working-class girls

The move towards the provision of education for working-class girls has to be seen in the light of institutionalised attitudes towards the education of working-class people in general. David Giddy, President of the Royal Society, speaking at the House of Commons on July 13th, 1807, argued that:

> Giving education to the labouring classes of the poor ... would ... be prejudicial to their morals and happiness: it would teach them to despise their lot in life.

That is, girls would not learn to be 'good servants' in accordance with their pre-determined rank in society. Furthermore, 'It would render them facetious and refractory ... insolent to their superiors.' The Rev. J. Twist in *The Policy of Educating the Poor* (1822) wrote of the absurdity of the lower classes being on an equal footing with their superiors, 'in respect of their right to mental improvement'. It was, he said, 'a dangerous notion'.

Despite such attitudes, a mass state schooling system did evolve. Raymond Williams (1961) has argued that the revolutionary idea of *education for all*, got its impetus from the rise of an organised working class demanding education, and from the pressure of a changing economy. The growth of capitalism and the importance of having a working class with a minimum of education and literacy is well documented.

Others argued that the state schooling system was set up with the intention of 'controlling' and containing the working classes (Purvis, 1980; Arnot, 1983; Sharp, 1976) in order to ensure the next generation of working-class children would accept 'life at the bottom of the heap' (Davin, 1987, p.143). The large number of working-class people in the rapidly expanding cities of the early nineteenth century was seen as a social and political threat to the ruling class (Simon, 1974). Both the Sunday School movement and the establishment of monitorial schools in the late eighteenth and early nineteenth century can be seen as attempts to control and contain them (Silver, 1965).

Evidence to support this line of argument can be readily found. For example, H. E. Oakley, a Manchester Inspector of Schools, 1879, was reported as saying, 'Schools need to foster immediate obedience and submission to authority rather than the vulgar and pernicious doctrine that one man is as good as another.' Oakley was not alone. Robert Lowe wrote, 'If the lower classes must now be educated ... they must be educated that they may appreciate and defer to a higher cultivation when they meet it' (1867, pp.8-10).

Another purpose of schooling, discussed in Part 1, was seen to be the imposition on working-class children of middle-class values and habits (Silver, 1965; Johnson, 1976; Hall, 1977). The state, 'suspicious of working-class adults' (Sharpe, 1976, p.17) and their morals (Davin, 1987), was to replace the deficient family and 'make up for the absence of morality and discipline in working-class homes' (Steedman, 1985, p.156). They would thus compensate working-class children for belonging to working-class families (Curtis and Blatchford, 1981). Teachers were to be 'moral entrepreneurs, missionaries', saving the working-classes 'from the worst excesses of themselves' (Grace, 1978, p.2).

Traditional historians have had little to say about working-class indigenous educational traditions and practices, possibly due to their lack of respect for and ignorance of them. Schools for their part have generally played a subordinate role in comparison to the educative role played by the home and family, particularly in transmitting the mores of a social class (Roberts, 1984).

Frith, writing about working-class resistance to forms of schooling before 1870, argued that national education was 'a matter of providing a particular form of education to a class which had (however unsystematically) alternative *forms* of learning available' (1977, p.85). It has been suggested that self-educating initiatives within the working classes were seen as dangerous – so state-financed education was imposed.

Unfortunately, information on the history of working-class people's demands for education is hard to find but Richard Johnson noted the significance of the working-class movement's shift from opposing provided forms of education, to agitating for educational provisions through the state. In the process alternative forms were discredited, destroyed (Hall and Jefferson, 1976) or adapted. The agitation for access to education was based 'on the assumption that only through access to existing or improved forms of state-provided schooling could advancement for working-class individuals be facilitated' (Sharpe *et al*, 1989). The state, for its part, used its power to create the structures which led to the identification of education with schooling and the validity of only 'certificated' forms of education.

There appears to be no historical analysis of how compulsory education came to be accepted (Lee, 1989). Clearly there were, and still are, working-class parents who objected. One still relevant reason is the need for children, particularly girls, in the home. Carol Adams records a teacher's story from '*The Referendum', Women Teachers 'Franchise Union Pamphlet* 1891: 'I had to evade sundry missiles thrown at me by irate parents who would rather have had their children running errands and washing up things in the home than wasting their time in school ...' (1982, pp.40-41). This view continues to be offered in working-class schools as an explanation for why parents so often condone girls' absence. An understanding of such forms of resistance suggest a different perspective from which to view the educational system.

The 1870 Education Act: working-class children in school

The Newcastle Commission, inquiring into popular education in 1858, discovered that 'relatively few children went to school' (Sharpe, 1976, p.13). Although the 1870 Education Act made full-time elementary education a possibility for working-class children attendance was not made compulsory until 1880 and not free until 1891 (Purvis, 1981). Free compulsory secondary education was not introduced until 1948.

The opening up of education in the years after 1880 – when my grandparents were children – made working-class children socially visible. In a school context the Chairman of the London School Board, in 1870 reported:

> Tens of thousands of children in our schools are ... grossly ignorant ... the only thing we can do is to look to their cleanliness and give them habits of order. (Adams, 1982)

Many children shocked the teachers, inspectors, visitors, social investigators (p.40). Ignorance and lack of cleanliness were major concerns. Charles Booth in *Life and Labour of the London Poor* (1902) reported on children who were 'ragged, ill-kempt and squalid in appearance ... stunted in growth, with faces old beyond their years ... tokens of penury and bad conditions at home'. Regimes of cleanliness and order, like domestic training, were ways of gaining and maintaining control (Steedman, 1990).

The physical condition of children in relation to the schooling task was also of great concern. For instance, a committee on Physical Deterioration, set up in 1904, reported on the cruelty of subjecting half-starved children to the process of education (NUT 1870-1970). There was also particular concern for part-time *workers* – whose work was approved as part of their class status.

> Many of the girls are half dead with fatigue and drop asleep over their work in the afternoon... it seems almost inhuman to make them ... work. (Headmistress speaking at the Association of Teachers' Domestic Science Conference, 1910)

Despite such expressions of concern many teachers had difficulty in empathising with working-class children who were 'so very unlike themselves ... tired, dirty, old before their time' and whose faces showed 'only an absence of childhood' (Steedman, 1987, p.124). This absence made it difficult to place working-class children, particularly girls, 'on the dividing line between childhood and adulthood' (Steedman, 1990, p.24). *The Quarterly Review*, 1877, reported,

> The habits and ideas of children of the lower classes would, in all probability, prove a considerable shock to the sensibilities of ladies who came into contact with them for the first time. (Adams, 1982, p.87)

Such factors contributed to the debate about whether it was 'genteel' for middle-class women to become elementary school teachers. College-educated women, in particular, avoided teaching in state-financed elementary schools which catered almost exclusively for working-class children. These schools were mostly serviced by working-class pupil teachers trained 'to maintain order rather than to expand minds or possibilities' (Miller, 1992, p.4). Trained elementary teachers, usually from lower middle-class or upper-working class backgrounds, were later to replace them.

What is important for the women in this study is that the reactions and attitudes outlined above relate to generations of people in our families. It was our parents, grandparents and great-grandparents that were being described as 'ragged', 'ill-kept', 'dirty', 'sickly', 'half-starved', 'half dead with fatigue', 'grossly ignorant', 'old beyond their years'. This is evidence of class exploitation. It was they with whom teachers could not identify or empathise and who were thought to be a shock to the sensibilities of *ladies*. This history is our history and it continues to inform us that we are perceived as inferior beings.

The curriculum: our subordination affirmed

The 1870 Act did not attempt to establish the principle of equal education for all social classes or to establish an equal education for boys and girls. Working-class children did not receive an education in common with middle class children, nor did working-class girls receive the same education as working-class boys.

State education bought a renewed emphasis on education for working-class girls, not for employment but for 'motherhood'. 'Grants were ... made for the teaching of cookery and laundry work' (Purvis, 1981, Note

7, p.111). Elementary schools, where the majority of working-class children went, offered girls the 3 Rs and cookery and needlework skills – which could be used both in domestic situations and in various forms of waged labour such as domestic service. There were few opportunities to become proficient in any other area.

Ann Davin's (1987) research on Board School texts used with working-class girls in Board Schools (1870-1902) illustrates how gender and class positions, through family and domestic ideology, were reinforced within the schooling process. Stories within these texts were 'set in a static, hierarchical world, where fulfilment and contentment ... [came] through keeping one's place and doings one's duty' (p.144). For instance, 'listening to one's husband as well as to class superiors; being a 'good tidy wife' ... industrious and content'. Other virtues modelled were: patience, humility, modesty, obedience, unselfishness, punctuality, tidiness (p.145).

The texts, Davin states, informed working-class girls that if they were 'tidy and diligent at home' they would be rewarded with 'good places in service' (p.145). Work in general was recommended endlessly. Girls were told: 'a life of labour is much pleasanter than a life of idleness' (Jarrold, 1871, pp.23-24). However, it was made clear that the 'good woman's work would be in the home – their own or someone else's – and that, 'great mistakes are made by those longing to 'better themselves', such as, 'when a girl who is only fitted for housework thinks that because she has been well educated at school, she ought to be a lady's maid' (Grant, 1871, p.45). Only boys could have aspirations. A working-class girl's ultimate aspiration, according to the texts, was 'either a good place, and the trust and respect of their mistress, or a good husband.' Such attitudes partly explain why many girls, whose abilities and education should have led them on to better jobs, found themselves forced to enter domestic service despite its potential exploitation – a point made by Pam Taylor.

What is important is that although working-class girls may not have believed, remembered or internalised the messages in these texts, this does not detract from the fact that the behaviours being advocated and the situations presented as natural and unchangeable constituted a form of indoctrination which was aimed at conditioning working-class girls to accept oppressive class and gender role positions. As late as 1926 the Haddow Report emphasised women's place in the home and the need for working-class girls to be taught housecraft, because the health, happiness and prosperity of the nation depended on it.

Although subjects like cookery, laundry work and domestic science were intended to help girls become better housewives the outcomes were not always the desired ones. There has been little reported evidence of working-class girls' resistance, though school log books and autobiographies do offer some insight. The school log books of North Lambert elementary school (May 1887), for instance, contained a list of 22 girls sent by the 'cooking instructor' to the head for misconduct, 'talking and idleness'. Grace Foakes in *My Part of the River* recalled taking a housewifery course – sweeping, dusting, making beds, bathing a life-size doll – and how, when the teacher left the room, they would sweep dirt under the mats, throw the pillows about, jump on the bed and drown the doll. Joanne Bourke (1991) in *Working-Class Cultures in Britain 1890-1960*, painted a very different picture of working-class girls' attitudes to domestic education. Significantly her information is not taken from working-class girls and women but official records.

Resistance was related to perceived relevance. Carol Adams cites one woman and her resentment at having to learn to starch white collars when none of the men in her family wore a collar (1982, p.44) and another at school in the 1890s, who repeatedly practised stitches but never learnt to make a garment (p.43). The usefulness of the cookery lessons could also be questioned. Many families had no oven, or gas stove, or utensils to make the dishes and no money to buy the ingredients (p.46). As Johnson pointed out, this

> discrepancy between institutional criteria and everyday 'lived' agendas ... is the most important reason for unequal educational outcomes, especially for the regular relative educational failures of working-class women. (1989, p.107)

While working-class girls received this diet of cookery and sewing, middle-class grammar school girls were learning 'a range of languages, literature, history and artistic accomplishments necessary for their future marital life' – as perfect women (Arnot, 1983, p.78). In the fee-paying secondary schools of the 1890s and 1900s domestic science was only taken by the lower streams who tended also to be pupils in the lower social classes (Hunt, 1984).

Improved opportunities for working-class girls' and women's education often was not supported by middle-class women. Ladies' 'philanthropist initiatives were often diametrically opposed to the emancipation of women in the social classes beneath them' (Summers, 1979, p.24). Clara Collet in *Memorandum on the Education of Working-class Girls*, 1894, was against girls from working-class homes pursuing an 'academic education'. Their education, she argued, was 'deliberately and rightly directed to fitting them for the social life which they will most probably lead'. She warned of the danger in

> promoting the secondary education of girls of the working classes along the same lines as those pursued by the girls of the middle classes, even the exceptionally able, because they would face 'social and domestic tribulation.' (Booth Labour and Life of the People, 1891)

Even the most feminist reformers maintained a conservative attitude towards education for working-class girls and women. Campaigns demanding the right to enter prestigious, male-dominated universities, for instance, were never intended to include working-class women, who were often defined as 'ignorant and incapable of learning the most basic knowledge' (Purvis, 1987a, p.264).

The 1900s mirrors today

The changes that occurred in education reinforced and polarized the differences between middle-class and working-class girls and women (Purvis, 1987): for instance, two distinct educational systems developed, elementary for working-class and secondary for middle-class children (Silver, 1974). The 1902 Education Act officially translated what had become 'middle-class education' into 'secondary education' which 'remained very much a middle-class enclave and even a middle-class status symbol' (Hunt, 1984, p.27). Availability was in accordance with parental purchasing power so working-class children *en masse* were excluded from what was largely the preserve of fee payers. With the free place system only making a tiny dent, working-class children were denied access to higher education.

The belief that schooling should be related to a possible future – though pre-determined – lifestyle (a belief held in the secondary-modern school I entered in the 1960s) was based on the expectation that most children would take up occupations similar to those of their parents and neighbours. These were jobs 'largely in factories or low-prestige service work' and, therefore, it was thought that an academic education would be of little use to them (Griggs, 1989, p.55, p.57).

The system was wrong, wrote the editor of the *TES* in 1915. It was hugely wasteful allowing only a minority of working-class children to pass the selection examination, holding in check any tendency towards meritocracy. It was not just selection that excluded working-class children but also poverty. My mother, for instance, got a scholarship to secondary school in the late 1920s. Her father suffered from TB for five years and died when she was ten. She tells me over and over again sixty years after the event, 'We couldn't afford the uniform'. It is her little *burning coal of hurt* which smoulders and at times flares up ferociously, fuelled by years and years of what I perceived to be bitter resentment that others should have the opportunity she did not. What made it worse was that her brother was able to go to a technical school until he was fourteen.

Working-class families have been more willing to support sons in taking up free secondary school places – to get better jobs – denying the same opportunities to their daughters. The attitude of many parents was that 'girls didn't need educating even if a scholarship had been won' (Bourke, 1991, p.120). This practice coincide with *official* views of the role of working-class girls and women echoed in education reports reinforcing a domestic ideology.

The 1944 Education Act

The 1944 Act, like the 1902 and 1918 Act, came at the end of a war. It was at such times that the physical and mental health of the working-classes and 'the appalling social conditions in which many slum children were being brought up' was noticed (NUT, 1870-1970, p.84).

When World War Two started, the State education system was providing 'unequal opportunities in schools of unequal social standing ... giving courses of unequal length under unequal conditions' (Ronald Gould, President of the NUT, 1943). An overwhelming proportion of working-class children were being educated in elementary schools. Their inferior buildings and resources, lack of graduate teachers and limited curriculum, compared badly with the better resourced secondary grammar and fee-paying schools, attended mostly by children from middle-class backgrounds. The 1944 Education Act was 'a response to a surge of popular feeling that after the war Britain would have to become a caring democracy' (NUT, 1993, p.17). It was anticipated that if secondary schools were free and their entrance based solely upon competitive examination, large numbers of working-class children would be successful and this would bring about far-reaching social changes (Griggs, 1989). Fifty five years on that has yet to happen!

Whilst secondary schooling was to be compulsory and free for all, there was no prospect of a common secondary experience for all children, nor any serious challenge to the 'socially divisive private sector' (Griggs, 1989, p.58). Independent schools at once raised fees emphasising the spirit of social exclusiveness (Barnard, 1963). State secondary schools were to be either selective, offering chances of public examination, or non-selective. In this way the Act cemented the idea of an elite academic education for a few and a *modern* education for the majority – in inadequately staffed and badly equipped modern schools to which the bulk of working-class children would be sent.

Like many other post-war working-class girls, I was a member of the first generation in my family to receive a secondary education. In 1960 I joined my sister at the local secondary-modern school where all children from the working-class community in which I lived went. No-one expected anything different.

As young children we were not aware that the selection tests we took at eleven were weighted against us, or that the test created self-validating divisions.

> Since we have simple tests for discovering children's natures (and there are luckily only two varieties of these) we can perfectly easily tailor the school-

> ing they get to suit these natures. Such a position accords a pretty self-fulfilling and pessimistic function to education, and the fact that this process of division has always produced a high correlation with the division between middle-class and working-class children simply serves to confirm the appropriateness of the division in the first place. (Miller, 1992, p.15)

The secondary-modern schools we were sent to were to cater for children 'only interested in the moment' and for whom 'abstractions mean little ' (MaClure, 1986, p.202). Such arguments were used to justify 75 per cent of the school population leaving school having taken no academic qualifications thereby ensuring working-class inferiority both in the schooling system and in the future labour force.

Like our mothers and grandmothers at elementary school, we working-class girls were to receive an education based on the domestic ideology of the 'good woman' as class-related gender differences continued to be expounded. For instance, in 1948, the year I was born, John Newsom, then a school inspector, wrote about women having needs 'based on their particular physiology and their social and economic position' and that their 'fundamental common experience' was that of home-maker. We learned cookery and needlework and the boys woodwork and metal work. Like our mothers and grandmothers it was expected that we would leave school at the legal minimum age, without qualifications. The only job choices that would be available to us were certain skilled and unskilled jobs characterised by their low status, poor pay and little chance of further educational achievement. No one suggested to us that social or economic deprivation – *not* a lack of intelligence – placed millions of us in this position. Yet the evidence was there in official documents. For instance, *Half Our Future* described the health and social problems of decaying centres of big cities – my own background.

A few working-class children were given a grammar school place. This was seen as the route to salvation for high achieving working-class pupils. Yet *The Early Leaving Report*, 1954, reported that of 'approximately 16,000 children who in 1946 entered grammar schools throughout England from ... [semi-skilled and unskilled families] about 9,000 failed to get three passes at Ordinary level'. Of these about 5,000 left school before the end of their fifth year. Only five percent got two A levels (MaClure, 1986). Clearly, *getting into* grammar school was not enough.

The introduction of comprehensive education in the 1960s, my own somewhat less than glamorous escape route from a secondary-modern school in Coventry, has been described as 'a means of ameliorating the more brutal inequalities in society without really changing the base structure of capitalism' (Wilby, 1977), as well as a way of maintaining the 'smooth functioning of the existing social order' (Simon, 1988, pp.29-39). Certainly my comprehensive school, purpose built in the late 1950s, was, in practice, a grammar school and secondary-modern school strung together. The only significantly different features were the architectural design and the wearing of black gowns by senior male staff. (It was at least a decade later before I came to understand what these symbolise. At the time I just saw them as an oddity; a topic of humour in children's comics.) However, this school, or should I say the qualifications it offered, was the starting point for change in my life.

Thirty years on, I am still the only member of my family to have entered higher education. This is not accidental, nor simply a question of 'ability'; it is a feature of oppression.

What can we learn from others about our past?

History involves interpretation. Some things are revealed and others remain hidden. In this study recorded historical events have not been in question, but their selection, interpretation, and the importance given to them are. Whilst acknowledging the official version of the history of the development of state education for the working classes, I have tried to challenge the *common sense* notion of schooling as, for example, good in itself. It has not civilised the uncivilised masses, nor given working-class children opportunities and benefits previously unavailable to them. Nor have the masses passively accepted the education provided. There *has* been resistance, though resistance is recorded in few mainstream accounts, accounts which are unilateral overarching explanations (Lee, 1987).

The State aimed at incorporating all social groups into its schools. Some would have us believe that this has been achieved. Yet evidence from working-class schools relating to apathy, disruption, truancy, early leaving, exclusions – all disaffiliations from the official agenda – would suggest that assimilation has not been perceived as being in these students' interest. Indeed, it could be argued that state schools have done little more than foster individual ambition and advancement, producing 'social mobility for a few within the existing structure' (Sharpe, 1989, p.5).

Given the limited sources of evidence from which to analyse the position of working-class girls and women in relation to state education and given that such analysis is central to an understanding of the current educational achievements of working-class girls and women, autobiographical accounts of working-class girls and women make an important contribution to historical documentation and present a challenge to existing accounts.

Chapter 2

A Sociological Perspective – Educational failure of post-war working-class children

Introduction

A sociological perspective, writes C. Wright Mills, enables us to make sense of our fate by seeing it within the framework of the history of society (1959, p.6). Accordingly I turned to the discipline of sociology and, in particular, the sociology of education, in my on-going search to make sense of the complex relations between education, self-worth and working-class women. Within this discipline a series of negative labels emerged: culturally-deprived, linguistically-deficient, lower class, etc. These were used to describe working-class people as problematic and pathological and to explain away their persistent educational failure. Whilst the pros and cons of this kind of labelling have stimulated academic debate, proportionately few academics had to deal personally with the social and psychological consequences of being labelled in this way.

When I was at school in the 1950s and 60s I was not consciously aware of *being* working-class – the label and I met at a time when I was, supposedly, being *educated out of my class*. What I was aware of, however, was a whole sequence of events, happenings, feelings that conveyed to me at a very early age that families like mine, and people like me, were somehow *lacking*, socially and mentally. A recent conversation with three women friends, all teachers, helped me to see how this awareness might have come about. Two of the women were discussing how, as children, they were ordered by their parents not to talk to children from the council estate lest they become like '*them*'. Maureen and I laughed.

We were by implication these children. Although we may have a sense of our undesirability in childhood, it is often not until it is made explicit in adulthood – by the *other* – that we recognise the negative impact of such class-based experiences.

An everyday sense of being different and of that difference being interpreted as inferior is painful to deal with in childhood and to recall in adulthood. A holiday postcard from a primary school teacher comes to mind. It arrived out of the blue. I vividly recall standing holding it and being overawed by the picture – a symbol of high culture – and taken aback by the act. 'Why to me?' (Though eleven years old I had never received a postcard, been on holiday, or travelled further than a few miles.) This gesture, though well-intended, raised within me an horrendously painful awareness of all those things I was not, had not done and did not have, personally, socially, materially.

It was at teachers' training college, studying Sociology, that I came across the term *working-class*. Even then I was not fully aware that it was me they were talking about. The affluent car workers and *deviant* working-class boys, as theorised by Lockwood and Goldthorpe, Willis and Hargreaves, were fairly alien themes to me. I could not relate them to the car workers I lived alongside in a major car-producing city, or the working-class boys I knew from secondary-modern school. I did not perceive this to be a problem in my studies. I had already learnt to discard my direct experience of the world as a source of information in the academic world. *They* were the authorities, the experts.

To explore the issues underlying these experiences I focus on education over the past fifty years. This chapter has three parts. Part 1 returns to the all-pervading myth of *education as an equaliser* of social conditions. Part 2 focuses on the educational failure of working-class children and the vast array of evidence and explanations for our failure. The work of Jan Lee, former working-class girl, teacher and teacher educator is important here (1980, 1987, 1989). Part 3 looks at the difficulties *successful* working-class students face in gaining access to and operating within higher education. In pursuing these themes I draw on evidence from various sources but concentrate on social explanations.

Part 1: Education as an equaliser – a dangerous post-war concept

A decade ago the Chief Education Officer of Manchester LEA, a miner's son, was reported as saying,

> If I ask myself what the education system has done for working-class children since the war ... the answer is not a lot. (Guardian, 12/12/89)

Nothing has changed. The British educational system has long been marked by sharp inequalities in educational outcomes for different social groups. Despite this the prevailing ideology is that education equalises conditions and opportunities. This has led some influential people to argue that access to social class groups should be opened up to each generation of 'competitors' rather than be abolished. Underlying this notion is a set of beliefs that working-class children are able to succeed simply on the basis of their ability and that opportunities for upward mobility – created by education in a capitalist society – are available to all working-class people. In this way the class structure was to be challenged. In reality it has cemented.

Equal opportunities, defined in terms of equal *access*, has not led to equal *outcomes* for different social and ethnic groups. In a speech to the Centre for Policy Studies in the early 90s, John Major was to describe equality of outcome as a 60s 'mania' for treating children 'as if they were identical' and thus deprived 'great cohorts ... of the opportunities they deserved'. What are these opportunities? Access to, and attainment in, educational institutions has always been dependent on class origins. Take attendance at 'a respectable boarding school' which is a 'sufficient social credential for later access to an advantageous social position' (Muller *et al.*, 1989, p.26) – which is certainly not accessible to the vast majority of working-class children.

The negative effects of schooling – 'to divide is to exclude'

Historically, equality of opportunity has meant allowing certain *bright* working-class children into grammar schools that recruit a disproportionately high percentage of their intake from non-manual backgrounds. Grammar schools do not offer ladders of opportunity for the majority of working-class children. Current government figures show the existing grammar schools to have an average 3.4 per cent of pupils eligible for free school meals and in some areas less than one per cent. The nation average for all schools is 18 per cent.

The decline in grammar schools in the eighties brought a noticeable increase in assisted places in independent schools. These were places intended for able, inner-city working-class children, yet fewer than ten per cent of children on the scheme had parents in manual jobs (Edwards *et al*, 1989). While the children's chances of success were more likely than if they had been in a comprehensive school, the risk of dropping out at sixteen was greater.[4]

Both grammar schools and assisted places involved 'unfair' competition-for-places. In ignoring inequalities, they failed to take account of the ways in which the education system – state and independent – privileged the already privileged. So moves to increase access did not reduce the existing inequalities for the eighty per cent of working-class children who attended non-selective schools (Reid, 1989).

Comprehensive schools were introduced from the 1960s to replace secondary-modern schools. Few were truly comprehensive. As Peter Newsam remarked about inner London, secondary education was not 'comprehensive' as a system and never had been. A large number of the schools were effectively secondary-moderns.[5]

In a recent review of the history of secondary education, Gary McCulloch argues that the system has a basic responsibility for failing the majority of its working-class pupils:

> it has undermined the potential of the majority, 'partly in the very act of classifying them as failures', and partly by negating a wide range of abilities and interests in favour of a narrow emphasis on form of ability expressed in academic examinations. (1998, p.1)

This has 'particular resonance in the 1990s' (p.2).

Despite the reality of the situation, working-class children are continually told that as long as they have the ability and show sufficient determination and perseverance, academic achievement is possible because they will be judged solely on their merit. No one tells them that prevailing definitions of *merit* are class-biased. A spokesperson for the

Qualifications and Curriculum Authority (QCA) has announced that, 'Pupils from middle-class families traditionally do better in exams'.[6] The linking of 'apparatuses of selection ... to mental measurement' (Walkerdine, 1991, p.183-184) and education to 'certificates' continues to support and legitimate different forms of schooling and ability groupings. These corresponded conveniently to social class groupings. In secondary schools streaming and setting on the results of tests have always ensured that the products of the old secondary-modern/grammar school distinctions remain with us, even in comprehensive schools, to which ninety per cent of students now go. This ensures the reproduction of class relations through education. It is a strong and enduring relationship that has long worked to the disadvantage of working-class children (Douglas, 1968; Hargreaves, 1967; Lacey 1970; Ball, 1981; Lee, 1987, 1989; Abrahams, 1995; McCulloch, 1998)

Although the trend in the late 1970s and the 80s was to move away from fixed ability grouping because it was known to lead to low self-esteem and social alienation, setting has rapidly re-appeared as a consequence of the introduction of the national curriculum and related assessments. Currently it is being promoted by the Labour government to meet, for instance, its end of Key Stage 2 literacy and numeracy targets for the year 2002.

Working-class children tend to be placed in lower streams and sets, so accentuating social class differences in academic performance (Abrahams, 1995; Walkerdine, 1991). Movement has always been minimal. Once allocated, children tend to take on the characteristics expected of them. Forecasts of ability made at the time of streaming and setting are to this extent self-fulfilling (Simon, 1993). Having been fed a negative image – by being assigned to low streams, sets or groups, whether in primary, non-selective or selective secondary schools – working-class children are encouraged to personalise their failure. They see their disadvantage as being due to their 'individual lack of intelligence, ambitions, effort' (Stanworth, 1983, p.15), or their families' inadequacies. No one tells them differently. It is an effective way of ensuring 'the legitimation and institutionalisation of the failure of the working-classes' (Lee, 1989, p.90).

Changes in education in the last decade have legitimated this stance. The government-imposed and centrally-controlled national curriculum, assessment system, and league tables, alongside the establishment of grant-maintained schools and the emphasis on greater parental choice, signalled the return of selective schooling within the secondary age range (Simon, 1988). Forty-seven per cent of the secondary schools opting out of local education authority (LEA) control in the first wave – September 1989 – had selective admissions policies. What followed was a further polarisation between schools in terms of reputation and social class intake. These educational reforms were militating against equality aims (Arnot *et. al*, 1999). It has now become apparent that once pupils' social background is taken into account, examination results in these schools were no better than in LEA schools. Whilst covert selection procedures on social and economic grounds have always existed – through informal pupil/parent interviews, complicated admission procedures, house purchases in desirable catchment areas – they were now being overtly promoted. Knowledgeable and affluent parents have always been able to use the system effectively in the interests of their children. Few choose to send their children to schools in disadvantaged areas. Whatever the initiative introduced, the groups most able to benefit are those from the most advantaged background (Willms and Echols, 1992; Simon, 1988).

Part 2 – The on-going educational failure of working-class children

The cumulative educational failure of working-class children is well documented (Davie *et al*., 1972; Essen and Wedge, 1983; Mortimer and Mortimer, 1987; Lee, 1989, Higginson, 1990; McCulloch, 1998). Even in the 1970s and 80s, inequalities in educational performance among children from different social backgrounds were identified as early as age 7 (*The Rutter Report*, 1972; *The ILEA Junior School Project*, 1986). In the 90s national standard assessment tests (SATs) data for 7-year-olds has also shown a clear relationship at a LEA level (McCallum, 1993) and at school level (NUT/Leeds University, 1993) with social class.

Recent research commissioned by Ealing council involving almost 5,000 and the first to track children's performance back to reception age pupils, found the lowest social groups consistently produced the lowest results in baseline assessment tests. At the end of Key Stage 2 over half the pupils scoring the lowest levels in English were eligible for free school meals. The research noted that children from more affluent backgrounds performed better and went on to the most successful schools, while the most needy pupils – those on free school meals – tended to end up in the worst schools. It concluded that poor social conditions must be tackled before pupil performance would rise.[7] The same researcher also noted that boroughs with the lowest proportions of households headed by unskilled or partly-skilled workers had the best results at Key Stage 2.

The gap appears to widen as children move up through school. Variance in performance between pupils is far wider at age 14. Analysis of national tests at 7, 11 and 14 also shows the difference between the best and worst schools with similar intakes increases from about two and a half years at age 7 to five years or more at 14.[8]

Despite rapid overall increases in GCSE qualifications, the gap between different social groups is widening (Sammons, 1994; Smith and Nobel, 1995). Data at LEA level showed GCSE results to have a stronger correlation with social background variables than SATs at age 7 (McCallum, 1993). According to Smith and Noble:

> Data from urban areas in 1993 shows that, in the poorest districts, comprehensive school pupils achieve on average approximately half the success rate in getting 5+higher grade GCSEs of comprehensive pupils in the most advantaged urban areas. (1995, p.133)

DFFE reports (1992-5) showed that the bottom thirty LEAs in the league table of GCSE performances are in substantially deprived urban areas. *Urban Trends* (1992) which looked at examination results between 1979-80 and 1989-90, noted a widening gap between deprived and better-off areas. More recent research using government data from the Youth Cohort Study (tracking 22,000 teenagers from 1988 onwards) also notes that the learning gap is widening. The authors found that by 1996 eighty per cent of state-school pupils from professional families were gaining at least five good GCSEs. In households with no one employed it was twenty per cent. In unskilled manual families GCSE performance dropped from twenty four per cent in 1996 to twenty per cent in 1998. The report argues that disproportionate help is given to those from advantaged homes.[9] There is a 'twelvefold gap between the top and bottom twenty per cent of GCSE results' and a further lengthening of the 'long tail of underperformance' (McCulloch, 1998, p.151). What is more, the proportion of pupils in deprived LEAs leaving school with no graded GCSEs is often over fifty per cent above the national average (Smith and Nobel, 1995). Given this information it could be argued that schooling 'exacerbates' rather than diminishes class differences in achievement (Lee, 1989).

Post-code analysis confirms that high-performing schools are attracting a growing proportion of socially-advantaged pupils within local markets.[10] The most successful schools appear to be increasing the proportion of pupils gaining at least five A-C GCSE grades at three times the rate of the most disadvantaged pupils.

Though it is public knowledge that girls are currently out-performing boys at GCSE level, no statistics are ever produced on the performance of working-class girls. What we do know from the social make-up of schools is that gender difference does not reduce the class divide for working-class girls. Selective schools have very few working-class girls and the increasing number of girls entering higher education is a result of the growing success of middle-class girls. At the lowest end of attainment gender differences are negligible (Hillman and Pearce, 1998).

There has been a sharp increase in the number of young people staying on beyond the minimum school leaving age but those from poorer areas are *still* much more likely to leave school at the minimum age without qualifications. Consequently the staying-on rate in some authorities is as low as thirty-five per cent; in others it is as high as seventy-eight per cent (Smith and Nobel, 1995). This matters because, for instance, in 1997 the jobless rate for people with no qualifications was double that for people with five A-C grade GCSEs and those who stayed on at school earned on average forty per cent more than those who left at sixteen.[11]

Achievement at 16-plus has a strong relationship with social background and at the stage of entry to higher education the social imbalance is massive. Working-class students have yet to be assimilated into a culture where it is *normal* to stay on at school until 18 years of age.

Why do working-class children underachieve?

Since the 1960s considerable time and money has been spent trying to determine the reasons for the persistent failure of working-class children in the schooling system (Jan Lee, 1987). Explanations have been wide-ranging. Theories of genetic difference (Herrnstein and Murray, 1994), social, linguistic and cultural deprivation have all been used at various times. Social factors relating to aspects of home background such as parent education, occupation and work condition, unemployment, one-parent family status, health and diet, infant mortality, death rates, poverty, poor housing, family size and cultural factors – in particular language and socialisation – have been seen to be causal. They depress educational performance. The failure of Black middle- and working-class children has largely been attributed to the same causes. No straightforward linear pattern of cause and effect has been identified. What is apparent is that the effects of class also shape the patterns of performance of different groups of ethnic minority pupils (Gillborn and Gipps, 1996).

When I was at school, explanations of working-class educational failure relied heavily on concepts of social pathology in working-class families. It was assumed that those characterised as 'deprived' – the working-class and ethnic minority children – did not have what it took to adapt to the school's academic culture and values. The problem lay in our home and 'the cultural influences surrounding' it. This explained why we, the 'culturally deprived', the 'disadvantaged', the 'underprivileged', and more recently 'the underclass' fail to learn in school in spite of tireless efforts to educate us.

Attention was given to early socialisation, in particular mother-child relationships, as it was working-class mothers who were seen to be responsible for the pathology in their children. To remedy the deficiencies in our home background, however, it was believed that what was needed was compensatory education. Implicit in this decision was the belief that education could make a major difference to reducing social inequality.

The role of the school was to give us – the deprived – the means by which we could appropriate the school's academic culture. This led to a heavy emphasis on early linguistic development, which took no account of our own cultural and linguistic codes. Many of us failed. This approach allowed teachers to see things they found strange or difficult to understand – parts of our culture they were unfamiliar with – as being aspects of our deprivation, particularly our linguistic deprivation. The superiority of middle-class language has long been offered as a plausible explanation for why working-class children do so poorly in the education system. A wealth of theories and related research exists which looks, in particular, at the role of language in the acknowledged educational failure of both white and Black working-class children (Coleman *et al*, 1966; Brice Heath, 1983; Mason, 1986; Daniels and Lee, 1989).

During my student teacher days in the early 70s, arguments relating to cultural and linguistic deprivation were strongly debated (Labov, 1972; Bernstein, 1973; Rosen, 1972; *Bullock Report*, 1975) Working-class language was perceived as a deficiency of language. I actively engaged in these debates without really realising that they were referring to my family or me. Academic discourses place the problem *out there* – not *here* in the institution. Later on I read Bernstein's work, and *restricted code* became a label I attached to myself. It seemed to fit with my three out of ten spelling tests and four out of ten school essays. Recently, I was reminded of how emotive this label was for me; a colleague and friend asked me in mid conversation: 'elaborated – what's that other word that went with it?' 'Restricted', I responded automatically, quite taken aback that anyone could forget this word. Into my consciousness floated the not-so-old beliefs in my own linguistic inferiority. At the same time as registering my negative emotions of vulnerability, of exposure, I realised this forgotten word had no significant meaning to her. Why should it? It had never been used to describe her. We were for a moment strongly divided by our class experiences.

In the 1980s, research claiming to have contested the deficiency model continued (i) to identify the home as the reason for failure, and (ii) to argue that 'working-class culture provides a deficient basis for language and cognitive development' (Daniels and Lee, 1989, p.3). Harry Daniels and Jan Lee criticised the work of Gordon Wells (1981, 1987) on this account. Wells found that within a short time of being in school, class differences became apparent in children's literacy development and interpreted this as due largely to a deficiency in working-class homes, not as proof of the negative effect of schooling on working-class children (pp.3-4).

Daniels and Lee also critiqued the work of Tizard and Hughes (1984) who, unlike Wells, gave direct attention to deficiencies in the school as well as the home. The work, they argued, lacked an analysis of the inherent inequality of the 'social context of schooling' and, more specifically, sufficient account of differences in language style and educational approaches (pp.3, 7). Tizard and Hughes acknowledged that differences exist – social incongruities not cognitive deficiencies – and that 'class groups have differential access to the rules of what counts as a valid cultural style' but did not address the fact that schooling or school values need to change, so argued Daniels and Lee, judgements were being made that disadvantaged the working classes (p.4; p.12).

Up until now, the only way working-class children have succeeded within the schooling system has been to acquire the language, procedures, rules, expectations, etc. of the middle classes (Lee, 1989). It is not that these versions of knowledge, discourse, understanding, meaning, are cognitively and intellectually superior to those of the working classes, but simply that this group has the power to legitimate their versions as cognitively and intellectually superior, argues Lee. If we as working-class people accept the class-based judgement passed, particularly on our language, and strive to adapt and adopt the meaning system which school presses upon us, we sever ourselves from our own meaning system and may even develop a contempt for it. If we reject the language the school offers and retain the class-identifying power of our own language we lose the opportunity of escaping working-class oppression (Rosen, 1986). Success can only be achieved at the expense of working-class consciousness, culture, language and identity (Brice heath, 1983; Ashendon *et al.*, 1987; Lee 1989).

In summary, state 'institutionalised' education is an imposition at variance with working-class culture. Its use of selective mechanisms – streaming, setting, its knowledge boundaries, its intolerance of language and experience outside the range of formal education – has ensured that school fails to make any real connections with the lives of many working-class children. Their rejection of school norms and values and self-exclusion, through apathy, indiscipline, vandalism and truancy takes place in the context, and as a result of, their compulsory incorporation into a middle-class orientated system of education that does not work for them. As forms of containment have been eroded ('special schooling', remedial classes, sin-bins) (Tomlinson, 1982; Lee, 1989) and schools have been made more accountable for student failure, we have seen a huge rise in permanent exclusions, particularly in inner city and other poor areas. In the last four years they have tripled. Every year more than 12,000 children are excluded from school. While the majority are white working-class students, Black working-class students are six times more likely to be excluded (Gillborn and Gipps, 1996). The government's target to reduce the number by a third by 2002 is on one level ambitious and on another not ambitious enough.

The role of the teacher in legitimating the failure of working-class children

> We are these kids:
> the thickies,
> the toe rags,
> the wooden tops,
> the grots,
> the dregs,
> the divvies,
> the plodders,
> the doughnuts
> the no hopers,
> the nutcases,
> Who calls us this?

All the women in this study work in education and all but one is, or has been, an experienced teacher. Teaching was one of a narrow range of servicing occupations that educationally successful working-class girls were directed towards – we serviced working-class schools. While there are many hard-working teachers who are dedicated to helping working-class students there are also many colleagues whose negative attitudes militate against them. For it is in teaching that we persistently meet, with the 'D's' syndrome, the notion of 'deprived', 'disturbed', 'disaffected', 'disadvantaged' pupils from 'dysfunctional' and 'demoralised' families. It is here that concerns with compensating working-class children were and are voiced, the belief that teachers have to compensate for their pupils' extreme learning 'deficits', which are attributed to personal and family failing rather than structural inequalities. As one secondary deputy head publicly announced, we are 'trying to work with them and instil middle-class values'[12] Pupils justifiably are defensive when teachers' negative attitudes emerge: 'some teachers make comment about how I'm brought up and what my parents are like, but I don't think they have any right to say this' (a pupil's response on a Keele University Pupil Attitude Survey, 1997).

The mismatch between many teachers' values, attitudes and experience and that of their working-class pupils has been extensively documented (Willis, 1977; Ball, 1981; Lee, 1989) Ronald King's study (1978) included teachers' negative descriptions of children in a primary school with a working-class intake: 'you can't afford to take your eyes off them', 'not too bright', 'below average'. He also highlighted the fact that teachers distanced themselves from the children's behaviour, 'I never behaved like that when I was their age'. In the teachers' terms, the children were not as children should be, they had few 'ordinary' or 'normal' children' in their classes (pp.110-2). King argued that it was teachers' class perspective and position that facilitated the social structuring of the children's identities (Lee, 1980). This is something other researchers have commented on (Ashendon *et al.*, 1987). Both Carolyn Steedman (1985) and Walkerdine and Lucey (1989) have pointed out the difficulties women primary teachers may face in the 'act of identification' when implicitly being asked, as part of their role, to mother working-class children whose real mothers they regard as unable to provide educational models.

Since the 1970s researchers have argued that children from different class backgrounds receive differential treatment from teachers (Keddie, 1971; King 1978; Lee, 1987; Ashendon *et al.*, 1987) and that teachers' knowledge of working-class and deprived background affects, in subtle ways, their expectations and assessments of pupils. So much so that it is 'a matter of 'common sense' to know as a teacher that children of class IV and V parents are going to perform relatively badly compared with children of higher socio-economic groups' (Steedman, 1982, p.5). HMI reports in the 1980s identified low expectations of pupils – predominantly held by teachers, but also by the pupils and parents themselves – as being the *prime* cause of underachievement in socially disadvantaged areas and the dominant explanation of poor performance. In the 1990s the Office For Standards in Education's (Ofsted) report on urban areas also blamed teachers for their acceptance of poor standards from pupils which they explain away as social deprivation. It was argued that schools were not providing any route out of ghetto areas of high unemployment, poor housing, overcrowded conditions, poverty and inadequate health care. Higher teacher expectation was identified as a point for action. Though higher teacher expectations are important they are not a substitute for the major structural changes needed.

Ofsted data shows that schools in deprived areas do worse in inspections that those in wealthy areas. Failing primary schools are overwhelmingly in areas where levels of poverty are high. The poorest third of primaries accounted for as many as seventy per cent of failing schools, whilst the poorest tenth made up nearly forty per cent (*TES*, 31/7/98). Research into 83 failing secondary schools in 1998 found that 59 had to cope with poverty levels over twice the national average. Not one of the failing secondary schools was in a prosperous area.[13]

Teachers in inner-city schools inspected by Ofsted and whose GCSE results were found to be below that of similar schools have protested that poor pupil performance does not inevitably mean poor teaching. This is true and there are many excellent teachers working in difficult schools. However, the implicit message in many media responses is that the real problem is the children and their parents. As one teacher wrote in the *Times Educational Supplement*, they don't 'behave in a socially acceptable way'. The teacher's choice of words: 'our kind of intake', 'a disturbed and disaffected child from a dysfunctional family with negative attitudes to school', 'is difficult to teach', are poignant.[14] What is missing from this and other such negative accounts is any expression of concern about the 'hardness' or 'unfairness' of the children's and their families' lives, or any statement that their poverty and related social problems urgently need addressing.

It has been argued that the majority of teachers uncritically comply with an unfair schooling process (Hartley, 1985; Pollard, 1985; Lee, 1987).

Jan Lee observed during her MA research in an ILEA primary school that

> ... many of the teachers indicated that they had never considered seriously the apparent failure or underachievement of working-class or black children in the education system. (1987, p.108)

She has since argued that teachers in general claim to be apolitical, denying their own social class origins and overtly that of their pupils and, in so doing, 'covertly collude' – albeit unconsciously – in denying the existence of structural inequalities and therefore social class (1989, p.106). This may simply be a reflection of the level of denial that operates in education at a local authority and national level. A great deal of research evidence exists that has shown that though teachers generally profess a classless view of society, in practice, their categorisations of children emanate from a specific class base (Lee, 1989). The outcome is to offer individualistic rather than social explanations, for working-class failure – the fault lies with the academic ability of the child or the parents' attitudes (Ashendon *et al.*, 1987).

Historically, those teaching working-class children have been drawn from the lower middle classes and the upper working classes seeking upward mobility. The vast majority of working-class people do not reach the status of a teacher, which in itself is a marker of the class structure in our society. Upwardly mobile people are more likely to feel the need to conform as closely as possible to what they know of middle-class standards (Miller, 1996). The desire for reward: money, status, life choices, alongside the desire to escape from the negative attributes assigned to lower-class people, assists in the necessary act of consensual assimilation which involves valuing the dominant culture and sacrificing one's own 'parent' culture even when the children you teach share that culture. A 'them' and 'us' culture is particularly important for those of us directed towards work which involves the regulation of working classes, be it teaching, policing, nursing, etc (Walkerdine, 1991).

The 'them' and 'us' culture is revealed in a multitude of contexts. In a school review I undertook in a working-class secondary school in south-west Essex, a number of the teachers said they would not send their children to the school. What are we as teachers covertly saying about the children in a school and ourselves as teachers when we are willing to teach there, but not to have our own children attend? The message is not always covert. I have listened to a number of teachers – some close friends – talk in a highly derogatory and stereotyping way about the working-class children they have chosen to teach. Given that some have taught in working-class areas for twenty years or more, I find myself asking, 'Why do they do it, when clearly they are uncomfortable with the clientele?' Could the deficiency label be being projected on to pupils? After all, my own reasons for teaching in working-class areas were a mixture of missionary zeal and a belief that I would not be able to fit in a middle-class school. For those not fully assimilated, there will always be a sense of culture and class incongruity and uneasiness with the relationship.

Jan Lee has strongly argued that the class dimension of the teaching profession is crucial to an understanding and explanation of the unequal process of schooling:

> It is primarily the teachers' class position in society and vis-a-vis the pupils ... which enables the operation of a divisive schooling system (1989, pp.104-105).

This belief led her to challenge middle-class students' and teachers' – and by implication teacher educators' – unquestioning acceptance that they are where they are on the basis of merit, 'in a just competitive system'.

Schooling: where are we now?

There is national concern about the overall low educational standards in Britain (a result of poor performance by mostly working-class children) and the unprecedented rate of legislative change by the Conservative government from the late 1980s was designed to shift the schooling system towards a more market-based approach: to 'choice', 'standards', 'accountability'. One major effect has been to reinforce and strengthen relative social class (and ethnic) advantages and disadvantages (Ball, 1990; Ball *et al* 1994).

Choice in an already unequal world has meant little for most working-class parents and their children. It has simply promoted the practice of selection and differention. Schools became more rather than less polarised in terms of reputation and social class and ethnic intake. In the 1990s the gulf between the weakest and strongest schools grew, aided by the creation of grant-maintained (GM) schools. These often made little positive difference to working-class children's lives as they were less likely to serve poor neighbourhoods. At the same time working-class parents were rarely connected to networks of information and influence that would enable them to understand the complicated admissions procedures, operate appeals, and present a 'good image' when dealing with schools outside working-class areas. In practice, there was a reduction of the number of pupils from poorer families in grant-maintained schools, a reflection of the increasing trend to segregate school communities by social background. The fact that local authority schools catered for fifty per cent more children on free meals than grant maintained schools, highlights the effectiveness of the exclusion of working-class children from GM schools.[15]

Growing social segregation, through concentrating socially disadvantaged children in an evermore limited number of increasingly unpopular 'sink' schools (Smith and Nobel, 1995) particularly in inner cities reduces the opportunities for working-class children still further. 'Sink schools' and 'working-class pupils' are synonymous whereas a sink school of middle-class pupils is inconceivable.

Equally damaging was the laying down of 'universal' educational standards for a socially and racially divided nation, based on the assumption that society is – or should be – unitary. In ignoring all alternative forms of knowledge and understanding the government was treating different social and racial groups as inferior. The focus was on national identity. 'What counts as valid knowledge' has always been a highly contentious area and part of the schooling process itself has been – via academic institutionalisation of knowledge – to render this contentious area both unproblematic and unquestionable. We now have a national curriculum which counts as knowledge and dictates how knowledge is organised. It has little bearing on any present-day 'common culture' and remains very much at 'odds with the way knowledge is organised, used and passed on in working-class people's lives' (Ashendon, *et al.*, 1987). The curriculum – introduced to raise standards – is enforced by assessment procedures that are supposedly neutral and fair. In reality, another value-laden assessment system is being used to legitimate the continued *failure* of the mass of working-class children (Lee, 1989).

With the current emphasis on individual responsibility – parent, pupil, school – rather than on social factors, differences continue to be 'individualised' out of sight. Yet individual achievement is not the problem, it is group under-achievement that is the issue. Individualism is simply being used to turn attention away from the link between social inequalities and educational performance. Social inequalities have to be addressed. The perennial argument that some children from highly disadvantaged backgrounds are successful will not do. Nor will the recent school effectiveness emphasis on 'value added'. The focus needs to be firmly on the position of start and finish.

Despite past attempts to remove class from the education agenda – the relationship between educational performance and social conditions becoming a proscribed topic in public policy debate in the 1980s – the issues always re-emerge. The National Commission of Education Report acknowledged that the 'most serious 'shortcoming' of education was 'its failure to enable ... a large majority of young people to obtain as much from their education as they are capable of achieving (1993, p.2). In the Her Majesty's Inspector's (HMI), 1993, study of urban areas, terms such as 'deprived' and 'under-privileged' were once again used to explain away both class and racial differences in public examination results. The Labour government's White Paper *Excellence in Schools* (1997) also acknowledged that the principal problem of the education system is its failure to cater adequately for the 'majority of pupils' and that this failure has 'deep and historic roots'. It confirmed the need to 'overcome economic and social disadvantage' (p.3) and recognised 'the spiral of disadvantage, in which alienation from, or failure within, the education system is passed from one generation to the next'. It declares 'zero tolerance [of] underperformance' (p.5). Prominent is its aim to promote diversity, even though it has done nothing to reduce inequalities in admission to school. Given the deep-seated tendency in favour of social differentiation in secondary education 'it is doubtful whether the diversity advocated ... will achieve these aims'. Division, hierarchy and social inequality have been basic continuities in education provision, as the private and state school divide illustrates (McCulloch, 1998, p.6-7). The goal of diversity in the past century has been of central importance in maintaining social differentiation (McCulloch, 1998, p.159). We have one of the most polarised school systems outside the United States. It is a system where school success is intimately related to class background. *The Excellence in Cities* £350 million package to help urban schools is likely to exacerbate this polarisation through the status symbols of specialist and beacon schools and learning centres (Johnson, 1999). Restructuring the system has not made an impact in the past, partly because practice refutes the theory. The class system has always reasserted itself. Labour has introduced an unprecedented array of initiatives ranging from improving social conditions in communities, to school-based learning mentors, to Educational Action Zones, setting and accelerated learning. We must wait to see the outcome.

Part 3 – Access to higher education since the 1960s: differential class chances

> For many millions of people it isn't a question of being first in a thousand generations to go to university; it's simply being the first in a thousand generations to get a few days' training a year (David Chaytor, Labour MP, TES, 26/3/99)

There are still those who believe free secondary schooling for all and improved standards of living have resulted in many working-class families sending their children to grammar schools and on to university (Smith and Nobel, 1995). Yet major longitudinal studies have consistently demonstrated the significant differences in attainment levels, particularly in terms of public examination results and entry into higher education for different class backgrounds (Sammons, 1995).

Over the past forty years gains in the number of higher education places by working-class people have been shamefully low. As early as the Robins Report of 1963, the proportion of children from non-manual home backgrounds obtaining places in higher education was six times as great as for children with manual home backgrounds. Yet the threefold expansion of higher education that followed did nothing to alter this situation. John Farrant (1981) calculated that between 1962 and 1977 – when the women in this study entered higher education – there had been a seven point five per cent increase in middle-class student numbers in higher education, but only a one point eight per cent increase in working-class student numbers.

Despite further unprecedented expansion in student numbers in the late 1980s and early 1990s, this pattern of inequality did not change. Expansions have not brought greater equality of access. In 1992 the non-manual classes (I, II, IIIn) formed seventy one per cent of applicants and received seventy five per cent of university acceptances. Those in the manual classes (III, IV, V) formed twenty one per cent of the applicants and received eighteen per cent of the acceptances. One per cent of class V applied and were allocated one per cent of the places. The UCCA booklet which held this data stated, 'When ... applicants of similar performance are being compared, any apparent bias largely disappears' (1993, p.6). No mention was made of the glaring differences in representation by the various class groups! Sadly the acceptance figures for 1998 were exactly the same as those for 1992.

Ron Dearing's inquiry into higher education in 1998 reported that twenty years of expansion and the doubling of student numbers had made comparatively little impact on the proportion of entrants coming from lower socio-economic backgrounds. The numbers rose by less than five per cent between 1985-1996, despite comprehensive education. Diana Warwick, chief executive of the Committee of Vice Chancellors and Principals (CVCP), pointed out at a recent conference, that currently eighty six per cent of teenagers from low-income groups do not go to university or college, whilst eighty percent from higher-incomes do.[16]

Until very recently, the nearest higher education has come to affirmative action is the development of access courses for mature students. Research suggests, however, that those under-represented – or excluded – groups were not necessarily the ones to benefit from access. For instance, Roseanne Benn and Rob Burton's research suggests that access was taken up mostly by women from social classes I and II (1993, p.17). If we look at the part-time alternative routes which working-class people are thought to pursue, again we find that opportunities tend to be most heavily exploited by those from middle-class backgrounds or seeking middle-class status, (Tight, 1991) as the Open University has reported.

It seems whatever the initiative introduced, the students who benefit most are those from the most advantaged background.

If we separate out working-class women we find that historically their under-representation has been greater than for men because the resources required for working-class children to overcome the obstacles to a university place were rarely expended on behalf of girls. In the late 80s, Reid (1989) calculated that women in social class V, my own social class group, had point eight of one per cent chance of getting accepted at a university and a one point two per cent chance of any form of higher education. Data presented by The Commission of Social Justice, contextualises this:

> Only 1 per cent of women whose fathers are from social class V hold an undergraduate degree or equivalent, compared with 41 per cent of men with fathers from social class 1. (1993, p.14)

In 1998 women in class V got one point six per cent of places (boys two per cent), a rise of point four of one percent over ten years.

For the professional middle-classes, higher education has become a standard expectation and is seen as 'something within the grasp of *all* their children' whilst among the working classes higher education remains 'an exceptional experience' (Scott, 1990, p.28), particularly for thc white working-class. Modood's (1993) survey comparing ethnic minority students found the only ethnic group who were under-represented in the 17-21 year olds in Britain applying to higher education institutions in the early 90s were the white group. That is, the white working-classes. Dearing also identified 'Black men' and 'Muslim women' as under-represented. This information has to be seen in the context of Britain having the lowest rate of entry into higher education in Europe and higher education being a way out of the poverty trap. As Jan Schmitt, Centre for Economic Performance, LSE, pointed out, the 'unemployment rate for workers with no qualifications is almost five times that for workers with a university degree'.[17]

The Dearing Report highlighted the fact that universities have a moral obligation to bring more working-class students into higher education as a way of increasing social equity in Britain and not wasting so much talent. Government plans to monitor numbers, drop-out rates and school background are to determine whether institutions are seriously trying to widen access.[18]

One of the main problems is said to be 'the lack of demand' from disadvantaged groups. Working-class areas often lack any effective grapevine culture or general awareness about the possibilities of higher education for children or adults. Few people have any contact with anyone who has attended higher education, so do not know how the system works and do not see its benefits.[19] Those who do gain entry are often older and are concentrated in particular institutions and subject areas.

Working-class students' experience of higher education

> The working-class student pupil who 'makes it' to university is deemed to have succeeded. (Reay, 1998a, p.13)

The incidents described below must have taken place at least thirty years ago, but they have not been forgotten.

> I come from a part of South Wales which I always regarded as classless ... In my first week at college in the Midlands I went for a tutorial with another girl. The lecturer ... turned to us and said, 'What do your fathers do for a living'? Madeline replied that her father was a research physicist ... I said that my father had died when I was nine years old and that he had worked ... at the local steelworks.
>
> From that moment on I was totally excluded from the conversation. I'd never met anything like that before and found it extremely bewildering and hurtful ... It was the first time in my life that I'd felt I was unacceptable – not me particularly but my background.

A second event is described:

> She suddenly turned on me and said, 'I have been Vice Principal of this college for more than twenty years and I never expected to have as our senior student (I was Vice-President of the Students Union) a working-class Welsh girl like you.' ... The girl in the next room said she'd been kept awake all night by my sobbing ... I still cry at the memory.

She finished her letter by saying:

> I had a distinction in education at college and have taken two diplomas and a B.Ed Degree. I've never gone for any promotion. I can hear them say, 'who's this working-class Welsh girl then'?

This woman's story highlights two key aspects (i) the life-long impact on self-worth of negative labelling and (ii) the false belief that once accepted into a higher education institution, working-class people are automatically on an equal footing with middle-class peers.

There is as yet little research on the difficulties working-class students' experience in higher education. Hilary Metcalf's (1993) literature review, *Non-Traditional Students' Experience of Higher Education* noted that, although aspects relate to class directly (for instance, culture and financial differences) and *indirectly* (for instance, under-representation) there is actually little evidence of their effects. Institutions of higher education – research institutions – have shown little interest in carrying out research, or setting out 'policies or practices directly affecting working-class students' experience in higher education' (Metcalf, 1993, p.17). Jane Haggis's personal experience as a working-class student illustrates this:

> My encounter with university 'knowledge' brought the discovery that working-class people were not 'there' within the academy as participants or subjects but as 'others' and 'ordinary people' to be studied and observed. (1990, p.68)

A similar sentiment is expressed by Diane Reay, 'the working-classes are either out there as objects of study or insider in their 'proper' place as cleaners, porters, and waitresses' (1998a, p.16).

A few small studies in the late 80s and early 90s look at working-class students' experiences. Howieson's (1991) study of mature students at Edinburgh University reported that the university was perceived as accommodating middle and upper-class school-leavers and unwelcoming to working-class students. Edwards (1990) in her study of women students with children reported that white, working-class women found their institution to be 'male' and 'middle-class' dominated. In Ainley's (1992) study working-class students saw their university experience as a cultural apprenticeship, an introduction into middle-class habits and culture the establishment expected. In Weil's (1986) study of working-class mature students, the students repeatedly expressed disappointment over being unable to voice their experience or having it denied. They felt aspects of their experience were made invisible or were redefined in their tutors' terms. Edwards' research drew similar conclusions, pointing out that the values and experiences put forward by academics as 'working-class' did not always match with the experience of working-class students. 'Academia is far more likely to be about the negation of working-class identities than validation and acceptance', observes Diane Reay (1998a, p.12).

These small pieces of research seem to be suggesting that, from a working-class students' perspective, higher education institutions are still geared to middle and upper class students' needs and are relatively unwelcoming to working-class students and the knowledge they bring. Researcher Diane Reay has written of her experience as a working-class girl at university. After battling to get into university she discovers, 'learning for working-class students is simultaneously about learning to be middle-class' (Reay, 1982a, p.12) and struggles with this. She also becomes aware 'that the working-classes have no claim on 'real' knowledge' (1998a, p.17). Beverly Skeggs expresses similar sentiments, 'When I arrived at university I realised I'd got it all wrong. The things at which I excelled were completely undervalued and many of the things that were valued I had not even known about' (1996, p.190).

Working-class girls who become academics continue to express a sense of unease, of feeling an outsider in academic institutions. Ignoring for the moment the 'oxymoronic puzzle' of a working-class academic there is emerging a small amount of autobiographical and biographical literature from people working within the academy. In *Voices of Academics from the Working Classes*, a number of authors speak of cultural clashes which serve to reinforce the impostor syndrome for academics from working-class backgrounds (Dens *et al*, 1997). What resonates throughout the volume *Working-class Women in the Academy* is an ambivalence of the position and a sense of alienation and marginality caused by the women's shift in status (Barney Dews *et al*, 1995).

Diane Reay points to a tendency for educated working class women to be on the 'lowest rung' in the academy and for their acceptance to be provisional. 'We few working-class women who achieve academic status know our status is provisional upon our continuing conformity. We may challenge but only so far' (1998a, p.16). She adds, 'it is acceptable for us to occupy the bottom rung, but impudent to presume more' (p.17).

Again, we see the reproduction of class relations being maintained through education.

The low rates of access to higher education for students and academics and the devaluing and exclusion of working-class experience, knowledge and insight are problematic for individuals and for society. On a personal level there is a denial of a central aspect of self-identity, on an academic level a narrow range of perspectives and on a social level massive human waste.

Conclusion

This chapter relates how although education over the past fifty years has been promoted as the means to social equality, it clearly has not achieved this function. Social class forms the basis for differentiation, segregation and failure in education. The education system continues to favour the already privileged and to fail the underprivileged. We know that nine per cent of students – in independent and grammar schools – dominate entrance to all Britain's traditional universities and therefore its elite professions and institutions. We also know that the bottom thirty LEAs in the league table of GCSE performances are all in substantially deprived urban areas.

'Deprived' working-class children who fail or 'underachieve' *en masse* in the state education system have their disadvantage ignored. Their failure is personalised, which causes huge psychological harm. On a school level it is their individual lack of intelligence, interest, effort that explains their failure; on a national level it is the problem of an individual school. In both cases the onus is on them to 'right the *lack*' (Walkerdine, 1991) in themselves.

The all-pervasive social pathology model – inadequate working-class homes, language and culture – is still with us. It continues to distract attention from the ideological purpose of perceiving working-class values, behaviour, etc. as 'deficient' instead of 'different' (Lee, 1989) and from a serious analysis of the structural conditions which promote differences, exploitation and oppression. Even those who conform and master institutionalised knowledge go on to face inequalities in higher education and the job market.

In the last decade the living standards of the poor have dropped (Oppenheim, 1993; Kumar, 1993). A study by the Treasury (1999) found that a quarter of the population now lives in poverty, three times as many as twenty years ago. Note the forty per cent rise in the number of children receiving free school meals in England during 1991 to 1993 alone and the rise of children born to families on or below the poverty line to four point two million, (thirty per cent) (Smith and Nobel, 1995). A report from the Jospeh Rowntree Foundation (1998)[20] states that a third of households in 1997 had no working adults and more than two and a half million children are growing up in 'work-less households'. This is important given that children's own future economic prospects are essentially determined by the economic status of the adults in their family.

Although poverty is not a cause of underachievement the things that go hand in hand with poverty are: poor mental and physical health, and parental unemployment. On one end of the scale we have death rates in poorer regions being 80,000 a year higher than in richer regions.[21] On the other end, we have issues of insufficient money for clothing, school meals, transport, school trips and activities, books. This affects school attendance and staying on, along with missing school because of illness or over-tiredness, or lack of support at home.

Recent studies on the serious consequences of low income remind us that barriers to learning remain in place (Wilkinson, 1994; Kumar, 1993) as we have seen in the context of access and choice. The educational inequalities – both in terms of opportunity and outcomes – are as wide as ever, with some evidence that the gap is growing (Smith and Nobel, 1995). In an increasingly fragmented and divided education system, reflecting a more fractured and wider social and economic structure, it is hard to see what would make it possible for children from working-class families to achieve equality of outcome. Not least because it is a truism that it is considered 'far too expensive to improve the educational standards of working-class children significantly' (Sir Angus Maude, one of the architects of Thatcherism, reported in the *Observer*, 2/1/83).

Chapter 3

A Psychological Perspective: making the working-classes invisible

> The role that psychology plays in legitimising the oppression of this society is by no means minor. (Brooks, 1973, p.317)

Introduction

The discipline of psychology presents us with universal laws based on very general explanations – thus separating the psychic from the social. This act has prevented social class from being seen as a structure of experience. I have encountered this when counsellors have silenced my attempts to relate negative feelings about myself to my working-class background. The roots of psychic problems, they imply, lie in the family narrative, not in one's class background. Yet counselling is itself a class-based practice, using a set of procedures learnt from generalisations about, for instance, what families should be like (Wright, 1992; Crawford, 1992). Denial of and indifference to the psyches of working-class people is a manifestation of classism.

This chapter divides into three parts. In Part 1, I explore the impact of 'otherness' on working-class people's sense of self-worth, considering a number of concepts: (i) *ordinariness*, an adjective which positions working-class people as members of a subordinate group, the masses; (ii) *the gaze*, the perception of working-class people as the deficient 'other'; (iii) *psychological simplicity* and *sameness* (Steedman, 1986), negative attributes imposed on working-class people. As Valerie Walkerdine asks, and this study tries to illustrate, 'What is the relationship between those fictions and fantasies and the psychic life of the oppressed?' (1995, p.323)

In Part 2 I look at a variety of classed psychological discourses within developmental psychology and psychoanalysis which marginalise or pathologise working-class accounts and centralise and universalise middle-class accounts. The work of Carolyn Steedman (1982; 1986) and Valerie Walkerdine and Helen Lucey (1989) is central. They are educated working-class women who have expressed anger at the class specificity of existing 'normative' theories and the exclusion of working-class lives from mainstream psychology texts.

Walkerdine and Lucey take a deconstructionist approach and analysed and re-interpreted transcripts from the work of Tizard and Hughes on pre-school working-class and middle-class children and their mothers. Steedman, on the other hand, take an historical perspective and used evidence from reports of nineteenth-century investigations of working-class children to question, for instance, the universality of Freud's psychoanalytic theory. These women validate their work by acknowledging and drawing upon their own working-class childhood experiences and in doing so have 'made a significant contribution to the understanding of the working-class female psyche that traditional psychological theories have assumed are included within notions of universality' (Plummer 1999; Segal, 1987).

Because fathers were central figures in the lives of the women in my study, in Part 3 I look briefly at literature on fathers and call into question the theorised father.

Part 1 – The impact of class on working-class people's self-esteem

As children we learn our place within the established hierarchies of the social world. Our place is defined by other people who impose on us definitions and values relating to gender, class, race etc,. It is from others that we learn whether 'we belong to the upper, middle or working-class, whether we are male or female, Black or white and whether such characteristics make us feel good or despise and denigrate ourselves' (Rowe, 1988, p.22). Outlined below are examples of the way some of us have learnt, through lived experiences, that we belong to the working-classes and that this group is both homogeneous and inferior.

(i) Ordinariness – constructed in relation to middle- and upper-class experiences

Ordinary people in literary and in sociology texts are the masses (Carey, 1992; Walkerdine, 1991). John Carey (1992) in *Intellectuals and the Masses: Pride and Prejudice among the Literary Intelligentsia 1880-1930*, talked about writers of the early twentieth century (whose class hardly needs stating) and their contempt for the emergent masses (working-class people), for their coarse minds and spiritual ignobility, suburban housing, cheap newspapers, tinned fruit and, worst of all, their recently-acquired education and social mobility which were eroding civilised standards. It was Carey's argument that these literary elite (Wyndham Lewis; Virginia Woolf; William Yeats) boosted their own self-esteem by viciously stereotyping the lower classes and holding them in contempt.

Working-class people have grown up with these attitudes; they have been part of our daily learning experiences. Valerie Walkerdine, for instance, has talked about her experience of being ordinary and having, through education, entered the world of the middle-classes in the seventies, a world 'peopled by those who designated themselves as special'. She argues for the need to reclaim that 'ordinariness' (1985, p.64), for in it 'lies a childhood like so many, and yet all too easily explained away in a pathologisation of difference' (p.65). Working-class difference signifies pathology, 'it is 'Other' to the middle-class orientation', says Walkerdine (1996, p.36).

(ii) The Critical Gaze – ordinary people seen through class-biased spectacles

Walkerdine tells a story to explain middle-class friends' fascination in gazing at ordinary people (working families). She tells us:

> We passed a row of cafes where ordinary working families were eating fish and chips, off plastic tables, with tomato sauce. 'How can they do it?' How to reply that they had been me, that I liked tomato sauce? (p.65)

The question these friends (people designating themselves as special) desired an answer to, Walkerdine states, was 'what was it like to *be* like that, the fantasized Other' (p.65). The positioning of working-class people as the object of fantasies and of fears is found in a multitude of texts: historical documents, novels, autobiographies. These fantasies and the repulsion and fear they embody, have the effect of pathologising and 'marginalising' the lived experiences of working-class people. What are subtle differences in social practices – often economically determined – become shame-based, as Marion McMahon relates in her MA thesis:

> In the home of my grade six teacher I was helping his wife peel potatoes for dinner ... I got a tea towel and tucked it into the top of my pants, like my mother did ... [she] called to her husband and two friends to come into the kitchen and see what an astonishing thing I had done with the tea towel. (1987, p.12)

McMahon tells us that her audience laughed, hardly able to believe the story, but the proof was standing silently in front of them. This was her first lesson in humiliation – one of many to come – informing her she belonged to the 'wrong class'. Here we see how the 'materiality of Otherness' operates to form 'social exclusion and subjective fragmentation' (Blackman, 1996, p.376).

Stories of the fantasied other have a point of commonality; the story tellers see themselves as 'un'ordinary, that is, superior to those they designate as ordinary, that is inferior; a manifestation of the unequal power relationship between the two. What the stories actually reveal is an insight into the middle- and upper-class psyche, its own fears and fantasies. (Satre writes of *the look* fundamentally objectifying; Freud the *drive to* look for mastery; Lacan *the gaze*, fundamentally oriented towards a lack.) The psyches of those gazed upon are always left unexplored; a consequence of the process of attributing psychological simplicity to working-class people.

(iii) The attribution of psychological simplicity and sameness to working-class people

The attribution of psychological simplicity and sameness to generations of working-class people has been highlighted by Carolyn Steedman in *Landscape For A Good Woman* (1986). Here Steedman condemns the tradition of cultural criticism for making 'solid and concrete the absence of psychological individuality – of subjectivity' (p.10). She offers a number of reasons for this. First, that the shaping of 'emotional and psychological selfhood' is constructed by and through the *testimonies* of people who are 'in a central relationship to the dominant culture' – psychology and psychoanalysis are based on stories of middle-class, white experiences (p.11). Second, that the nostalgic writings of working-class scholarship boys ascribed to working-class people a simple, unproblematic, passive psychology so denying them a personal history and a developing consciousness (Hoggart, 1959; Seabrooks, 1982). Third, that sameness is identified in working-class autobiography – constrained as it is by conventional devices of the genre – giving romanticised accounts of poverty, solidarity, the power of the mother. Absent, for instance, is any discussion of psychology's theories, the development of class-consciousness, or an understanding of class as a learned position (p.13).

Part 2 – Socially-specific accounts which make up psychology's theoretical base

If we acknowledge that psychic development takes place within a social world and that this world is class, gender and race dominated, what insight can the discipline of psychology bring to an understanding of the psychic development of white, working-class girls? How do working-class girls become psychologically prepared for the 'positions set for them' in a world which is hierarchically ordered, politically, socially and economically, (Spelman, 1990, p.94) and their place is at the bottom of the hierarchy?

(i) Developmental psychology and psychoanalysis

In *The Tidy House*, Steedman looked at existing theories of child development from an historical and social perspective and concluded that Western developmental psychology was based on 'the testimony of a limited number of middle- and upper-class children' (1982, p.84). Its roots lie in observations of inhabitants of the royal and aristocratic nurseries of the seventeenth and eighteenth centuries, the diaries of upper-middle-class women of the early nineteenth-century, and in the accounts of middle-class male academics of the late nineteenth century. She also observed that much of it has been based on conversation with, and observation of, little boys. Girls' development was seen in relation to that of boys. This has meant that the experiences of working-class children, particularly girls, are absent from developmental psychology's theories of childhood (p.110).

In *Landscape for a Good Woman*, Steedman illustrates the centrality of middle-class stories and the marginality of working-class stories in the development of psychoanalysis and argues strongly that it matters whether one 'reshapes the past' from an experience of affluence or poverty (p.5). She is critical of psychoanalysis which has constructed itself around socially-specific personal accounts. This specificity is illustrated through her comparison of data from Mayhew's nineteenth-century interviews with working-class girls (in particular, the little watercress girl) with data from psychoanalysis (for example, Freud's middle-class, female client, Dora). These two young girls, separated by age, class, time, geography and the content of their stories are held together, argues Steedman, by 'the dichotomous nature of their two narratives and by the way in which one illuminates the other' (1986, p.127).

Steedman tells us, 'When a thing is presented in Dora's story, it takes on a universe of meaning: a jewel case ... a closed door, a pair of pearl earrings' and 'the story is already there to tell' (pp.137-138). In the little watercress girl's account, 'The things she spoke about (pieces of fur, the bunches of cress, the scrubbed floor) ... are not held together in figurative relationship to each other' (1986, p.138). The story has to be gleaned from her actual childhood, not a client's fantasies. In the narrative terms laid down by Freud in 'Fragment of an Analysis', says Steedman, the little watercress girl's story, 'does not fit', but the marginality of her story maintains the other's centrality (p.138).

The evidential base used in psychoanalysis to explore the experience of all women has been constructed from the experiences of middle-class (European) women (Wright, 1992). It ignores 'troublesome but necessary considerations such as class and ethnicity' (Brewer, 1996, p.40). Relatively few working-class people become psychotherapists, or indeed, psychotherapists' clients (and are not, therefore, part of their research data) and few psychotherapists have any knowledge or interest in the lived experience of being working-class. Yet at the same time, as psychoanalyst Franz Fanon has commented in the context of Black people, people 'have to attend to the woundedness of their psyches' in order to liberate themselves (bell hooks, 1991, p.13). Telling one's story is a way of doing this. Yet as Steedman acknowledges, this is problematic. In telling her working-class story to middle-class friends she found them caught 'in a terrible exclusion' – the existence of poverty and marginality of experience – 'that measures out their own central relationship to the culture' (p.17).

(ii) 'All women': socially-specific accounts of mother/daughter relationships

There is a mass of popular literature on mothering; that is, on universalistic normalising accounts premised on the middle-class experience. Nancy Friday (1977), Kim Chernin (1985) and Collette Dowling (1989), for instance, draw upon theories from psychology (Freud, Lacan, Horney) and upon the experiences of women like themselves, to talk about mother/daughter relationships. Dowling's mothers are college and professional women, Friday's are academics, lawyers, journalists, gynaecologists, therapists and Chernin's are educated women who are her therapy clients. This relatively narrow group of women provides the data from which the authors' generalisations about all women are made. Lived experiences of racism and classism were not considered to be significant issues because they were not part of the white middle-class woman's experience.

The mothers identified are not materially, socially or culturally deprived. They are emotionally deprived. This is an important factor, for this is the basis on which the authors imply that women in general have some sort of shared experiences, the evidence lying in the production of daughters who lack self-esteem. Self-esteem, Dowling argues, is determined by our internalising of 'how we are perceived, what we are told, what feelings and attitudes are conveyed by the primary caretaker', mother (1989, p.179). This belief led her to state, 'Is it possible ... most women are still struggling with fundamental feelings of inferiority?' (p.14).

The implication here is that feelings of inferiority are experienced in relation to a universal norm. Yet as Simone de Beauvoir (1953) has argued, white middle-class women in the United States cannot be said to believe Black people are superior to them. In the same way one could argue that upper- and middle-class girls in Britain couldn't be said to believe working-class people are superior to them. Superiority and inferiority are social identities, which are not simply gender-related but also class- and race-related. Yet there is no recognition of this.

The social specificity of these accounts can be illustrated in other contexts. Take, for instance, the concepts of 'good' children and 'sacrificing mothers'. Dowling writes of parents wanting their children to reflect well on them 'when they look good, we look good' (1989, p.31). This, argues Alice Miller, leads mothers to project 'expectations, fears and plans' (1983, p.49) and produce what Steedman calls (and Miller implies) 'children who have been made good' (1986, p.105). Children are made good, however, 'within specific class and social circumstances' (p.107). Steedman illustrates this specificity by speaking of her own experience of growing up in a working-class family where mother is paying the price for her daughter's existence and expects to be paid back. You come to know, Steedman argues, 'that ... someone else has paid the price for you, and you have to pay it back' (p.105). The payment is as much economic as emotional. This experience of having 'to pay mother back' is class-based and does not sit well with, for instance, Chernin's generalisation that daughters try

> to assure themselves that their mother was happy with the sacrifices she made for [their] ... sake, whilst at the same time they are telling themselves there was no sacrifice. (1985, p.90)

The same message is conveyed in Dowling's story of feeling emotionally responsible for her mother. 'To what extent her burden was real and to what extent it lay in my imagination, a projection of my own loneliness is hard to know' (pp.119-120).

Steedman's, Chernin's and Dowling's accounts of mothers' sacrifices are different but they are related. Steedman is writing about mothers in working-class families letting their 'good' daughters know of their sacrifices and their expectation to be paid back – economically and emotionally, whereas Chernin and Dowling's accounts lead us to believe in that middle-class mothers sacrifice themselves for free and that although daughters recognise their mothers' sacrifice they deny it. At the same time, Chernin tells us, the most common type of mother-daughter relationship brought into her consulting room is one in which the mother is 'envious of the daughter's opportunity, her doing what she had wanted to do' (p.87). These are formally educated mothers. Many had gone on to higher education and had started on careers, but had 'chosen to renounce these as part of the self-sacrifice' (p.88). Chernin writes, 'Naturally, we want the best for our daughters, everything we were ourselves denied, and to this end we sacrifice ourselves unstintingly' but there is a tension between this altruistic statement and the lived reality which brings mothers to her:

> To envy one's child, to want what she has, to feel that her having it has been at one's own expense – what a cruel and terrible irony. (p.87)

One could ask why, if these mothers *naturally* wanted the best for their daughters, did they become envious rather than wishful or sad. And why did they perceive themselves as having sacrificed themselves? Were they motivated by altruism or were there other complex reasons such as fear of being independent, of male disapproval? The class specificity of Chernin's mothers and Chernin's interpretation is revealed in the following statement,

> If economic necessity ... shaped the mother's life, she would have had powerful aid in subduing her discontent and unhappiness with the institution of motherhood. (p.90)

So successful daughters of women who had no choice but to work out of economic necessity do not call up 'the older woman's envy and resentment' by reminding them of their failure (p.91). Walkerdine's description of her working-class mother's envy, and my own experience, provide evidence to the contrary:

> aspects of greed and envy in my desire for something more, something different from the opportunities never open to my mother and for a life that she could never have dared hope for. This produced inside her great envy of me. (Walkerdine, 1991, p.150)

The dominant cultural view is that mothers should be self-sacrificing martyrs (Wright, 1992; Spelman, 1990) and daughters dutiful. Those who are not are pathologised. It is in the stories of educated working-class women like Steedman, Walkerdine and Lucey and the women in this book that we find counter-evidence.

Pam Trevithick, drawing on the experiences of her own working-class background and the workshops she led on 'Unconsciousness Raising

With Working-class Women', highlights this when she describes some of the unresolved feelings working-class women have expressed in the context of mother/daughter relations. For example, we are:

> angry with our mothers ... for allowing themselves to be mistreated and for not protecting us from the oppression that they knew so well. We blame them for not handling our father better, for not defending us at school, for not showing us how to belong ...
>
> bitter that we lost our childhoods too soon when we were asked to 'mother' our mothers or brothers and sisters and we are sad for ourselves and our mothers that we could not have a life without poverty and hardship ... disappointed that she could not be the 'ideal' mother in the 'ideal' home ... (pp.76-77)

Where would such a description fit in the framework of mother/daughter relationships outlined by Dowling, Chernin, Friday etc.? Their texts illustrate how racial and class identity is masked. As white, middle-class women, they have not seen themselves in terms of a class or race but as merely women. They have 'set out and detail the specificity of their lives' (Walkerdine and Lucey, 1989, p.44) as women who unquestioningly accept themselves as the norm, thus failing to acknowledge the lives of most women and, albeit implicitly, collude in the oppression of other groups of women. Women do not all share the same mother or daughter experiences, for class and race strongly influence our experience of what it is to be a mother and a daughter.

Some like de Beauvoir in *The Second Sex* (1953) tried to get around this issue by contrasting the situation of women with that of Blacks, Jews, the working-class. This approach fails to address the fact that we live in a world in which there is racism and classism so women's class and race matters (Spelman, 1990). Consequently it is important to be sceptical about any account that talks about women en masse whilst failing to take into consideration class and race (Joseph, 1991; Braxton, 1989; Frakenberg, 1993) oppression and exploitation.

(iii) An historical perspective on working-class mother/daughter relationships

Recognising the absence of considerations of a working-class context from many texts on child psychology, child analysis or sociological descriptions of childhood, Steedman turned to the responses of working-class girls recorded in the late nineteenth-century parliamentary inquiries into child labour. These lives – mirroring those of the grandparents and great-grandparents of women in this study – can offer 'a deeper understanding of modern working-class girlhood today than can the normative accounts of development that make up classic child psychology' (1982, p.109; 1990).

What Steedman discovers in these accounts is a history of the obligatory and reciprocal economic ties that working-class daughters have with their mothers. These girls grew up with a *sophisticated* notion of the economic basis of family life and this economic understanding gave them a sense of self. A daughter's primary identification with a mother figure – that modern psychological accounts have presented – was 'elaborated' by the recognition of an economic mother/daughter duality which working-class boys did not appear to have.

> In becoming a worker like her mother and in her precise understanding of the terms on which she was sent out to work, in her detailed knowledge of how money was got and laid out, the girl showed an economic identification with her mother. (Steedman, 1986, p.90)

At the same time daughters were aware that economic and social circumstances made them a burden, 'a difficult item of expenditure'. The ambivalence of being wanted and being resented – and the economic understanding that arises from it – a sense of obligation and reciprocation – are not unique to working-class childhood, suggests Steedman, but working-class life-styles may make this knowledge more accessible to working-class girls and make working-class girls more able to articulate this perception (p.90). Steedman and also Walkerdine and Lucey highlight this point as evidence of working-class children having access to information denied their middle-class peers (Brewer, 1996) such as the vital part money played in their parents' and their own lives. Evidence of the continuity of historical experience and the class specificity of this kind of economic duality can be found in Walkerdine and Lucey's work and in the accounts that follow.

Current psychologically simplistic descriptions of working-class girls acting out a family role that is almost theirs – of mother – says Steedman, miss 'the angry sense of debt, of payment due that earlier economic relationships between mothers and daughters in working-class households' had (1982, p.126). Steedman cites Kathleen Woodward's (1983) *Jipping Street,* where the author acknowledges that what she felt for her working-class mother was an 'attachment and identification' that was 'an angry and hateful reckoning of what she owed', an emotion Steedman shared (1982, p.127). This debt relates to the mother who tells you 'how hard it was to have you ... the impossible contradiction of being both desired and a burden' (1986, pp.16-17). Where, asks Steedman, is the literature on mothers which tells you that, 'whilst one exists, one also need not have been, that things might be better if one wasn't there at all'? (1986, p.96).

As a working-class girl I recognised what Carolyn Steedman means when she talks about working-class girls being burdens, being resented, as a consequence of economic and social circumstances. 'Never have children dear ... they ruin your life,' said Steedman's mother; 'If it wasn't for you,' said mine. Could it be that 'it is *ordinary* not to want your children ... normal to find them a nuisance?' asks Steedman (1986, p.17). Such accounts jar with the current idealised notions of mothers' love. Until these things are theorised, modern accounts of mothering will bear little relation to working-class experience, despite claims to encompass it.

(iv) Normality and pathology: child rearing practices as pathologies

"The family' is implicitly given centrality in most theories of normal child development' (Phoenix, 1987, p.52). The family in question is, however – as outlined above – a highly specific social construction, the *idealised* white, middle-class, nuclear family. Father is the economic provider, mother is at home seeing to the needs of the children, providing 'a form of parental care that is difficult for any working-class parent to offer' (bell hooks, 1985, p.140). Accounts based on this image render invisible Black and white working-class groups, whilst making them 'visible in pathological categories like 'father absent' households' (Phoenix, 1987, p.60) and 'latch key' children (Plummer, 1999).

Psychology has always been in the business of defining itself via pathologies and class has entered psychological categories as a way of socially regulating normality and pathology. Since normalisation hinges on the detection of pathologies, the targets for intervention in child rearing have inevitably been poor, working-class and ethnic minority mothers (Walkerdine, 1991; Tizard, 1986). The fact that what constitutes good mothering is different in different social groups tends to be ignored. For instance, few working-class mothers would consider the upper and middle-class practice of sending their children to boarding school as good mothering.

Looking at interpretations of class differences in parental child-rearing values, Walkerdine and Lucey (1989) challenged what counts as evidence of good mothering. Central to their argument is the belief that the notion of good mothering produced and sustained by psychology has tended to validate middle-class practices and pathologise working-class ones, albeit subtly. Claims to *truths* about mothering (Chodorow, 1978) are a form of regulation, they argue. Working-class women are regulated through being measured in relation to idealised motherhood.

The research work of Tizard and Hughes (1984) sought to normalise and revalue working-class child-rearing practices by describing these practices as *different* rather than *deficient.* Walkerdine and Lucey analyse their transcripts of four-year-old girls and their mothers. They show how their experiences as women from working-class backgrounds led them to notice different things, or to interpret the same things in a different way from the authors. For instance, the data on working-class and middle-class home-life indicated that working-class mothers were more likely to regulate and discipline their daughters in an open and overt way. They did this to demonstrate to their children that they were the 'supreme authority' (p.107), to make it clear that domestic work had to be done at and within a specific time and to let their young children know they were to be self-reliant and not interfere with this job (p.78).

They also noted that working-class mothers were mostly involved in low-paid, part-time work. Most had heavy domestic responsibilities, lived on little money, often in bad housing conditions and they experienced the world as a frightening place (p.160). Consequently, they taught their daughters lessons in coping in an unpleasant and 'oppressive and unjust order' (p.138). Material necessity, for instance, led them to 'constantly tell their children that they cannot have what they want, when they want it' (p.115). In Tizard and Hughes' research, these mothers were seen to be abnormal, insensitive and pathological (p.30).

In middle-class homes domestic life was seen to be centred on the children: 'no overt regulation, no power battles, no insensitive sanctions' (p.24) but a sensitive mother fostering the illusion of the child's 'free will'. Pretending that people can operate of their own free will, Walkerdine and Lucey argue, is a feature of a social order which denies power, oppression and exploitation. In practice, power and conflict are *not*, as one is led to believe, dispersed or eliminated through intellectualising, they are simply suppressed (p.103). In the normalised view of psychoanalysis this is 'healthy adjustment' (p.105). Walkerdine and Lucey question this constructed position arguing that the intellectualising of middle-class mothering is a sham.

In their reading of Tizard and Hughes' research, Walkerdine and Lucey also find evidence of a hatred of, or violence towards, mothers. Acts of violence and violent emotions – which all too frequently are theorised as a pathology of the Black or white working-classes – were most commonly displayed in children's attempts to control and regulate mothers (p.119). 'Twice as many middle-class girls expressed direct violence towards their mothers, or actually hit them', than working-class girls (p.122). These emotions 'shatter myths of harmony' (p.119) in middle-class homes. Yet, as Walkerdine and Lucey point out, the 'possibility of authoritarianism; of violence about to erupt, of rows and fights between mother and daughter' were linked only with working-class homes in the Tizard and Hughes text (p.120). In Walkerdine and Lucey's view, working-class girls seemed to have a much clearer idea of where the boundaries of bad behaviour lay; partly because working-class mothers tended to adopt the stance of positional power, warning or threatening them, and making it quite clear when they were angry (pp.130-131). Working-class resolutions of violence, they argue, have to be seen in relation to 'its place (and its opposite place in middle-class denials) in a violent and oppressive order' (p.138). In contrast, most of the middle-class mothers in the research intellectualised *the problem* or turned their own or their daughter's negative emotions into feelings. In this way acts of violence were denied.

There are, Walkerdine and Lucey conclude, no normal mothers. There are just different mothers and daughters struggling in 'families constituted in their difference from, and opposition to, each other' (p.152). These struggles have different psychic effects and 'it is the working-class mothers who had to be watched over above all others' (p.29). This is important to be aware of, particularly for those of us who have been assimilated in varying degrees into the middle-classes in adulthood. We have believed psychology's myths and yearned for the ideal middle-class mother, despite being aware that these myths called into question *everything* our working-class mothers ever tried to do for us.

Part 3 Fathers and daughters

The women I interviewed all talked about their fathers at greater length than their mothers. Little appears to have been written on father/daughter relationships in general and what has provides another set of myths. It is to these myths that I now turn.

Without doubt the relationship with father is enormously important, said Nancy Friday (1977, p.65). This is a viewpoint shared by William Appleton (1981) author of *Fathers and Daughters: A Father's Powerful Influence on a Woman's Life*. The back cover of his book states, father 'is the first man in her life. For much of her childhood she is his little girl and he is her hero.' But what about those of us who were not father's little girl and for whom father is not a hero? Inside I read, 'If there is one universal truth found in the many women I have studied, it is that *no man will love you as your father did when you were a child*' (p.179). This view sits uneasily with the absent father described in so many women's life accounts.

Other idealised generalisations are offered by Appleton: 'From age six to puberty ... he ... begins to be interested in her school work and to teach her' (p.12); traditionally girls have got their assertiveness and career strengths from their fathers (pp.195-196). But what of the millions of fathers who have no career – for example, manual workers, the unemployed; who could not give their daughters undivided attention or become involved with her school work?

And who are the eighty-one women he interviewed? The author tells us, 'I selected them at random, based on their willingness to be interviewed, from classes and seminars I taught, social gatherings I attended and places where I work and consult' (p.ix). Is this a random selection? Who attended his classes? With whom did he socialise? I am suspicious that his selection is class and race specific. Has Appleton provided us with a model of the *idealised* white, middle-class father?

The myth of a universal father can be found in de Beauvoir's psychic patterns of father-daughter relationships. She talks about a particular stage in the development of a little girl's subjectivity, where father's life has *mysterious prestige.* This is denoted by the hours he spent at home, the room where he worked, the objects around him, his pursuits, his hobbies – all sacred in character – and by the fact that he was the responsible head of the family. De Beauvoir is talking about idealised white, middle-class men, yet the social specificity of this goes unacknowledged.

'The father as patriarch, apparently invulnerable, in control', says Ursula Owen, 'is one of our most powerful mythologies' (1983, p.9). Fathers are seen to represent *social power* and that some do is apparent in Owen's book *Fathers: Reflections by Daughters.* Here fathers are journalists, writers, managing directors, doctors, officers and lawyers, men who wear bowler hats in the city, jet off to America or the Middle East and provide the funding for governesses and nannies. Sara Maitland, one of the women writing in the text, says of her father that he handed on to us what he had received from his family, 'education, pride, class privileges and class responsibility, a wealth of belonging as much as of belongings' (p.37).

There is a strong image in Owen's and de Beauvoir's texts of fathers 'moving in another world which obliges them constantly to leave home'. In practice this meant they were 'often absent, especially during a child's early years'. This reality sits uneasily with the notion of fathers as 'the essential protectors' (p.12), unless we take on the Freudian view, 'His absence as well as his presence structures the home; his position is sacred' (Harris, 1984, p.61), a view shared by Juliet Mitchell (1984). The middle-class father in the texts presented as being all fathers, is the father against whom working-class fathers are measured and found wanting. Working-class men do not hold prestigious positions in the work-force, nor fund governesses and nannies in the home. Nor do they have a 'mysterious prestige', class privilege or wealth to hand on to their daughters. Capitalism and the material conditions of class do not allow the patriarchal model to be achieved in working-class life.

Working-class women are conscious of coming from a culture where men are oppressive and in some homes a working-class man's power manifests itself as control, imposed through anger or violence. This gives him his meaning as father. We are also aware of coming from a culture where the men in our families are oppressed. They may be 'giants in some homes' controlling women and children through ownership, says Steedman, but their position in the home is not supported 'by recognition of social status and power outside it' (p.75). They are not, 'gods of patriarchy outside the home, but pathetic and often powerless figures' (Walkerdine and Lucey, 1989, p.94). Working-class men's position is not confirmed by the social world.

Working-class daughters learn class positioning from an early age. For instance, they learn to recognise father's subordinate position in the world outside the home and that 'the world is a hard and dangerous place', particularly for father (Brewer, 1996, p.409). As many know from experience, the harsh realities of his life result in harsh material consequences. Sandy Brewer says her own father 'literally worked himself to death' (1996, p.406). A father who is powerless, vulnerable and suffers daily humiliation in the outside world is 'not the vilified patriarch' (Walkerdine, 1996, p.358).

The conflicting emotions of working-class daughters – of growing up with the oppressor and the oppressed – are revealed in Pam Trevithick's description of the unresolved and painful feelings working-class women carry from childhood. They talked of anger, loathing, fear, bitterness and rage and were at the same time disarmed and sad that father earned too little and placed the burden of making ends meet on mother. Locked into fear, he had become weak, indecisive, anxious and over-dependent on mother, a bully that had been bullied and humiliated 'to the point of numbness' by those with power or authority over him. He had not been strong enough to stand up to their oppression and protect his daughter from 'the anguish of being treated as inferior in a thousand settings'. A man with so little to show for a lifetime of toil and struggle that they wondered 'at the end of the day whether ... [he] really ever had much male privilege' (1988, pp.77-78).

Such accounts disrupt the central story in which the daughter's life confirms her belief in masculine superiority. A father who is a relatively unimportant and powerless man 'cannot present the case for patriarchy embodied in his own person' (Steedman, 1986, p.79).

Conclusion

I have tried to highlight some of the subtle ways in which working-class people come to be positioned as an inferior group. First, through being labelled *ordinary* by a self-appointed superior other; second, through *the gaze*, where daily acts of working-class people are interpreted as pathological and third, through the attribution of psychological simplicity and sameness. Implicit in these positionings are unacknowledged inequalities of power that ensure that the voices of working-class people do not get heard. Hence, the centrality of the idealised middle-class experiences in developmental psychology and the marginality of working-class versions.

An exploration of the theoretical base of current child psychology and psychoanalysis indicates that although a great deal has been written particularly about mother/daughter relationships, there is scant discussion about how class and race impinge both on family life and the construction of gender subjectivity. 'So-called *truths* – universalisms which may appear to be true – are not necessarily true, as has been demonstrated when talking about women (and men) of different classes and ethnic groups. 'Using the white, middle-class woman's experiences to argue, for example, that 'this is how it is for women' denies the lived experiences of other kinds of disadvantage and oppression' (Plummer, 1999; Ussher, 1991; Spelman, 1990). The experiences of one social group, however valid, cannot be said to represent all experiences. That they are accepted as representative may explain why many of us feel we are a bundle of contradictions. We do not fit the white middle-class idealised model used to define who we are. It is understandable, for instance, why 'Black women have not regarded psychoanalysis as central to their self-understanding (Ussher, 1991) and why – through fiction or autobiography – they have engaged with *contradictions*, not universalisms'. Such a stance is useful, too, for white, working-class women in acknowledging and validating their struggles and experiences (Plummer 1999).

In mainstream accounts of fathers, a relatively unexplored area, we find the idealised middle-class father against whom the working-class father is found wanting. Significantly it is the educated daughters of working-class fathers who have begun to challenge such accounts', coming to their father's defence, highlighting both the harshness of his life as an oppressed worker – there is no romanticised notion of the working man here – and his weakness as oppressive ogre or overly dependent man in thc home. An interesting avenue for further exploration would be how this reality fits with the notion that 'traditionally, girls have got their assertiveness and career strengths from their fathers.'

Working-class girls of different racial groups experience in different ways the disjuncture between their parents' power over them as children and their parents' lack of social power. These contradictions have to be reconciled as children learn about their social world in the different contexts they experience (Phoenix, 1987). To be of value developmental accounts must take account of structural factors: participation in the employment market, household structures, the operation of class bias and racism.

Chapter 4
Analytical Frameworks

> Why ... is it the case that everything ever written about class is always targeting one class, (usually written by the other) ...? (Walkerdine, 1996, p.356).

Introduction: establishing the class parameters

What it means to be working-class, educated and female remains a largely untheorised area. Theoretical perspectives and frameworks developed in the post-war years – the life span of the women in this study – progress from grand theories of class analysis dealing with the masses, to empirical research – interested in social mobility, the family, underachievement, through to interactionist approaches – critiquing the education system and curricula from a class perspective, to feminism, which brought the family back into focus and put gender at the centre of its concerns – often at the expense of class analysis – through to post-modernism and post-structuralism – privileging multiple sites of power. These perspectives are analysed in terms of their potential to describe and explain the lived experiences of educated working-class women like myself – in particular how we acquire our class and gender identity within a society which is classist, sexist and racist.

The new left, new right and many feminist intellectuals have argued that social class is out-dated, reductionist, of declining significance as a source of identity (Pahl, 1989; Saunders, 1987), and that it no longer contributes usefully to current social analysis (see Bates and Riseborough, 1993; Phonenix and Tizard, 1996; Walkerdine, 1996). Recent post-structuralist debates 'both within and outside feminism' have also made clear that 'class categories fail to capture the complexities of contemporary social life' (Reay, 1996, p.58). It is 'a grand category of modernity, rather than one which accords with fragmented post-modern subjects' (Walkerdine, 1996, p.355).

Pakulski and Walters refer to the disappearance of class discourses as an indication of the demise of class (1996, p.667). The lack of any collective expression of class interests, they argue, is 'confirming evidence of the current unimportance of social class' (1996, p.675). But as Diane Reay points out, 'discourses of classlessness are in effect class discourses' when they 'operate in class interests.' Discourses of classlessness, like market discourses asserting 'freedom of choice for all', act 'in the interests of the privileged in society' by enabling them to deny or dismiss their social advantage (1998, p.261). Contemporary academic discourses marginalising 'the ways in which social class contributes to social identities' (p.272) do the same. Class – like race and gender – signifies a specific type of power relation (Brah, 1994). It is the articulation of power that enables the more privileged in society to silence disadvantaged and exploited groups.

Sandy Brewer talks of the 'shifting sands of class positioning', noting the dramatic social and technological changes in the last two centuries. She argues that it is now

> problematic to speak of the working-class or of being working-class because such definitions or identities might be based on outdated systems of social classification or on a psychological need to establish a sense of belonging and to be able to locate oneself in relation to an established set of social values even if they are felt to be under threat by personal and societal changes. (1996, pp.402-403)

Traditional theories and methods of assessment of social class have long been subjected to critical scrutiny for the 'crude ways in which it is operationalised' (Phoenix and Tizard, 1996, p.429). Historians and sociologists continue to grapple with the theoretical difficulties and the usefulness of the concept of social class for social analysis. A great deal of confusion and ambiguity remains, both about what class means and its relationship with, for example, income, education, cultural values, beliefs, power; its association with hierarchy, status, structures of material inequality; its potential social force. Furthermore, social class is only one system of social stratification, additional difficulties in 'operationalising it' come from 'considerations of the intersection of 'race', gender and social class' (Phoenix and Tizard, 1996, p.429; Brah, 1996; Gilroy, 1994). It is widely acknowledged that conventional class analysis is unable to deal with the situation of women, of racial groups, or of the age differentiation of labour markets (See Bates and Riseborough, 1993; Collins, 1990; Phillips, 1992).

Within a quantitative research context, class analysis has been narrowly defined in terms of occupational categories, as in the Registrar General's classification, or multivariate, as in Goldthorpe and Marshall's (1992) scheme. Here there is no theory of history, of class exploitation, or of class-based collective action (Holton and Turner, 1994). Certain researchers have argued that class cannot be reduced to a set of statistical attributes (Reay, 1998a) and some have defined the working-class as those who share working-class culture. E.P. Thompson (1963) argued that class position requires a form of political consciousness where class is an embodiment of common traits, experiences and values. Others have taken into account working-class respondents' views: as a working definition: Elizabeth Roberts (1984), for instance, uses manual occupations and limited economic standing.

Whilst the concept of class is 'riddled with definition problems' and complex attempts to theorise it have been inadequate in their application to social analysis, social class remains an important 'axis of social stratification' (Phoenix and Tizard, 1996, p.429). Phoenix and Tizard's study of the identities of young Londoners makes this apparent. Middle-class young people felt insecure lest people from the working classes resented their relatively privileged life styles (p.439).

This book demonstrates how social class still affects people's life chances and it remains central to social analysis precisely because it differentiates 'people's lives and experiences' (p.427) culturally, specifically and differently (Marshall *et al*, 1988; Reay, 1996, 1998a). It remains 'one of the major filters through which individuals make sense of the world' (Reay, 1996, p.58).

The exclusion of women in analytical frameworks defining class

A great deal has been written about class but the 'nature and scope' of that writing is problematic (Walkerdine, 1996, p.355). It is well documented that the bulk of pre- and post-war writing came from the dominant class, gender and racial group. Functionalism, empiricism, conflict theory, cultural analyses were all developed by white, middle-class male academics. This group's taken-for-granted but unacknowledged power position enabled them confidently to present their theories of class – rarely backed up by research and notably abstract – as the authoritative view. These theories could only be questioned through rational debate within the academic community consisting largely of other white, middle-class academic males claiming class, race and gender neutrality (Plummer, 1999).

Feminist researchers exposed the patriarchal and sexist biases of academic knowledge and practices such as the exclusion of women as public knowledge-makers. They revealed how the research questions asked were those that appeared problematic from the social perspective of white, middle-class men; how the language and forms of expression used systematically favoured male ways and how the primacy of analysis and conceptual development – naming and valuing – reflected male psychology. Most importantly, they showed that the ways that mainstream social science research had been applied made it difficult to describe and understand the realities of women's lives or their experiences.

Moves to alleviate inequality were initially concerned with the removal of gender bias. At a research level, this often meant adding the work of white, middle-class female academics to existing research as opposed to challenging fundamental theoretical assumptions and ways of carrying out research (Plummer, 1999). As a consequence, feminist theory was criticised for being too firmly based on male models which embodied 'the values and power divisions of sexist society' (Stanley and Wise, 1983, p.96). Millett (1969), Firestone (1970), Mitchell (1975), for instance, in their effort to tackle the issue of female powerlessness within the constraints of historical and structural analysis all adopted grand theories (Warren, 1988) which encompass an unacknowledged class and race specificity. Significantly, it is these theories that have travelled through time. Marshall outlines their characteristics:

> highly developed conceptually – not very revealing about their perceptual bases, highly referenced to support their often linear arguments and so on ... not very different in form from positivist writing. (1990, pp.2-4)

Grand theories are not the only form of analysis to have travelled well, to still be widely used in research and to demonstrate 'patriarchal biases and cultural assumptions about women' (Benn and Burton, 1993, p.19); class stratification is another (Goldthorpe and Llewellyn, 1987; Hayes and Miller, 1995). Take for instance, the marginalisation or exclusion of women through researchers' 'conventional' use of the Registrar General's classification. Class was reduced to an occupational category and women were placed in class groups according to their father's or husband's occupation. The underlying assumption was that the family is a rational unit of analysis with complete class equivalence within (Plummer, 1999; Goldthorpe and Marshall, 1992; Benn and Burton, 1993). These simple categories based on the male labour market overlooked the complexities inherent in the relationship between class, race and gender (Brah, 1996; Gilroy, 1994).

Feminists have continued to debate whether the family or the individual is the appropriate basic unit in class analysis. Michelle Barrett and Mary McIntosh (1982) have argued that the family is a class institution which gives each of us our initial class position. Phoenix and Tizard have argued that 'With increasing numbers of lone parent households, higher rates of women's participation in the labour market and the often different social class locations of women's and men's occupations ... ' it is 'indefensible' for stratification theorists to continue making 'the family' the unit of analysis (1996, p.429). A joint classification of men and women living in the same household has been suggested.

The Registrar General's system was not designed to deal with the current 'flexible' labour markets with their unemployment, discrimination in employment, the increase and pattern of women's employment (Crompton, 1993). It ignores socio-economic standing, class experience and subjectivity, issues of racial discrimination and difference, for instance, the disproportionate unemployment of Black people (Jones,

1993). Black women are more likely than white to have male partners in a 'lower' occupational group than themselves (Mirza, 1997). Furthermore, there is significant disjuncture between official methods of classifying people and the beliefs of those being classified but because it is simple to apply and allows comparison between many research studies (Phoenix and Tizard, 1996), researchers continually reproduce and focus on men's rather than on women's class position (Lampard, 1995; Evans, 1996).

Abbott and Sapsford (1987) maintained that the way forward was not to add women to a model which was developed along the dimensions important to men's lives and referring to the structure of male employment but to incorporate women in their own right so permitting different insights to emerge. Roseanne Benn and Rob Burton (1993), who looked at working-class women's entry into higher education via Access schemes, found that when women were classified in social class groups in their own right, access to higher education for working-class women was shown to be even less likely than indicated by previous low figures provided via the Registrar General's classification (Plummer, 1999). Ivan Reid offered an explanation for such a finding that the Registrar General's classification was not able to deal with:

> Students who succeed may be classified as working-class via their fathers' occupation, but have middle-class educated mothers and grandparents and come from educationally responsive and supportive, materially well-off, small families. (1989, p.177)

If we limit the class debate to the economic sphere alone, then, women are marginalised. Occupation measurements neglect 'wider dimensions of social action and economic power, including any discussion of the contribution of gender to economic inequality' (Holton and Turner, 1994, p.804). There is also 'a neglect of the myriad ways in which social class differences contribute to social inequalities' (Reay, 1998, p.259). For a comprehensive picture of the impact of social class today (Prandy and Bottero, 1995; Prandy and Blackburn, 1997) we need additional sources of information.

Another major theoretical approach adopted by male researchers and 'developed to explain the experiences of mainly white and working-class men' (Griffin, 1987, p.218) was cultural analysis. This approach emerged in the late 70s and 80s and incorporated youth culture studies, ethnography studies and conflict theory concerned with class reproduction via education.

Within schooling contexts, attempts were made to describe and account for the cultural practices of oppressed pupils by focusing on the interconnections between lived cultures, determining structural forces and the way the active consent of the working-classes to their domination was achieved. But, as Arnot and Weiner reported:

> Schools ... [were] investigated in terms of the preparation of male pupils for male occupational and vocational destinations. Access to higher education, social mobility, class conflict and school counter-cultures were discussed predominantly in terms of white, male working-class youth, as the group most subject to class control and educational disadvantage. (1987, p.12)

However, conflict theorists like Bowles and Gintis (1976) although arguing that 'the experiences of schooling prepare children for their experience of the labour force', failed to offer any understanding of how schools provided different experiences for boys and girls. For them sexual divisions of labour were not significantly a product of schooling but rather of the family.

Paul Willis's ethnographical account of working-class boys and the factory floor – underpinned by the theories of Bowles and Gintis – illustrated that, despite their overt resistance to the authority of the school, anti-school subcultures accepted their position as unskilled labour, so reinforcing their subordination. His account was criticised by Angela McRobbie for failing to 'integrate ... observations of masculinity and patriarchal culture into the context of the working-class family'. The inclusion of women, she argued, would have enabled the 'link between the lads' hard outer image and their private experiences – relations with parents, siblings, and girlfriends' – to be explored (1980, p.41). Male researchers showed themselves 'to be blind to the relativism of their own perspectives' (Acker, 1981, p.96).

This strong focus on male working-class culture was also observable in John Clarke's *et al.* text *Working Class Culture: Studies in history and theory* (1979), which listed twenty-four working-class cultural studies.

The focus of these studies, said the authors, was partly to do with the emergence of a generation of scholarship boys and girls. 'Who were the scholarship girls?' I wondered as all twenty-four authors were male. The list included the classic texts of Hoggart (1959), Williams (1961), E.P. Thompson (1963), Young and Willmott, (1957), Goldthorpe and Lockwood (1968) – all familiar names. The inclusion of 'and girls' was significant at another level. Of the ten case studies and theoretical essays in Clarke's text, nine were written by men and about men. This may partly explain why women like myself, brought up at that time in a working-class culture find it difficult believe that books like this are about us (Plummer, 1999).

Interestingly, three years earlier, along with Rachel Powell, Clarke critiqued the concept of marginality as being inadequate in its application to research on girls. The book their article appeared in was Stuart Hall's and Tony Jefferson's *Resistance through Rituals* (1976), a collection of largely ethnographic research articles focusing on post-war youth sub-cultures. Here again, Youth was predictably masculine and deviant. For instance, Tony Jefferson dealt with Teddy Boys, Dick Hebdige with Mods (male by implication – scooters, mod/rocker clashes, 'wide boys'), Rastas and Rudies; John Clarke talked about Skinheads; Paul Corrigan looked at the (male) street-corner culture; Paul Willis presented motorbike boys and Chas Critcher commented on (male) mugging. There were two articles about girls (McRobbie and Garber; Powell and Clarke), again tucked at the back and again the only articles written by women. The irony of marginalising an article about marginalisation seems to have been missed by the editors.

A perception of the working-class male youth as a deviant or troublesome other made them a fascinating research topic for numerous white, middle-class male academics who profited greatly from writing up their research – sensational accounts of the 'stereotyped' lived experiences of young working-class males. The working-class boys' actual lives were little affected by such arguably unrepresentative and distorted accounts. Whilst what they did and said was reported, it was often decontextualised and used to sensationalise or lighten up dense texts, or to make a political point on behalf of the author. Rarely were youths' views used to make or argue a point in their own right.

The voice of the academic dominated these texts and more often than not emitted a language that alienated the subjects of study and rendered them powerless to respond. Yet the power relationship in these seemingly irreversible, and arguably exploitative class relationships went unacknowledged (Plummer, 1999). Twenty years on, male academics have become less interested in these lives. Yet life for working-class boys has become more oppressive and the main educational concern is still boys' (largely working-class boys) underachievement. The mass of failing working-class girls, as in the past, continues to be ignored.

Female academics have shown comparatively little interest in the lives of working-class boys or girls. They were however interested in these male youth studies as evidence of patriarchy. Girls (if visible at all, for the lads regarded women as inferior) were seen as 'birds', 'scrubbers' or 'hangers on' (Llewellyn, 1981, p.42). Male researchers uncritically reproduced these views (Plummer, 1999).

Historically, working-class girls have not been regarded as worthy subjects of research. There were few small-scale studies which could be set alongside Willis's lads, or ethnographies of 'girls at school in the Hargreaves/Lacey mould' (Llewellyn, 1981, p.42). This was partly because girls were not seen as so confrontational and flashy (Fuller, 1980). Deviant behaviour such as 'indifference' or 'withdrawal', more common amongst working-class girls and conforming working-class boys, received little research attention.

Including women: working-class girls and femininity

Feminists focusing on the ideology and culture of femininity in the seventies and early eighties tried to theorise the characteristics of the female experience. The few studies of working-class girls' lives, limited though those were, made class divisions visible. Working-class girls were found to be in subordinate positions in the gender and the class hierarchy, oppressed both within class and by class.

Angela McRobbie was one of a very small number of researchers to focus on what being working-class meant to working-class girls. In her research she noted that working-class girls were distrustful and even hostile to outsiders (the Other), including herself. Interestingly she makes no reference to her own class position but relates the girls' suspicion and their shunning of outside interference of any sort to their 'being female' and inhabiting a culture of femininity' (1978, p.101).

The culture of working-class girls, McRobbie argued, could be seen as a response to the material limitations imposed on them as a result of their class position, but also as an index of, and response to, their sexual oppression as women (p.108). This view was shared by Katherine Clarricoates (1981), who argued that although most women were pressured towards a feminine role, working-class girls had it forced upon them earlier. For instance, they were less likely to be encouraged to extend childhood by opting for educational achievement. Community values, school expectations and often the family worked against them going on to higher education and having a career. Marriage and a family with, perhaps, part-time work was much more likely.

Working-class girls married and had children earlier than middle-class women. Clarricoates suggested this was 'an attempt to escape the tedium of boring, mundane jobs' (1981, p.40), whilst McRobbie described working-class girls as envisaging an unexciting future life. They endorsed the traditional female role and femininity simply because it seemed 'perfectly natural' and so accepted the oppressive features of their lives as both intransigent and unavoidable facts of life (1978, p.97). The author's choice of words like 'unexciting', 'mundane', 'boring' to describe working-class lives – and the implied passive acceptance of those lives – blots out the lived experience of oppression: the painful physical and emotional struggle for survival that has to be endured (Plummer, 1999).

Llewellyn (1981) argued that the concept of femininity provided working-class girls with a weapon to fight a class-determined education by inverting the 'hierarchy of productive over domestic labour'. They could reject the frustrations of school life and meaningless employment and search for emotional and personal fulfilment in domestic life and motherhood. The effect, said Llewellyn, was similar to working-class lads' resistance in undermining the 'mental/manual' hierarchy, though what was left in place was the hierarchy of male over female. Whether they were 'fighting' a class-determined education or submitting to it is debatable. What is not is that working-class girls have not escaped 'meaningless' employment: they are the millions of low-paid women workers (Plummer, 1999).

Rosemary Deem suggested that 'focusing upon domestic life for personal fulfilment' may partially explain why women (by which she means mostly working-class women) were 'prepared to accept employment in the worst, lowest-paid jobs within the secondary labour market' (1981, p.17). This notion of domestic life as personal fulfilment for working-class women is highly questionable. Being dependent on a working-class male is in itself an economically and emotionally risky position, one which reinforces working-class women's dual subordination. Working-class girls, it is argued, were required to be feminine, 'to be submissive, subordinate to their men, dependent and domestic'. This is a 'sharp disjuncture from the imperatives of their daily lives' where they needed to 'aggressively struggle for actual survival' (Anyon, 1983, p.20). Seen in this context, the concept of femininity alone is inadequate to explain why working-class girls continue to be women at the bottom of the pile (Plummer, 1999).

Michelle Stanworth (1983) made reference to a self-perpetuating cycle, whereby the narrow range of opportunities open to working-class women in previous generations weighed down the ambitions of girls in the present (See also Bates, 1990). Images of what working-class women are and what they might be were integral elements in girls' decisions about their educational futures. A lack of knowledge about alternatives and ignorance of status, wages and positions relative to other sorts of workers, she argued, contributed to their acceptance of their circumstances. These class-based and gender-related factors can help explain why those who have aspired to be upwardly mobile – in relation to their parents – have often found themselves in a female occupation ghetto that many middle-class women of the same ability or achievements have avoided.

Femininity, working-class girls and schooling

Research on working-class girls and schooling, like that on boys, tended to present all working-class girls as anti-school. McRobbie, referring to the disadvantaged position of working-class girls in the schooling system, argued that their academic failure was legitimated because they were female. Llewellyn agreed that femininity as constructed within schools did not encourage achievement or ambition in the academic world. Schools prepared pupils for their positions in the labour force, which needed working-class girls to be adaptable, pliable and docile – feminine attributes – but with marginal skills. As argued in Chapter 1, femininity within education has always been class specific. In more recent years, it is middle-class girls who mostly make up over half the university population.

McRobbie described working-class girls' under-achievement as being expressed in class, sex and 'anti-school' articulations; the girls knew themselves to be failures in terms of the school's criteria of success. They were allocated to the curriculum streams of the 'less able', to receive a basic training in non-examination courses, commerce, typing and everyday life skills. The images constructed of commercial stream girls – by both teachers and students – were those of dumb classes and tarts (Middleton, 1987).

Working-class girls, McRobbie found, occupied an antagonistic relation to snobs, swots, old-fashioned, conformists, who were most likely to be middle-class girls. The constructs of academic and commercial types have always related closely to social class groupings. Llewellyn (1981) interpreted this stance as working-class girls judging academic success 'unfeminine'. This working-class girl would argue that the 'unfeminine' did not relate to the academic but to class-related issues of prolonged childhood symbolised by, for example, school uniform and not being allowed to wear make-up at eighteen.

Research at this time showed girls in lower streams taking up an oppositional stance by discarding the official ideology for girls in school: neatness, diligence, appliance, femininity, passivity, behaviour required for assimilation, and adopting defensive and aggressive gestures as weapons, exaggerating the feminine – even sexual – stereotype: dressing-up, making-up, smoking, swearing (acts symbolising adulthood) to invert the purpose of schooling. That is, they focused on the social at the expense of the academic (McRobbie, 1976; Middleton,

1987). In using their sexuality girls were 'expressing a class relation, in albeit traditionally feminine terms', argued McRobbie (p.104). Kessler *et al*., however, found that some working-class girls exhibited behaviour that was 'quite like the boys', behaviour which confirmed and even exaggerated boys' masculinity and which violated conventional femininity. It was, they argued, more like a protest 'against femininity' than a 'confirmation' of it. Girls were challenging 'their subordination as women' (1985, pp.226-267). This response is one that has emerged from more recent studies on working-class girls, though such studies are still very sparse.

Arnot *et al*, (1999) reviewing the educational progress of working-class girls over time note that studies in the early 80s offered images of white working-class girls as overly preoccupied with romance (Wallace, 1987), caring little for educational success or secure long term employment. This I would argue was a means of escape from the realities of their pre-determined life, high dependency on men on low incomes (See Chapter 6). School did not provide routes to alternative life styles – most working-class girls were school failures. In the mid 80s working-class girls were perceived to strongly identify with female work and qualifications were less important to them than a good job (Griffin, 1985). Again this is a realistic response to what life offered. Those of us who have watched our fathers 'work themselves towards death' in manual jobs would not want to take up working-class male roles and male professional roles were never an option. In the 1990s, as Arnot *et al* point out, there has been a shift in the tolerance of the inevitability of domestic drudgery and women's subordination as wives and mothers (Sharp, 1994; McLaren, 1996). This has come along with the decline of manual work. Unemployed men can not keep their side of the unwritten domestic 'bargain', to be the provider. Working-class girls still choose to leave school as soon as possible and take jobs in the 'realm of women's work' (Sharpe, 1994). They opt for security rather than resisting family conventions, note Arnot *et al,* 1999. As I argue in Chapters 6-9, for many working-class girls the price of 'breaking away' is too high to pay, something middle-class girls are not required to do.

Feminism's approach to gender and class theory in the 1970s and 80s

> Perhaps one of the deadliest and least resistible of seductions for feminists is their seduction by theorists, by theories, by the theoretical. (Miller, 1990, p.8)

Class inequality needed to be examineded in the light of women's experiences but analyses of gender divisions were developing separately from those of class. Numerous attempts have been made to combine concepts of class and gender – capitalism and patriarchy – and more recently, concepts of colonialism to address racial divisions. There remains, nevertheless, a great deal of conflict over how these forms of oppression and their inter-relationships are to be explained.

In the late 1970s and 80s a few attempts were made to graft on or in some way incorporate inequalities (predominantly racial and sexual divisions) to existing explanations of class inequalities. Michelle Barrett (1987) looked at the alternative ways the relationship between gender and class had been articulated (Delphy, 1984; Burton, 1985; Segal, 1987) and identified four different theoretical positions. The Marxist position, where gender was not a separable element of class relations, took the family as the basic unit of which classes were composed. This left unanswered many questions (Hart, 1989; Abbott and Sapsford, 1989). For instance, if women and men were united in the class struggle 'why was it that women were paid less, given less power and were provided with fewer opportunities in the work place'; 'how was the position of women in the home and their low status there to be accounted for?' A second position was that gender division constituted a system of oppression that was wholly independent of class division. The assumption was that the meaning of gender identity and experiences of sexism, for instance, were the same for all women 'as women'. The strongest formulation of this position was the argument that gender division comes analytically before class division, patriarchy being the root cause of women's oppression and capitalism being a product of patriarchy.

Feminist accounts which refuse to take on the class and gender differences among women simply mirror male accounts which refuse to take differences between men and women seriously. Claims that theories constructed by one group of women are adequate to describe all women's lives are too simplistic.

A third position was that capitalism and patriarchy were two identifiably separate structures historically co-existing in particular societies; a domestic mode of production with its own mechanism of exploitation co-existing alongside an exploitative capitalist mode of production. This did not account for why patriarchy and capitalism impose more limitations upon the lives of white working-class women and women of colour, than those of white middle-class women. The fourth position was that women constitute an identifiable social class. Christine Delphy and Diana Leonard (1993), radical feminists taking a Marxist approach to material relations, describe men and women as economic classes. One class subordinates the other, and exploits it for its work; women are exploited because men appropriate their labour. The assumption here is that women do not exploit each other. They do. There are women who oppress less powerful women than themselves (Ussher, 1990, p.255).

These frameworks rely upon a particular image of power as constraining those who do not "fit" the white, male, middle-class subjectivity which capitalism and patriarchy rely upon in order to function (Blackman, 1996).

Feminism and education

Research methods and approaches adopted by feminist researchers to investigate gender and class inequalities in education have been diverse and contradictory, based as they are on conflicting theoretical perspectives which relate to the theoretical positions identified by Barrett: Liberal feminist, Radical feminist, Marxist or Socialist feminist. These varying perspectives have been important in determining the form research has taken and what aspects of inequality have been addressed.

Educational research and practice under the heading of Liberal feminism (Sayers, 1986; De Beauvoir, 1953) fell within the normative paradigm and had some of the following characteristics: usually quantitative; based on functionalist assumptions; used devices such as sex-role stereotyping; adopted an implicitly behaviourist theory of socialisation (Middleton, 1984); had its roots in the development of the free market economy and was the discourse of equal rights, of feminists seeking equality with men within a capitalist hierarchy. Liberal feminists were the first to focus on the considerable divergence between the educational routes taken by girls and boys and exposed patterns of gender differentiation (Arnot and Weiner, 1987) and their consequences for male and female training, access to higher education, the professions and work opportunities. They also drew to the attention of educational policy-makers the continuation of male and female occupational patterns within a sex-segregated labour market which placed women at a distinct disadvantage when compared with men (Deem, 1984; Burgess, 1990). What Liberal Feminists failed to do was: to account for the persistence of certain roles and patterns of male domination; question the historical/material basis of sex stereotypes; acknowledge the impact of class or race on gender. Their concern over equitability diverted attention away from *how* education legitimated and preserved the class and race structure. For example, discussion of girls' underachievement rarely considered the different achievements of middle- and working-class girls and little attention was paid to the routing of working-class girls – white and Black – into non-examination streams. More importantly, there was no expressed desire to change the current social structure to benefit other groups of women.

In contrast to Liberal feminist notions of disadvantaged women, the more radical perspectives on women – aired by classical Marxists and Socialist feminists and Radical feminists – maintained that women were oppressed and that this oppression was structural (Middleton, 1984).

Radical feminism re-shaped the political agenda to include the power relations between men and women and their legitimation and reproduction through schooling. The strength of the approach lay in its descriptive powers of patriarchy and patriarchal educational knowledge and its generation of theory grounded in experience. Researchers looking at the school as a site for the reproduction of patriarchy – male interests, dominance and control – debated the patriarchal biases of academic subjects; the social construction of femininity in the process of classroom interaction; sexist language as a means of male control; the perception and organisation of gender conformity and deviation in primary schools; the nature of patriarchal power in the academic profession itself; and the androcentricity of the male-dominated academic disciplines. They failed to address gender and class relations and over-emphasised sexuality and male/female power relations without adequate consideration of how these relations were shaped by the dynamics of, for example, white power.

Marxist and Socialist feminism emerged from a dissatisfaction with Radical feminism's emphasis on description and a recognition that Marxism did not adequately explain the specific nature of women's oppression under capitalist patriarchy (Barret, 1987; Segal, 1987). The problem was how to merge explanations of class and gender in education, given that sociological and Marxist accounts of the education system had excluded any systematic consideration of gender or of the role of the education system in creating a highly sex-segregated labour force. Marxist categories of class 'juxtaposed with, or transposed on to, feminist categories of gender', were, however, to prove problematic (Barrett, 1987, p.55).

Michelle Barrett attempted to develop a Marxist feminist perspective on how a gender-divided work-force came about, but was doubtful whether a method which sought to understand education and training processes in terms of the reproduction of relations of dominance and subordination could be applied to the question of gender:

> It would be difficult to argue, for instance, that the qualifications and skills imparted to a girl at a major independent school would in any sense 'equip' her for a place in the division of labour that was subordinate to that of a working-class boy who left school at the minimum age with no formal qualifications. (1987, p.58)

This crucial point – central to this research – has been ignored in much feminist writing. Women have a dual relation to the class structure, Barrett argued. In the context of white, working-class women they may be directly exploited 'by capital' via their own wage-labour and indirectly exploited by their 'vicarious dependence on the wage of a male breadwinner' (p.58).

Critics of the Marxist/socialist feminism position have argued that a class analysis based on an economic explanation cannot offer a sufficiently specific account of other kinds of oppression.

Although feminism has successfully challenged theories, theorists and theoretically based research in terms of limited insight when it comes to issues of gender inequality, it has not dealt with the way gender, class and race interrelate and so has been as excluding as the traditional class theories it has criticised. For instance, 'feminists have nothing to say about the situation of working-class women in the 1990s' (Cole and Hill, 1995, p.175). Its omissions make questionable the generalisability of the theory it has generated. I am not suggesting that we ignore or invalidate these insights but rather that we acknowledge what level of understanding they can offer to particular social groups when the situation of one group of women has been confused with the situation of all women. Take, for example, Julia Stanley's comment in her research text, 'like most people over 40, I went to a small, single-sex, selective school – in this case a direct grant grammar school' (1989, p.1). Most women over 40 went to secondary-modern schools (Plummer, 1999).

Many women have turned to the history of mainstream feminism for further insight into the conditions of their lives to find there is no mention of women like themselves. This has partly come about because feminist theories and research itself has been racially and culturally specific. In taking their own white, middle-classed experiences for granted, feminist writers have marginalised or excluded the lived experiences of most women. As Ussher has pointed out, to the majority of women, placed outside the normative framework, the 'white middle-class feminist' may have little to say. 'She will be perceived as representative of the dominant elite, who act to alienate working-class women in innumerable ways' (1990, p.225). 'Why is it so difficult to get middle-class women to talk or write about their lives as classed?' asks Walkerdine (1996, p.402). Similar arguments have been put forward for race, for the experiences of Black women, (Carby, 1987; Amos and Parmar, 1987) and racism in society has been ignored by feminism, as Black women have forcibly argued. It is significant that the racism of white women in the women's movement was a major reason why Black and Third World women have not identified with contemporary feminism in large numbers (Smith, 1983).

As Diane Reay suggests, 'raising issues of social class within feminism' feels like an act of betrayal, or 'ignorance' (1998, p.259). This is perhaps because the feminist movement has yet to acknowledge its own class and race perspectives and its fears of the differences between women

(Walkerdine, 1990). The challenge of difference, Reay argues, 'exposes relations that those in dominant positions would rather not acknowledge or have to deal with' (1996, p.444). Women do not talk about themselves as oppressors but it is not incidental that less powerful groups of women in our society are neither part of the dominant communication system, nor part of the academic debate. While less powerful groups of women remain invisible or marginal, power differentials between women are maintained (Plummer, 1999).

Conclusion

Structuralist explanations of society, capitalism and patriarchy and more recently colonialism have presented groups as homogeneous, accounted for in terms of single factors (working-class people's oppression, women's oppression, Black people's oppression). This has inhibited analysis of the inter-relationships of class, race and gender (Brah, 1994; Paechter and Weiner, 1996) and done little to increase our understanding of the complexity of difference and the effect difference has on people's psyche (Plummer, 1999). To look at the specifics of class, race and gender identities we need specific accounts which can be used collectively to re-frame and refine overarching theories.

Post-modern and post-structuralist approaches have moved us away from simply relying on these over-arching theories in which class, gender and race are given universals, towards an 'examination of the way in which stratification and difference is produced historically' (Walkerdine, 1996, p.358). Whilst it could be argued that these constitute yet another effective 'new' middle-class strategy for 'shifting' and 'denying ' class power differentials (Reay, 1998) they do allows us to acknowledge ...

> the difficulty of theorising women, either as a single class or solely in relation to accepted accounts of class (even within competing analyses) [whilst acknowledging that women live] their lives within deeply known allegiances to class and race and within quite specific relations to other women and with men. (Miller, 1990, p.48)

Things that have been largely overlooked by 'macro, modernist' explanatory frameworks' (Paechter and Weiner, 1996, p.269) can be researched at a micro-level, including the power relationships between women ... that feminism has been reluctant and ... ill-equipped to do' (p.270). This does not mean we should abandon overarching theories. Without them we are unable to explain, analyse and prioritise, for instance, post-modernism's blindness to inequalities and injustices (Reay, 1996, p.454).

Walkerdine, in her editorial introduction to *Feminism* and *Psychology* points out that there is an increase in the number of feminist academics who having grown up in working-class families and are now beginning to write 'experientially about class and to analyse it' from a subjective and psychological point of view, rather than an essentially economic one. In this way, class, as a subject, is coming increasingly on to a feminist agenda 'as a significant issue for the understanding of culture, feminine subjectivity and identity' (1996, p.355). A number of recent studies looking at women's relationships to class and gender equalities highlight the need to 'explore women's sense of class and how it is enacted in different contexts' (Reay, 1998, p.259; Hey, 1997; Reinfelder, 1997). It is important to note however that:

> current feminist work which examines the intersections of class and gender is almost exclusively written by feminist academics from working-class backgrounds and is not reflected in the concerns of mainstream feminisms. (Reay, 1998, p.260)

Prevailing contemporary academic discourses marginalise 'the ways in which social class contributes to social identities' (Reay, 1998, p.272) and mainstream feminism ignores social class as an important social division (Skeggs, 1995).

Chapter 5
Addressing an imbalance

> I can find no account in academic literature of how class forms on a daily basis the complex and contradictory subjectivity of a woman like myself. (Martindale, 1992, p.323)

Did other educated working-class women around me feel in alien territory servicing education? Is this a feature of having a structural relationship to education which is fraught with dilemmas and contradictions, past and present?

Traditionally working-class history has been located in research models that are saturated with the meanings of those who speak about rather than experience working-class life. As we have seen it is the 'Other' who has held up the magnifying glass to the working classes and reported back what they see. All lives are interpreted and explained through dominant white, middle-class discourses. There is no discourse that legitimates working-class people's personal knowledge and no 'public forums' in which they can give their account (Reay, 1998, p.268). What is more, telling stories of our past experiences, which are always explicitly contextualised in concrete situations and with associated thought and feelings, can be uncomfortable (Plummer *et al.*, 1993).

What can we discover when working-class people whose lives class theory claims to describe and explain, actively take part in the construction and re-construction of this theory? 'Voices that are informed by insider knowledge of working-class culture rarely inform academic writing' (Reay, 1996, p.64). Wanting to address this issue, I sought to discover 'what the collection, interpretation and publication of educated working-class women's narratives – at present largely absent from the public domain – could tell us about female, working-class lives that existing class analysis can not' (Plummer, 1999).

There exists no 'paradigm' for a 'working class' stance – a contradiction in terms (Reay, 1996). As already highlighted, the 'barriers to talking or writing about a working-class past' are forceful (Reay, 1998a, p.15) for 'speaking the realities we know we have lived requires that we transcend the subtleties of taboo and the limits of discretion' (Lewis, 1993, p.54). As a way of enabling 'ordinary people' to make sense of their lives and overcome their feeling of powerlessness I link history and biography together. It is an approach that can be found in literature demonstrating the experience of racism from a Black female perspective. I use it to highlight and make significant the lived experiences of a group of educated working-class women who have been 'educated out of their class'. In exploring how class, and the inequalities it generates, are lived in gendered and raced ways, the approach brings together stands of thought which have historically been studied separately. The stories being told are used as a way of finding out and validating experiences and emotions which have their origins in class experience.

The research

My research focused on the conflicts a group of working-class girls faced when they attempted to make use of the education system to escape their destiny, foretold in their working-class mothers' and grandmothers' lives. Taking adult views of childhood raises a number of issues: 'What does being working-class mean to women who were once working-class girls?'; 'What happens to 'the self' that is a working-class girl when educational success (and later occupation) labels you a middle-class woman?' and 'How does this process impact on our self-identity and self-worth?' Our experience of education and in particular higher education disconnected us from our social origins. In positions of class and race privilege, we can now pass as middle class, so we can hardly claim that our perspective on social class is that of the disadvantaged working-class girl. Nevertheless our experiences of once being precisely that and all the inequalities that implies, still powerfully affects our sense of identity and daily experiences.

Working with memories/self-construction

Childhood memories reflect our struggles with the social order and say much about the social order in which we constitute ourselves. Individuals are their memories, since memories are the building blocks for a theory of self. In talking about our specific experiences we create a self-identity, consciously or subconsciously (Rosenwald *et al*, 1992). The self is a valuable source of information to derive insight into complex psychological issues set in specific historical, social and political contexts. The personal stories we tell of our lives – the way we select, construct and describe our realities – throw light on how we construct our sense of self in relation to our gender, class and ethnic backgrounds. Some socially constructed meanings are specific to working-class girls, as this book illustrates.

The stories we tell are not 'a mirror of a world out there', nor an exact record, (Riessman, 1993) they are incomplete, internally inconsistent, subjective and contain an inevitable bias, both in their selection and presentation of content (Stanley, 1993, p.48). It is the nature of the bias in research that is important (Crawford *et al*, 1992, p.153).

Collecting data

The research looks at the development of class awareness for a small group of white, educated working-class women, from various religious backgrounds (Catholic, Jewish, Church of England) and ethnic backgrounds (Irish, Eastern European, English, Italian), who were working-class girls in the post-war years – spanning the 1940s to 1970s. The group is one to which I belong.

Class is taken to be complex, dynamic and embodied in real people and in real contexts. The interviewed women identified themselves as coming from a working-class background. Using individuals' perceptions, I accepted the class label the women gave themselves as a marker of their awareness of their class position. This allowed diversity within the group to emerge within a shared class history of working-class girls (insiders) who had become educated working-class women (outsiders) (Plummer, 1999). We had points of commonality: we had lived in working-class neighbourhoods (poor housing, rented accommodation) and our parents had left school at fourteen for traditionally working-class jobs (dockers, cleaners, labourers). A central feature of our childhood experience was poverty, though this was experienced at different levels.

The Self as researcher and researched

> A text written as if the researcher had no autobiographical presence would constitute a deception about the epistemological status of the research. Such a study lacks validity. (Connelly and Clandinin, 1992, p.11)

My past and present experience of class strongly influenced the research approach I took and my part in it. Rather than take on the conceptual frameworks and relevances of disciplines that cannot deal with personal experiences – and discard my own experience as a source of reliable information – I deliberately chose an autobiographical/biographical approach. It enabled me to enter the space behind the magnifying glass as one of the subjects of my research, thus allowing the authority of my own class experience – which prompted the research and drove me to look beyond existing class theories – to be recognised. Most importantly, this role as participant minimised the risk of class betrayal. Writing about other educated working-class women's lives and not my own would have been yet another form of class exploitation.

Friends – a source of data

I wanted to collect data from people who were the 'experts' on the experiences of educationally successful working-class girls: educated working-class women who knew and understood what it was to be a working-class girl. This group is generally invisible in the world of education, unless the women choose to reveal this identity. We change our dress, voice, behaviour – all the things that marked us out.

The women in this research were women I knew, women who had acknowledged their class backgrounds. Interestingly our class related conversations had been based on the educational implications of socio-economic background, not on personal experience. Were we maintaining the hidden self from subtle labellings of inferiority? Why else would we stay silent about such an important part of ourselves? For people to reveal aspects of themselves, the 'hidden', the 'secretive', the 'silenced,' the kind of class experiences I was wanting to explore and make explicit – there has to be trust. Within friendship the essential ingredient is trust, which shifts the emphasis away from an 'objective, neutral, dispassionate' stance (Thomas, 1992, p.14). Yet in academia, accounts achieve legitimacy only to the extent the authors succeed in distancing themselves from the actual experience encountered. We are not rational and objective experts with no interests and no positions. 'The least we can do is make these evident' (Ussher, 1990, p.9). In research practice it is considered more reliable, objective, legitimate to question people you do not know than to question people you know, especially friends. This is taboo. Telling friends some things about oneself may be considered too risky (Grument, 1987). But we tell many things to friends that we would not tell to others. The meaning of 'friend', after all, contains expectations of confidentiality, trust, openness, interpersonal intimacy, confession, which, if violated, damage friendships (Plummer, 1999). With these friends, people I trusted, I shared aspects of my own 'constructed/reconstructed' working-class childhood experiences within the family, and then school. I had written at length in a language that was distinctly personal, recalling events, experiences and feelings relating to such matters as social and economic deprivation, conflictual relationships, intimidation and failure in school. The writing process itself made me aware of how difficult it was to access and articulate aspects of self that one has learned to cover up, deny, or want to forget. As educated working-class women we are shaped by middle-class norms, labelled and tucked into middle-class definitions and the structures of our suppressed childhood oppression are not always apparent. Remembering a disadvantaged past may be a struggle for some because exposing a 'working-class 'I' borders on schizophrenia' (Reay, 1996, p.445).

Exploring my own history first and sharing it – the task I was setting other women – was invaluable. It informed my understanding of the narratives and the issues around sharing aspects of working-class childhood. We come from a background where anything that was said or did was judged, often as inadequate. In the act of using 'I' or 'we' the protective distance is removed (Plummer *et al.*, 1993). Consequently, 'self-disclosure' is a risky, even dangerous business. We risk objectifying ourselves and our families, of conforming to deficit models and providing ammunition to fuel continuing pathologisation (Reay, 1996, p.453).

Contrarily, exposing aspects of one's own working class life can position you as an equal with those with similar experiences. It establishes your authority in the subject and provides a safe environment for women to explore this aspect of their childhood. It is only with a friend that one can say in private what one is not supposed to say in public, the unspeakable (Plummer *et al.*, 1993). When this knowledge is taken into the public arena issues of vulnerability, of danger arise once more. It is for this reason that I anonymised the women. I focus on collective and conflicting issues not individual lives. This removes danger to the individual but it does not prevent objectification of working-class people's lives.

Interviews

The interviews about family and then school were very loosely structured, open and informal – much like our relationships. Each woman structured her own narratives – telling her story in whatever way she chose, moving at her own pace and setting her own limits on what information she wanted or was willing to share. They all remained, as I had, totally in control at all times of what they revealed about their early lives. This seemed wholly appropriate in accessing knowledge that is not generally talked about even in working-class families. And talking about the family to others outside is strictly taboo for fear of public exposure.

In the interviews I avoided discussing aspects of my autobiographical stories unless directly asked to do so, not wanting the women to feel they had to talk about the issues I had raised. I was keen to find out how they had experienced their early working-class lives and how these experiences framed their now middle-class worlds. This proved valuable because it allowed me to question some of my own views. For example, in my mind fathers were not of central importance in working-class girls' lives. This was not the case for other women, for whom centrality was not necessarily determined by father's availability.

I responded to and followed up issues raised by the women. This was a key element in the reciprocal nature of the research procedures and the everyday way we related as equals. Occasionally, as happens in conversations, I found myself butting-in and voicing my opinion. Sometimes my probing of a meaning – as the transcripts reveal – was more of a prod. Fortunately, these were usually ignored. The women rarely halted or digressed and they left questions unanswered which they consciously – or subconsciously – did not wish to respond to.

In transcribing I noted that we – in varying degrees – slipped in and out of using spoken, working-class grammatical structures: incomplete sentences, re-affirmations, like 'you know', 'sort of like'; terms which have been taken as evidence of the language deprivation of a restricted code user. But here it showed how comfortable we were with each other. We were safe, our guard was down, we knew the other would not equate our intelligence with the grammatical structure we uttered: a rare moment. Each woman was given her transcript copy to alter anything she felt was inaccurate or wanted removed. No one changed their scripts or the grammatical structure of their speech. Nor did they raise this as an issue – other than to say they were aware of it (Plummer, 1999). Throughout our lives we have had to demonstrate our knowledge of an 'elaborated code' in order to succeed – even in situations where this has been inefficient and/or unnecessary. It is precisely for this reason that I did not 'correct' the grammatical structure of our speech when using quotes. We are using the language of our class background, a hidden part of the educated working-class self.

Selecting, interpreting and writing-up

Taking each transcript of home and school experiences, I drew a demarcation line determined by a change in theme. The content determined the label. Emerging themes within and across transcripts and themes implicit within the data were noted. The content of each woman's story was summarised by eliminating repetitions and sequencing events chronologically. Using substantive key themes I wrote a collective story which reflects broad categories of experience and privileges the most striking and frequent elements of the discourse. The central theme is relationships, particularly between mother/daughter, father/daughter, peer and teacher/pupil. The main criteria for selecting data for objectification was sameness and difference – between women, specifically in relation to social class – and conflict and contradictions, within and across transcripts. Class, for working-class girls, is intrinsically tied up with an awareness of difference but this allowed me to note what difference our 'differences' made. I also experimented with polarities, for example, power/powerless, economic provider/non-provider, dependent/ independent and placed responses within these categories. The issues that emerged are not universal or eternal but are grounded in the lived experiences of the women in this book. These specific accounts do not claim to hold universal truths for all educated working-class women. Many versions of childhood working-class life are complicated by where individuals are positioned within the working classes. To conflate one set of experiences with the very different experiences of other women from working-class backgrounds is to ignore difference (Reay, 1998a).

Making sense of one's data is a personal process and though I take up the position of an insider, the text is still my interpretation of accounts: mine and others. In identifying with the women in my research I do not eliminate the implications of Walkerdine's query, 'How far is it possible for ... [any] observer to 'speak for' the observed?' (1991, p.195). As with all research, the accounts are read through the researcher's experience. The researcher's social background influences what is said (Walkerdine and Lucey, 1989). This is denied in positivist science. It brings with it dangers of proximity and risks of conflating varied experiences with my own. There is a 'thin dividing line' between the understandings of similar experiences that 'respondents bring to the research process and the element of exploitation implicit in mixing up one's own personal history with very different working-class experiences' (Reay 1999, p.65). Accessing the domains of meaning generated by others will always be difficult as there are many possible readings of interview transcripts. In an attempt to minimise distortions I present a plural text – a collection of different voices and experiences – which is not synthesised into a consensus. The accounts confirm and challenge each other.

Validity – notions of truth

Can subjective accounts be valid beyond individual interpretation? What has passed for rationality, truth and objectivity has long been contested ground. Life history as research is about understanding how the research process illuminates our ways of knowing (Munro, 1991). It 'is to be regarded as providing insights into the subjective perspective of an 'individual" (Ribbens, 1993, p.87), in this instance, individuals whose class experiences are denied or ignored by mainstream research. The academy however has traditionally demonstrated a limited tolerance for lived experience, easily dismissed as 'anecdotal', and in some quarters intolerance is so great that it is an affront to scholarly sensibilities (Brodkey, 1987). It is somewhat ironic that it is devalued and neglected as a form of research precisely because of its principal strength: those being written about present the evidence.

In the hierarchies of knowledge what we know as working-class children is 'relegated to the realms of the intuitive' (Reay, 1996, p.63). Where it is viewed as inferior and unacceptable by intellectuals. It has never counted as 'knowledge' or it is always at the bottom of the knowledge hierarchy (Lynch and O'Neil, 1994, p.32). This book sets out to disturb the knowledge hierarchy which is itself problematic for we educated working-class women have learned to understand our class experience through middle-class ways of knowing at cost to the working-class ways of knowing we bring with us (Luttrell, 1992). In the absence of a working-class paradigm the accounts themselves will be understood and made sense of within the confines of dominant middle-class discourses which will determine their legitimacy.

The accounts are valid in their specificity, not as representative samples of universally agreed categories. They bring in to the public domain knowledge which is both difficult to obtain and devalued. It differs little from mainstream research in that research is by its nature preoccupied with matters which are partial, contested, inter-subjective and illusory – as is all truth (Munro, 1991). In practice, most accounts compound imagination and fact but this does not 'weaken the usefulness of a text for prospective analysis' (Holloway, 1989, p.15). All data is open to question and there are multiple versions of all truths (Purvis, 1987).

Again the important question is not whether the research is biased but in whose interest it is biased (Plummer, 1999). All research is 'shaped by who we look at, from where we look, and why we are looking in the first place' (Wheatley, 1994, p.422). In formal academic writing this subtext is masked by the seeming impartiality of the text (Pile and Thrift, 1995). Similarly 'past experiences are continually worked out by academics' without acknowledgement or even recognition (Reay, 1998a, p.15). Academia is a social location where particular 'truths' are told (Walkerdine, 1990) and other truths such as those that emerge here need to be brought in from the margins.

Part II

In the introduction to this book I referred to the psychological and emotional impact of education on working-class girls, particularly in relation to home/school conflicts. The next three chapters examine this theme using the childhood experiences of six educated working-class women who achieved academic success – in the traditional sense of formal qualifications. Although there has been significant social, economic and political change over the last fifty years, what these women have to say about their family life and school experiences tells us more about the issues working-class girls face today that any existing theory. We get a different perspective on class and gender identities from those embedded in contemporary academic discourses. There are none of the certainties of conventional middle-class positionings.

Drawing on the stories we told, I pay particular attention to the aspects of our childhood experiences that led us to identify with and construct ourselves as coming from a working-class background. Specific areas of tension and conflict – both within and between home and school – are identified and the impact these had on our relative failure in school is detailed. Our educational achievements are discussed and the negative effect they had on our self-identity and self-esteem when we had been led to believe that for able children education was a social equaliser. Consequently, I explore family relationships, parental support, the impact of peers and the demands of schools, especially the level of academic success expected of working-class students.

Remember that, at one level class oppression has to do with the individual psyche. Society is located inside our heads, that is, in our socially located and structured understanding of 'myself, 'me-as-a-person" (Ribbens, 1993, p.88). On another, it is a major social issue concerning the political and economic institutions of society. As Popkewitz has it, to understand where individuality begins, one must first understand the ways in which history and social structures impinge upon our choices (1988, pp.379-400). There is a 'tension between the individual as an active social agent, the product of a given 'life history' capable of making positive decisions and choices, and the individual as influenced by specific social structures and ideologies' (Griffin, 1987, p.216).

In using autobiographical accounts, the chapters focus on personal experiences but these experiences relate to historical and structural phenomena. It is important to keep wider historical, social, cultural, economic, and political influences in view.

Chapter 6
Life in a Working-Class Family

What do we mean when we say we come from a working-class background?

Most people do not articulate how the sociological category of class has shaped their life. Evidence is there, nevertheless, in the stories we tell – or don't tell – about our lives (Richardson, 1990). From the women's texts I first identify aspects of class difference and illustrate how concepts of class and class positions are learned through specific experiences and *in relation* to *others* in general.

The women in this study all identified themselves as from a working-class background. In our experience, class position is historical and situational, not fixed or universal – for instance, through our educational achievements we have, or are perceived to have, marginally shifted class position. Whilst the model of a class continuum with working-class at one end and middle-class, or upper-class, at the other – with a few people moving up and down (Richardson, 1990) – may underlie our stories, what we focus on is difference and perceived relational positionings. Using three of the women's texts, I identify perceived indicators of class position – which are also shifting – and demonstrate that class awareness is a learning process. Class mobility and differences within the working classes become apparent.

As suggested in Chapter 5, talking about one's own working-class family to others raises notions of potential betrayal. 'You don't let other people know your business.' So I have been careful to protect individual families while still raising important family issues.

Social mobility: becoming aware of difference

> [There are] divisions within the working-class itself, between its respectable and upward-striving representatives and the poor ... (Campbell, 1984, p.46)

Housing areas (and now post codes) have been one crude indicator of people's class. This awareness of housing location as a class indicator is revealed in one woman's description of her family as moving up.'Up' meant out of a working-class area into a middle-class one and this denotes an awareness of hierarchy. In this instance, housing also symbolises sectarian differences:

> [A] working-class family ... with so many kids ... I mean I'm sure the neighbours must of ... 'cause it was very Protestant ... I'm sure they must of shit themselves when we arrived. Twelve children all trooping around the streets ... which was ... like a working-class tradition, but we were in a middle-class area.

Significant differences and distinctions are highlighted which are linked to socially allocated geographical spaces and traditions: a Catholic 'working-class family' in a 'Protestant' middle-class area'; children 'trooping around the streets', a 'working-class tradition'. There is also reference in the text to working-class families living in each others' houses. In the new place, unlike the old, J observed, 'there wasn't the sort of living in each others' houses that we were ... used to' [laughs]. Also implicit is the notion that Catholic working-class traditions – large families (another class indicator of the time), going in and out of each others' houses, children in the streets – made Protestant middle-class people anxious. When other Catholic families 'moved up', she notes, 'we turned it into quite a common area.'

This was an area of Belfast which was, presumably going through a period of social transition, its occupants changing from being predominantly middle-class, Protestant, nuclear families to predominantly working-class, Catholic, extended families. A middle-class area can absorb a few working-class families who 'move up', but the arrival of too many, she learns, turns the area into 'a common area'. Labelling an area 'common' because it is mainly occupied by working-class families – in this instance, Catholic families – implies an awareness or a learned belief that working-class Catholic families and the lives they lead are somehow seen as inferior.

Other class indicators emerged in the text. '[It] was only because dad worked in the shipyard that he could afford to buy a house up there.' Male occupations, particularly fathers', have traditionally been the marker of class position. J's father would be classified as a skilled or semi-skilled manual worker according to the textbook definitions, so categorised as working class. J uses different criteria to classify him. While she identifies her mother as coming 'from a very strong working-class background, a Catholic ghetto', she does not feel the same is necessarily true of her father.

> Dad actually lived in quite a nice house ... a huge big house ... behind and above a sort of butcher's shop ... I think they were quite well-off really ... so he wasn't really working-class.

Further details in her text suggest that what J identifies as evidence of her father's middle-class origins, others would perceive to be characteristics of the 'respectable' working-class family. This is evident in other aspects of her family history.

> You couldn't really call us working class, not really ... We sort of lived out the area ... we were always relatively well-dressed ... and education was [important].

In addition to housing location, cultural practices in childhood, father's occupation, parents' family of origin, two more indicators of class positioning arise: dress and education. The phrase 'relatively well-dressed' is interesting. She was, after all, one of twelve children. Her family's only income was her father's wage. In her early teens he lost his job in the shipyard, was unemployed and finally took a low-waged, unskilled job. By then, only one of the children was at work. Money was short. Saying she was well-dressed, her clothes handed on from older sisters, was possibly a reference to cleanliness – a marker of the respectable working-class family (see Bourke, 1994). In terms of education she was talking about the importance of making the best of state-funded education, as private education would not have been an option.

Perception of a family's level of poverty touches upon another important indicator of class position, income. Whilst on the one hand J feels, that

> We weren't poor that you didn't ever have any money, but there wasn't a lot of money to go around. You got what you needed to survive sort of thing and that was it.'

She adds,

> Money didn't appear to be a problem, although it must have been for my mum ... We weren't sort of made aware of it ... I think that it's mum sort of like being a wizard.

J put her family's economic survival down to her mother's remarkable money management skills. Yet at the same time she recalls that her mother 'spent a lot of time paying people, borrowing from people', that there was the 'Provident cheque as well' and that a lot of their 'clothes were bought from the shop round the corner ... on tick.'

Having only 'what you needed to survive' and yet not perceiving yourself as being poor, is a feature of working-class life, a part of working-class people's social conditioning. Poverty is relative. There is always another family worse off than yours. Furthermore, to acknowledge you were poor in a society that blames poor families for their poverty means blaming your working-class parents. They had not worked hard enough or taken advantage of the opportunities offered to them. If we accepted this, what would it say about them, about us?

The other women interviewed unquestioningly described themselves as coming from working-class backgrounds but there was evidence of social mobility in two families, one upward and one downward. These women's stories, as the first, further illustrate the relativity of poverty and the diversity of those defining themselves as working class.

Upwardly mobility was identified in terms of father's changing occupations. The one upwardly mobile father, a lift operator and electrician before the war, became a bank messenger after the war and gained bank manager status on retirement. His daughter K talks about him making the switch from blue to white collar worker and infers that the Masons may have been influential in this rise. The younger of two children, born and brought up in a council and later privately rented flat in the east of London, she describes her childhood as a time when her father was poorly paid. She recalls him having to work in the City during the day and clean the bank underneath their rented flat at night. This, she says, was necessary for the family's survival. K describes her father as 'a conventional working-class father', explaining that he would try and do everything for her. '*If I wanted a bike he would work overtime to get me a bike.*' Not all the women would see this as characteristic of 'a conventional working-class father'.

What was unique in this story is the part cultural activities play in signalling a person's class position: opera, ballet, piano lessons. K told me her parents, 'used to sing together and ... be at amateur dramatics' and that she had ballet and piano lessons. Such pursuits are not generally associated with a working-class life style though they do indicate a desire for upward social mobility, a mirroring of the middle classes. K ascribes these activities to the 'middle-classness' of her Italian mother, her cultural interests, which she acknowledges were unusual in a working-class family. '*We always had good music in the house ... we always had opera ... We always had that culture bit.*'

The upper-classness of opera is a very British notion. While K tells me that she did not think 'I'm poor', she did distinguish her family from others around her:

> There were a lot of people who were wealthy ... They lived in a different house to where I lived. They had big houses [laughs] ... I became aware of quite a high settlement of ... moneyed Jewish people ... Becoming aware of those kinds of differences ... When you don't live in a house, when you live in a flat ... you kind of perceive that difference.

Yet she was conscious of having things others did not. She recalls having a caravan when 'no-one else had a caravan in Devon' [laughs]. Her father's long working hours and her mother's 'nest egg' gained when her family's small asphalt business was sold, bought luxuries. She was also aware of being in rented accommodation, not private, a flat not a house, of having extras but not wealth. Money was, however, spent on sending her brother to private school – although the school was inappropriate for him. She notes the gender difference, a son's education took priority over a daughter's.

L grew up in private rented accommodation, in the east end of London. She tells me her parents came from 'families with money'; 'dad's relatives had 'loads of money' and mum's were 'very wealthy'. The parameters of this wealth are unclear. She believes that when her parents married they were disinherited, 'they didn't get a penny either of them.' As one of ten children, she described herself as growing up in conditions of extreme poverty, possibly a consequence of downward social mobility.

Looking closer – emerging indicators of social class positioning

Other traditional class indicators are evident in the stories we told of our childhood: parents' levels of education, housing conditions, health. All our parents were educated within the state education system. All but one received an elementary education, one a secondary education. They all left school at the age of fourteen so were restricted to the lowest end of the job market. With the exception of the father who had received three years of secondary education our parents worked in single-sex, unskilled, semi-skilled or skilled manual occupations. These were generally poorly paid dead-end jobs: labouring on building sites, the dockyards, in shipyards, factory work, domestic work, jobs done only by those who are the most financially insecure.

In terms of housing, we all began our early childhood in very cheap, privately rented accommodation and then moved into council housing or the lowest end of the private housing market, houses that only the working classes lived in. Overcrowded conditions, the lack of space and privacy were serious problems, ones which provoked family stress.

> I spent the first four years of my life in a derelict, ex-army Nissen hut in which my parents had squatted. It had no water, electricity or sanitation. We all slept in one room – my parents, my sister and I. When I was four, my parents bought a two-bedroomed house – with electricity, running water, an outside toilet, though no bathroom – in an inner city slum area. They were able to do this because my grandmother was the sitting tenant ... My sister and I continued to sleep in the same room as my parents until I was nine and she eleven. The other bedroom was occupied by my grandmother and younger brother.

> We were a family of twelve in four bedrooms. [Gran then] had to have one of the bedrooms, so that meant that we were all sort of shuffled around. I think most of us really resented it ... It caused a lot of family strain ... My whole childhood was bedrooms, millions of beds all squashed together.

> We were always overcrowded ... It's horrible ... you never had any privacy because you're all in the same room ... All our possessions were in cardboard boxes under the bed [parents and ten children in three bedrooms].

Health too is class-related. There is a direct correlation between health and people's level of wealth. At some stage in our childhood our mothers and fathers were highly likely to experience some kind of physical and/

or mental breakdown, manifesting itself in serious illnesses, drink problems, emotional withdrawal and depression; an outcome of their hard lives. As medical journals show, breakdowns continue to be a serious threat to health for many working-class people.

When recording our stories I was stunned by the frequency and severity of psychological and physical illness in our families and the huge impact this had on our lives. We can see this just by focusing on the nuclear families.

There was illness in my own family during my childhood in Coventry.

> My mother had tuberculosis when I was five and gave it to my baby brother. Both were taken into isolation wards. My sister and I went to live with an aunt and uncle who already had three children of their own. My grandma and my aunt's brother were also living with them in their small three-bed-roomed council house – six children and four adults.
>
> In the nine months she was in hospital I saw my mother once (behind a glass screen) and my father very occasionally. He was either working or at the hospital visiting my mother and brother. My mother came out of hospital after almost a year but was soon taken back in – for another three months – this time with yellow jaundice. My brother having developed meningitis, the treatment of which left him with epilepsy, remained in hospital. During this time my father developed pneumonia. He was off work for an extended period of time. My mother came out of hospital earlier than she should have to look after him, we three children and my sixty-year-old grandma. Because of money problems she also took on a job as a dinner-time bar-maid and continued with her evening job in a factory.

Other women told similar stories. R explained how her father had developed lumbago, then a slipped disc, and 'something happened to his neck'. This meant he was off work for 'a long time' and bringing no money into the home. She and her younger brother had both had polio and her younger brother had been temporarily paralysed. When she was nine her mother, who was working full-time as a cleaner and cook, had a nervous breakdown and went into hospital for six weeks. She tells me she, 'was sent to live with one family relative' and her younger brother 'sent to live with somebody else'. Her father worked long hours in a cement factory and so they saw little of him or each other.

B tells the story of her mother breaking down:

> A social worker thought it would be best if my dad's mother, who was badly bedridden, came out of hospital ... So my mum, at forty, with three kids under five ... the youngest six weeks old, moved into this flat with my bedridden grandma and she looked after her for two years.

Taking grandma was the condition of being given a council flat. Older working-class women had little means of supporting themselves. Her mother, not surprisingly, was unable to manage and she (aged 6) and her sister (aged 5) were temporarily sent from their home in South East London to a convent in Canterbury, a good way away – to ease the burden. Her parents made one visit.

K recalls being taken into an isolation hospital with meningitis when she was 8 or 9. She tells me, 'you were paralysed'. When she was 11 her mother, who had been 'incapacitated or ill for most of her life', died from a spinal injury acquired in her teens. She was 'in her thirties'.

Insiders learning about being fathers and mothers in working-class homes

> You can hear your parents in you [head] ... they're part of you aren't they.

One cannot talk about the women in this study – or working-class girls in general – without seeing class as a lived experience within the family. As young girls we experience the psychological and physical impact class has on our parents and our own lives. So we must set our educational experiences in this context to develop an understanding of home/school incongruities, so often spoken about but rarely analysed in texts. In the pages ahead, I try to explore our perceptions of fathers and mothers as central figures in our experience of working-class family life and as role models for the style of life we were destined to inherit.

The family is a notoriously difficult area of research. The women knew relatively little about their family history. As R states, 'It's what I don't know that is fascinating'. Working-class families do not keep historical records of their lives to pass on to future generations. Sources of information such as diaries, biographies, family portraits are not usually available. Our grandparents – a valuable source of information – tended to die at an early age. Those that lived on often preferred to forget rather than recall much of their earlier lives. As a consequence we have limited knowledge of what life was really like for our parents, grandparents, great-grandparents.

Learning about working-class men from our fathers: the 'good providers'

Working-class men as good providers: myth or reality? Official views of working-class families have traditionally been based on the father's position in the home.

> The authority of the working-class father within the household has been established as a tenet of cultural criticism, with Richard Hoggart, for instance, remarking in 1957 that 'the point of departure for an understanding of the position of the working-class father in his home, is that he is the boss there, the 'master of his own house". (Steedman, 1986, pp.72-73)

The implied authority of fathers in working-class homes is closely related to the notion of a family dependant on a man who is the breadwinner. We were brought up in families where it was accepted that it was the man's role to provide for women and children, his women and children. The laws and practices of the time, which, for instance, insisted that the homes, rented or mortgaged, could only be in the man's name, reinforced this position of authority. Women had no rights to the home.

We knew even as young children that our fathers, despite disliking what they were doing, worked hard mostly in factories, docks, on building sites. We talked about them 'working all the time' doing shift work, or labouring on building sites six days a week and sometimes twelve hours a day. This was true also for K's father who had a non-manual job ... '*All he seemed to do was work, I don't remember anything else ...*'

However, when your only income is through selling your labour – usually physical – and you are employed in the lowest paid and most unstable end of the job market, being a breadwinner or provider is an identity rather than a reality. Few working-class men were in occupations that paid enough or were secure enough to provide adequately for a family on a regular basis. Being a provider, therefore, was more about being in regular, full-time work, particularly at a time when work was short; working overtime at every opportunity and being seen to spend all your money on the family. One could be a good provider yet still not bring sufficient money into the home.

As children we grew up with the notion that our fathers were good providers. This was the image our mothers promoted. Only as adults did we question it.

> I learnt that despite my mother working my father was the provider, even though there were times when he earned nothing because he was seriously ill, temporarily laid off, or out of work. At these times he did not provide – my mother fulfilled this role.
>
> During my childhood I do recall him handing over his weekly wages (and all the responsibilities with it) to my mother who'd give him back pocket money and bus fares to work.

Handing over one's wages without any deductions was seen to be a marker of a 'good husband' in working-class families (Roberts, 1984, p.110). Although we believed father was 'a good provider', there is ambiguity in these beliefs. '*He'd spend [his] entire money on the rest of us and do without himself*', said one woman. Later, she said, '*If he hadn't been drinking we wouldn't have been so hard up ... He'd go on big binges ... he just drinks and drinks ... He'd always be first to the bar ... taken advantage of.*'

The same conflict appears in B's story. Her mother tells her that father was 'a good provider', but now she queries this: '*I can remember that not always being true ... I can remember his giving his weekly money. Sometimes it was as little as £2.00. That was not a lot in those days.*'

On one level it is true that our fathers were providers. They went to work, worked full-time, worked over-time when possible and earned more than working-class wives. Their provision, however, was rarely adequate or secure.

It is also true our fathers were discontented with their working lives and would have liked a lot more from life. L spoke of her downwardly mobile father at 14 having '*to go into the [family bakery] business ... It's often the way in Jewish families*', she states. She recalls that he *'went to work up to ... about seventy and resented every day of it*'. He was 'bright' and had wanted to do something else but he could not. As a consequence, she tells me, 'there's a lot of frustration there.' J spoke of her father going 'straight into an apprenticeship' through 'connections', and trying to educate himself further.

He's sort of like self-taught. He read a lot and he's very into history and geography and all and he even took himself off to night classes to do 'O' level English Language, which he never got.

Only K's upwardly mobile father improved his job prospects. At 11 he had won a scholarship and went to a secondary school, though he still had to leave at 14 'to go to work'. His daughter describes him as 'a very clever bloke', though she adds, 'He didn't realise he was bright.' She explains:

He wasn't academically bright ... You'd want something for a crossword and he'd know, something really obscure, that knowledge that comes from working-class men who avidly read Reader's Digest ... It's all that stuff, that body of knowledge that you don't get from anywhere else [laughs].

Years later he worked his way up to a managerial role in a bank. Her memory of him is one of him 'trying to prove himself'.

In the home

The majority of men believed that they proved their masculinity by never doing any domestic chore which could be construed as belonging to the sphere of women. (Roberts, 1984, p.116)

The instability of the male as provider did not affect the division of labour in our homes. We grew up in homes where it was taken for granted that men (whether fathers or brothers), the designated family providers, were waited upon by women (mothers and daughters) even if not in work and even when wives and daughters worked full-time.

Other than wash up occasionally, my father did nothing in the home during my childhood, despite the fact that my mother worked and despite the fact that at times he brought no income into the home.

He just went out to work and he provided for his family ... Just sort of there like comfortable; mum did ... everything. He never had any responsibilities ... When you look at it from her point of view his responsibility was to provide money, even at a stage when he stopped doing that ... He's been lazy really, he's sort of sat back and let her do everything.

It is true that our fathers, cast in the role of 'providers', opted out of offering their physical labour in the home by cleaning, shopping, cooking, child-care, but were they masters of the home?

Male dependency manifest as control, being 'the boss'

> If a man wasn't the 'boss' of the home 'he wasn't considered to be a man'. (Bourke, 1994, p.72)

I would argue that the strong division of roles in working-class families helped males cover up their dependency on women, a sign of weakness in working-class communities. Opting out of taking responsibility in the home, being on the periphery of the family physically and emotionally, masked our fathers' dependency on our mothers. Though I grew up with this model of male behaviour, it is only now that I realise my father had an investment in not taking responsibility. His physical helplessness in the home was feigned.

Another woman views her father's current behaviour now in a similar way. She tells me: '*Dad sort of he just drives the car ... he allows it to happen because it suits him ... He was just there in the background.*'

She says about her mother: '*she's carried him*' while '*he worked and provided the money*' and adds that although they had '*quite a strong relationship*' it was '*only because mum was prepared to shoulder everything ... She's done everything for him all along.*'

She recalls how when there were only seven children still at school, her mother started work:

> I always remember the first night she went, dad sat in that corner like this [gestures] ... and he missed her so much ... He doesn't know what to do with himself ... he just sits there looking very sad and miserable, mopes, grumps.

K watched her father 'completely cracking up' when her mother died when she was 11. Whereas previously he had been a distant man, he suddenly became emotionally demanding. He would, '*physically cry, fall apart, want you desperately just as a physical comfort ... Yet he'd never been like that before ... no personal dialogue, no emotional interaction.*' But the emotional barrier went up again immediately – he remarried six months later and quickly had another child. She recalls him saying, just before he died, '*Oh, you'll have to forgive me, I've always been so sentimental*', to which she now says: '*He was but ... the way he's dealt with it is by being very, you know, he's put the wall up ... so you didn't get emotion, otherwise he'd just collapse.*'

We talked about dependency among the current generation of our working-class families.

> My brother-in-law had told my sister he'd kill her if she left him. At the time, I felt there was an element of truth in this.
>
> Oh my brother says that ... used to follow my sister-in-law around ... I don't think she ever goes out on her own ... She couldn't speak to a neighbour, he'd sort of end up smashing the neighbours ... It was at that level ... that insecure.

Underneath these threats lies male dependency.

Other women became aware of their fathers' dependency when their mothers started to claim some independence. B recalls her mother saying that her father did not speak to her for months. Why? He had found out that she had been to the pictures with his sister. As Beatrix Campbell has pointed out, 'working-class men would not stand for a woman running around and doing things on her own' (1984, p.73). When the children had grown up and left, one father was full of disbelief when his wife flew off to Italy and America with her sister and brother-in-law. He refused to go. '*Up to the minute she got on the plane he did not believe that she would go without him*', his daughter tells me. On her return he was at the airport with bunches of flowers.

'They play such a small part in our life'

> The folklore of father/daughter relations ... asserts that there is a fondness, affection, a doting and even covetous attitude on the part of fathers towards daughters ... (Arcana, 1984, p.121)

A point of commonality in our stories is our fathers' physical and emotional unavailability and our inability to communicate with them, particularly as we reached our teens. The women talked about their fathers always being at work so I assumed they would feel that fathers were fairly insignificant in their lives.

> To me fathers (men) were physically and emotionally unavailable people. Because he was working very long hours, I hardly ever saw my father. When he was at home he positioned himself on the periphery of the family and for much of the time engrossed himself in a newspaper, or the television. It was as if he wasn't there. When I was fourteen I once had to travel alone on a bus with him. The uncomfortableness of the silence between us haunts me even now.

My mother would indeed say, 'I'll tell your father'. She was, as Juliet Mitchell (1975) has pointed out, referring to a 'symbolic father'. 'Fathers', as one of the women states, 'played such a small part in our lives'. So I was surprised when they appeared to be such central figures in the women's stories of childhood. In the case of one woman this was understandable; her relationship with her father was a fairly positive one. She describes him as '*Always in the background. He never came to the fore ... quite shy and sort of laid back ... [The girls] could always go and have a weep on his shoulder.*'

Like my father, her father was a man in the 'background'. She described him as 'shy', 'laid back', but someone whose shoulder you could 'weep on' if you were a girl. This softness was absent in the other father/daughter relationships. But there was also another side to the man: '*He never hit us really. Now and again he used to make a half-hearted attempt. When he did lose his temper, which wasn't very often ... you'd just disappear.*'

This other side is revealed also in her description of him as someone who was a '*blinkered Catholic ... It's black or white, there's very little grey'*, and someone who '*rants and raves and gets really up-tight about everything ... the police and the army and the Protestants and the this and the that.*'

My father repressed his emotions; hers seems to have projected his feelings onto the outside world. Some fathers project their aggressive feelings and emotions onto members of their family. This could be mistaken for being master of one's home.

Father was central in the other women's stories simply because of their negative childhood relationship.

> I hate my dad – I think he's evil ... he's a dictator, he's a tyrant. Didn't hit us ... it's verbal bullying with my dad ... [I have] visions of him sitting in a chair screaming at you all the time, especially my brother ... [He] screamed abuse all the time ... I just used to shake.

L acknowledges that her father 'was often very nice' to the outside world but as far as she was concerned, 'he was weak, self-absorbed and totally selfish.'

The fathers' aggression would emerge when daughters challenged their male authority. B perceived her early childhood relationship with her father as friendly but recalls that between the ages of 12 to 14 she came to see him as 'mentally cruel'. She remembers her first 'big blow-up':

> I didn't want to wake up ... I think it was too much of a shock and too hurtful ... I can remember going to bed ... and crying because of what he'd said and thinking, if only I didn't have to get up.

She mentions two specific incidents. The first was when her father gave her two sisters the money for an ice cream but not her. '*I found that very, very hurtful*', she tells me, and adds, '*He just didn't like me ... It didn't take long before ... I would go back ... I saw them [her parents] doing it all the time. They used to argue quite violently.*' The second incident occurred when father took on a domestic role:

> We'd gone to mass ... he'd cooked our breakfast ... I hated his cooking ... he never did it right ... I said ... 'Oh I'm not eating that the egg's cooked too much ... why did you have to do it'.

She reflects on the incident, '*I must have been very nasty ... that must of hurt him ... He came back at me ... as now, I would expect*'.

The depth of this father/daughter rift is revealed when the mother and daughters left her father. Her sisters (16 and 12) visited their father 'almost every night'; she aged 17 did not. She '*didn't go back once, didn't want to and couldn't understand why they were doing it ... I couldn't have done it and I shouldn't think he wanted me there anyway.*'

B links her father's aggression with drink, observing the '*cruelty came out more and more when he was drunk*'. '*He would go ... on and on*'. His routine, she tells me, was to '*come home from the pub and go to bed and get up and have a meal and go out again*' with drinking friends. When sober he was 'very withdrawn and very quiet', and spent 'a great deal of time in bed'.

Another woman had a similarly stormy relationship with her father. This started in early childhood.

> I've odd memories as a child where I actually threw things at him and he ... picked up some of my toys off the floor and threw them in the fire because they shouldn't have been there ... I picked up his newspaper and set fire to

> it [laughs] ... He'd say, 'How dare you! Vera, come and control this girl of yours.'

In such instances, she tells me, '*He'd clobber me ... or I'd run away and hide from him ... When he was drunk ... he'd hit out in anger and he'd strap us.*' She adds, '*He wasn't an easy person to live with for the vast majority of our childhood ... bad tempered ogre.*' It is of some significance that she also says, '*I don't think we had it any worse than a lot of kids had at that time*'. To be hit, even strapped, was seen as the norm.

She also talks about her fathers' drinking 'loosening his tongue',

> [He] finds it very difficult to express what he wants, unless he's fairly blotto ... He just rambles on, you can't shut him up.
>
> If he came in while we were still up, he'd become argumentative ... Most of the time we just left him and went to bed ... We had that sort of pattern with him during most of the period I can remember. Just a thoroughly bloody pain in the neck.

The intensity of the rows, highlighted when, for instance, neighbours called the police out 'on more than one occasion' and father 'in a drunken stupor' hitting her mother 'with such force ...' before he 'conked out ... sozzled on the floor.' After this attack on her mother when she was 18 she recalls telling him: '*if you ever put a finger on my mother it'll be the last thing you ever do ... You wouldn't have touched her if I'd been in the house*'. His reply, she tells me, was, '*No because you'd have picked up the nearest knife and put it in me.*' She adds, '*He knew I would have done it*'.

Fathers' attempts to control their daughters' sexuality

The area where the father's control over his daughter emerged at its strongest concerned their daughter's developing sexuality. As daughters moved into their teens, gender inequality in this area peaked. While this was when fathers emotionally distanced themselves, it was also the time daughters felt most constrained.

J, who felt she had a close relationship with her father, was aware she 'could never really talk to him'. She linked this realisation to her sexual development:

> It was the whole sex thing that ruined all of that ... He wanted to know what was wrong and I just couldn't have told him in a million years ... As far as I was concerned that was taboo.

My own father who was very quiet man, remained a distant figure but I became aware in my early teens that he was guardian of his daughters' virginity. A working-class girl's virginity was still an exchange commodity in the 1950s and 60s and attitudes towards premarital sex were condemnatory. There was some reason for concern. Working-class daughters did get pregnant very young and were more likely to give birth than their middle-class counterparts, just as today. This was true in our families. Only now that the numbers of very young mothers has increased has it become a concern to government.

I had far more freedom than most other women I knew, particularly those who were only or eldest daughters. The fact that my parents lived together without a marriage certificate – my mother having been briefly married before – and we three children were classified 'illegitimate' (more family secrets), may or may not, have influenced matters. Two of the women who were the only daughters had very severe limitations placed on them. One explains:

> He was using every conceivable means to stop me from getting out of the house ... was obsessed with [me] not coming into contact with boys ... I mean this was a joke seeing most of my family are made of men and boys ... They were alright because they were family ... He obviously just presumed I would just be led ... I would just end up pregnant.

Her birth, the reason for her father and mother marrying when they did, may have been at the root of her father's anxiety. She tells me that he had wanted to bring her up 'how girls were brought up in Eastern Europe when he was last there [pre-war]'. When she was 16, he was demanding that she be home by half past nine. Aged 18 and home from teacher training college, he'd tell her to 'make sure you're back in this house at eleven o'clock'. The irony was that in her teens she had locked her father out at night when he came home drunk.

K was defiant.

> I used to go through hell ... I was quite old, 15, 16; I'd have to be in at ten o'clock ... If something finished at half past ten, or eleven, most parents

> used to say, 'when it's finished I'll come and pick you up', he'd come at nine, half past nine...
>
> It completely backfired ... because I'd just make sure that ... whatever I couldn't do after ten o'clock I'd do before and I just used to lie, outrageous lies. I'd say I was baby-sitting round a friend's.

The notion of your father coming to 'pick you up' is totally alien to me and to at least one other of the women.

Though not discussed at length here, there were other ways in which fathers tried to take ownership of their daughters' sexuality which were violations of a daughter, not protection. I was taken aback when one of the women told me her father had said to her, 'come outside for five minutes I'll show you what it's all about.' Her response was, 'I knew what he meant. I just ignored him, he was always saying vile things.' In other stories issues of sexual abuse were raised – more family secrets – partly as a consequence of living in overcrowded homes.

Blaming or understanding our fathers

> ... the majority of us excuse them, make allowances for them. (Arcana, 1984, p.121)

As daughters we are critical of our fathers. L blamed her father for the fact that her mother became pregnant every couple of years, '*As far as I'm concerned that is my dad's responsibility and no-one can take that away*'. Two blamed their fathers for spending money on drink, as this brought increased poverty and shame. At the same time daughters could be all-forgiving, tolerant and self-blaming. Looking at our fathers' lived experiences and relating them to society's demands of, and impact on them, enables us to see their behaviour during our childhood in a social context. It helps us understand that blame does not lie solely with the individual. This is important when you belong to a social class that has a history of being exploited.

It is mothers who defend the fathers, telling their daughters of the fathers' hard lives: neglect, violence, poverty, persecution. My mother told me my father was beaten as a child, that his father was a gambler and alcoholic who spent most of his time away working on building sites. And that as a young teenager he was left by his mother. At 18 he went off to war. Another of the women knew much more about her father's earlier life; again from her mother. Her Eastern European father – whose own father had died when he was a child – was 'taken away from his mother [by German soldiers] screaming', at the age of 16, and sent to fight 'on the front line'. He never saw his mother again. When she was in her late teens the family got enough money together to travel to visit the mother's grave, ten years after she had died. She remarks:

> for the first time I realised what a trauma it had been for him, seeing his reactions at her grave-side ... to never be able to discuss that, because he didn't actually see his brothers and sister until she died ... For years and years when he was drunk he would get very maudlin about his mother ... He would be crying about ... how he never got to say goodbye to her ... she was the only person who loved him and understood him and none of us did and we didn't really care for him anyway, why didn't he run back ... and so on ... Huge psychological traumas.

She adds, then 'there was all the things that went on in the war which I know very little about', and the bigotry in England ...

> All the trauma of coming to an alien country, not being able to speak the language ... and the bigotry they had to contend with settling in England ... where people were trying to change their names.

In addition several of the fathers experienced persecution at work. When talking about her father, L tells me:

> I think he got quite persecuted when he was young for being Jewish and my dad was a coward ... I think my dad didn't keep it up [his Jewish religion] because he was frightened of people knowing he was Jewish. He didn't move into a Jewish area. No he took himself right out so that he was ostracised from everybody, which is quite strange because usually immigrants stick together.

One Catholic father was working in what was 'very much ... a Protestant ... stronghold', a shipyard left due to intimidation. His daughter remembers:

> It got to the stage where it was just so difficult, 'cause he's not really very brave' ... Once the tension got to him ... all these insinuations and intimidations and everything, he just left ... Quite difficult for him to take really.

Whereas these fathers' 'opt out' of conflict – which their daughters see as a sign of weakness – another father breaks down. His daughter links this to his inability to 'take teasing' and his 'very low opinion of himself'. R tells me, 'He calls himself an ignorant man.' In adulthood she has tried to help him.

> I've tried to make him see that if he could actually try and talk things through when he was sober he'd be able to try and solve a lot of the problems, but he just keeps things bottled up inside him.

In working-class communities 'it's not the man's thing to do, is it, to unburden yourself', she says. As a member of the family and, as an individual, she holds herself responsible for her father's poor self-image.

> We didn't understand ... we weren't terribly sympathetic ... We have probably made him feel this [low self-esteem] ... as part of the family ... [I] would hurl ... abuse at him. 'If you were a more educated civilised person' ... I meant it, [I had] no hesitation in saying things like that ... She [mother] always said to me my problem is that I don't understand him.

K explains her father's negative behaviour in terms of the pressures he faced.

> He used to get up at half-past-five, travel all the way to London, do his full job there, come back and then he would ... do his second job ... and he had a wife who was always ill ... Apart from anything else, it's bloody tough working. You don't have time for luxuries ... It's a luxury in'it ... worrying about psychological and emotional welfare.

She is right: emotional and psychological welfare was a luxury. In many working-class families it would still be thought self-indulgent. Just before his death, K's father asked her to forgive him for hitting her.

> He broke down ... He asked me to forgive him about it ... He said, 'I only hit you once ... please forgive me' ... I did ... but he didn't only hit me once, but it was the one time that he'd remembered ... I think he realised that being that strict was, I would say, the wrong thing to do.

Though she believed he was wrong to be so strict with her, she both forgives and justifies his behaviour.

> At the time they had a young baby, they wanted to sleep at night ... On reflection, I suppose the last thing they wanted was to wake up to some bloody daughter.

It is worth noting that few brothers shared their sisters' desire to forgive their fathers.

Learning from our mothers what life as a working-class woman entailed

As far as we were aware, we were to inherit our mother's lives, yet we spoke about them far less than about our fathers, even though we felt we knew them better. They and other working-class women around us were our role models, the only women (other than schoolteachers) we really met in childhood. We talked about their lack of educational and employment opportunities and the constraints placed on them by marriage and motherhood. We sympathised with the hardness of their lives, their relative powerlessness, and wondered whether things would have been different had they had been born in another era, or married someone else.

Education and work – missed opportunities

Even the mothers who did well in school were denied secondary education. Severe economic and social constraints forced them into what, traditionally, was seen as 'women's work', summed up by my mother as 'dirty work', 'boring work'. Our mothers cooked, cleaned, worked in factories or for the National Health Service caring for others – jobs only the working classes do, low-paid, often temporary or part-time and with no career opportunities and few employment rights.

At 14 my own mother worked in a weaving factory. When I was young she worked an evening shift in an electrical goods factory, cutting wires. In my teens, she was working in a pub at nights and weekends. Other mothers had taken on cleaning, shop work, 'hard work in factories – never anything skilled or specialised'. They accepted these 'fairly boring things just to bring the money in', poorly paid though they were. Working-class female respondents in Beatrix Campbell's (1984) *Wigan Pier* did the same. Only R's mother furthered her elementary education in later life, training for a typing/clerical post. She became highly committed to caring for people – in a mentally-handicapped people's home – another common route for working-class women. Another 'worked nights' and 'weekends' as a 'pink lady': 'auxiliaries that help the nurse'. She, 'was in her element', 'she loved it', J told me. It has been argued that working-class family life prepares women for low-status, low-paid caring roles demanding high levels of personal commitment. It is an extension of working-class women's role in the family (See Taylor, 1979; Campbell, 1984; Bates, 1993). The jobs our mothers took depended upon and exploited their labour and at the same time ensured that working-class women could never be economically independent.

'You had no choice' – marriage, motherhood and family secrets

> Didn't want her she [already] had nine children.
>
> You ... didn't have an illegitimate child; you married. You had no choice.

The women in our families were not expected to be providers, despite at times being the only providers. Instead, their central role was that of housewife and child bearer and carer. The social pressure to get married and have children was immense. Any other kind of behaviour was seen as abnormal. Indeed, deviations became family secrets. Those of us with mothers who bore children out of wedlock know this information to be a well-kept family secret. When, as middle-aged adults, we women asked our mothers why we were not told this information – gleaned from other relatives – they told us our fathers wanted the secret kept. R observed the moral code: '*You just didn't have an illegitimate child ... you married*'. You did not leave or divorce a husband either. The family controlled its own members. My mother for instance talked of her Uncle George marrying a woman who had been married before and how the family 'called this woman everything' and that she 'wasn't ever really admitted to the family'.

Once married, working-class women were destined to spend much of their lives child-rearing. My mother had three children – three too many, she would say. She told my sister and me many times throughout our childhood and adulthood, 'You had no choice in them days', and that, given a choice, she would not have had children at all.

One mother, a strict Catholic, had twelve children, 'one every eighteen months'. Recently she acknowledged her resentment to her daughter, who tells me, 'I know she does resent having all those children [but] it was interesting for her to admit it.' It is of some significance then that, when one of her younger daughters got pregnant, this mother tried to persuade her not to marry, despite her strong religious beliefs.

> As far as mum was concerned the damage had been done ... She could be swallowed up into the family; she didn't have to marry him. Everything would be OK.

The issue of women having to have too many children was raised by another of the women in the group, who talked about her mother's desire to have her tenth child aborted – another social taboo,

> My mum was having a baby every couple of years right the way through ... I can remember when my sister was conceived which was accidentally really ... she wasn't having any more. She asked the doctor for an abortion ... She didn't want her, she had nine children. She went to the doctor ... men in power it is. He said no ... she was in her change ... it's criminal.

Her mother 'nearly dies' giving birth to this baby. Fathering children was seen as proof of manhood in working-class communities. Control apparently lay in the hands of 'men in positions of power': fathers, husbands, doctors, priests, employers. For our mothers, their inadequate education, marriage, children, economic dependency on a man, added to by low-paid, low-status work all seemed inevitable – things over which they had scant control. Individually and collectively, these factors hugely constrained their lives, as in their own mothers' lives. Any deviation from this norm – remaining single, cohabiting, leaving one's husband, getting divorced, having an abortion or an illegitimate child, was strictly taboo, and so was having a formal education and a career. In working-class families we learn that this is our inheritance as working-class girls.

Hard lives for generations of working-class women

> She had a really hard life. (grandmother)

> It was hell. (mother)

An area of commonality in our stories was the hardness of our mothers' and grandmothers' lives, both in childhood and adulthood and this has been expressed by other working-class women. Grandmothers died in childbirth – one died in her mid-twenties giving birth to a fifth daughter. The grandfather remarried and fathered eight more children. This mother was then one of thirteen children. There was 'great hardship' in the family, says R. K's mother also lost her mother in childhood when she was giving birth to a fifth child. The Italian grandfather then married his wife's sister, 'keeping it in the family'.

A number of our grandmothers had no male provider and brought up their children on their own. J's granmother took care of thirteen grandchildren when one of her daughters died of cancer. My father's mother, who had ten children, left her husband but took some of the children with her – the rest living with the eldest daughter. My mother's mother brought up three children on her own. Her father, who had been too ill to work since my mother was 5, died six years later. Little money came into either home. Another of the women's mothers – one of five children – lost her father as a child. He was put in a mental home after an accident (another family secret).

Our mothers (like our fathers) were brought up in families where life was hard. They too went on to create their own families in which life was hard, a consequence of the continuing poverty trap. L speaking about her mother's life raising ten children, says, 'Her life was, I think, awful.' Another woman describes her mother's life as 'hell'. She tells me, 'She had a really hard life.' She recalls a time in her childhood when her mother, with five young children, spent nine months living in an old farm labourer's cottage while the father worked away and visited on weekends:

> A scullery ... no bigger than this table ... with a sink and my poor mother... Jesus! It must have been hell ... There was no washing facilities ... there was no running water ... the pump was ... up the road.

She recalls that when she was 13 her mother had to manage on her own again, now with twelve children. Her father had gone to England to find work. It was his 14-year-old daughter, not his wife, who wrote, '*Come home ... mum ... [is] finding it difficult to cope*'.

It is interesting that educated working-class men have not talked about working-class women's oppression. This aspect has been ignored while virtues have been romanticised.

Working-class mothers in the home

'The story of the working-class mother's domestic power is present in many literary and sociological sources' (Kohn, 1971, pp.323-338). We challenge that story,

> That romantic bit in working-class circles ... that ... covers up the discrimination or the difference between males and females ... The idea that the women are really in control ... When you actually look at it and go into detail ... 'what power do they have?' Usually ... in very limited sorts of areas.

The attribution of power in the home to working-class women is historical. It usually refers to their dominant role in organising the household, child-rearing, and controlling the finances. Looking at working-class women's role in the home between 1890-1950 Elizabeth Roberts noted that the areas where women exerted significant power were moral and economic control (1984, p.110), powers which were all exercised firmly in the perceived interest of their families. But it could also be argued that women's responsibility for such matters has arisen from working-class men's lack of interest or irresponsibility, rather than from the dominance of working-class women.

In our texts there is plenty of evidence of mothers exercising control in the home, but is this a demonstration of their power? As a child I saw my mother as extremely powerful. For instance, she controlled the money and made all the day-to-day financial decisions. What appeared to be power was really control. K's text contains examples of the control her mother and stepmother exercised in the home. For instance, she recalled an aunt telling her, 'God your mother was so fussy around the house.' An obsessively clean and tidy house is a form of control (Chernin, 1985). About her stepmother she says, '*She was so regimented that you knew every night what you were going to have to eat ... Tuesday you had that and Wednesday that.*' Dictating what will be eaten and when is another form of control being played out.

Discipline, as administered by mothers, was also centred on control. L talks about her mother's 'rigidity' and 'coldness' and its impact on her. She tells me:

> My mum was rigid – if she said something ... she couldn't change it ... it would be 'do as you're told or out' ... You'd get belted when you were young, 'um I think you were beaten into submission ... We'd all go to bed with the light off and we'd all do this for that reason ... There were always threats hanging over your head. You had no power over anything you did, it was survival.

Interestingly, she suggests her mother's behaviour, '*might of been her way of coping, that those were the only rules that she could actually live by*'.

Another daughter describes her mother as the disciplinarian. She gives the example of one of her sisters being caught smoking at school. She tells me, '*I can remember us all being lined up coming home from school*' and added, '*Mum was always yelling at yer and cuffing you and smacking you and all that sort of thing. She did all the discipline.*'

Two women talked about their mothers having strict control over their attendance at church. One tells of her mother's rigid insistence, '*As far as she's concerned ... her duty as a Catholic mother is to bring her children up in the Catholic faith*'. She insisted on their going to church while they lived at home, even as adults. Going to church was linked with courting respectability. It divided you from the rougher working-classes. 'Respectability', Beatrix Campbell observes, 'has been crucial in the control of women, their domestication, dependency and subordination' (1984, p.220).

In our homes, respectability was sought in various ways: having a clean home; being a good money manager; disciplining your children; attending church. These are the areas mothers tried to control. There were other elements too: for instance, never being hit by your husband, never letting others know your business. One woman recalls an incident where her older brother lost his temper with her and her sister while her parents were out. There was so much noise, she says, that, '*the next door neighbour thought dad had been beating mum up*'. She describes her mother's reaction:

> Anything rather than let the neighbour know what was going on and she was so devastated ... 'and your father's never ever raised... his hand to me' ... My poor ... mum crying ... I'd never ever seen her cry before.

The status of the housewife was linked to maintaining the privacy of her home (Bourke, 1996). The issue of women as controllers and controlled is perhaps best illustrated by looking at aspects of the mother's power in relation to father. When we do this, ambiguities start to emerge. Strengths that often arise out of desperate and frustrating situations could be interpreted as evidence of power. Take one woman's account of her mother's attempts both to gain and maintain power when dealing with her husband's drink problem. She would say, 'If he can't make it upstairs' that's his problem.' She 'would try ... berating him'. She would lock 'the drink away'. She would get 'totally exasperated'. She would 'leave him to find his own way home'. Were these acts of empowerment or of control and self-protection? It was when he was drunk that he hit her.

This seemingly powerless woman with 'a very mild sort of demeanour' found within herself the power to defend this same man from working-class male colleagues at the factory. Father had felt he was being persecuted at work and had begun to break down. It was mother who *'went to the people involved and tackled them about it ... Left them in no uncertain terms that they either put up, or shut up*', her daughter tells me. This was not the act of a powerless woman, rather it exemplified the double-bind working-class women find themselves in. Their understanding of the impossible demands society places on working-class men is influential in their acceptance and tolerance of undesirable behaviour in the home and their defence of the man outside the home.

This ambiguity appears in another story of the mother/father's power relationship. Although there is evidence of her father behaving aggressively:

> My mum and dad used to argue all the time ... my dad used to hit her ... I can remember him hitting her when she was pregnant, I can remember her storming out into the night ...

there is also evidence of her mother doing so. She recalls her mother

> ... standing there with a rolling pin ... and hitting him [her father] over the head ... I can't remember what happened, but I do have that image in my head of her waiting behind the door.

Her mother, she tells me, 'was frightened'.

B recalled that her mother once told her how lonely she was; a consequence of her father's control and jealousy. 'She found that really difficult. Her actual words were something like "coming from such a big family".' Evidence of her feelings of powerlessness and perhaps desperation can be found in the way the mother uses the father's treatment of his daughters not of herself as a means of chastising him when he is drunk. '*You've got three lovely daughters and you come home and behave like this.*'

This lonely, seemingly powerless woman does, nevertheless, take her three young daughters on holiday on her own, albeit to a place she has been to before. Father 'would never come, he would stay at home, or come for the day', his daughter tells me. She also leaves him, if only for six months, '*We came home from school one night and he'd been drunk and particularly bad and ... she said get your things we're going*'.

Our working-class mothers, though placed in economically, socially and politically subordinate positions, were often able to summon up a range of strengths which enabled them to have *some* control – at least in the home. One strategy was to take the caring role to the extreme: to become a 'martyr'.

K describes her stepmother as 'a martyr'. She ...

> married someone who she knew was dying ... one of these martyrish women [laughs], takes on lost causes ... She takes on this bloke with two neurotic kids ... If you were to say to her 'what do you want to do?' ... she'll say, 'I don't mind dear I want to do what makes your father happy'. I'd never know what she wanted ... 'as long as your father's happy that's all I want'.

The notion of mother as a martyr is also revealed in other stories:

> She collects waifs and strays. Ever since I can remember we've had a hanger-on, somebody who hasn't got anybody else ... all women ... all ... had no-one else to go to ... They're usually unmarried ... women who've been looking after old parents ... Old school teachers that everybody else hated, she'd end up looking after them.

One could argue that being a martyr, being indispensable, collecting others around you symbolises a dependency on and therefore a need for control of others.

'Where else could they go?' – marrying the wrong man

We inherited conflicting messages about women and marriage. As one woman states, women 'are fed that it's in their interest to get married' but 'when you look at the alternatives ...' they are limited and 'the only significance it has is that it has made them ... against all evidence ... see it as a safety haven'.

The message J received from her mother about marriage was that '*It's the woman that has to give if you want your marriage to succeed. You're just gonna have to give*'. If you are not '*prepared to give ... well it won't succeed ... It's that sort of simple and she's very matter of fact about it*', her daughter tells me. I was fed the message 'if you do not have children the man will leave you'. Other women in this study received other messages. Some, aware of their mother's unhappiness, believed the problem was simply that mother had married the wrong man. Two tell me that when they were children they couldn't understand why their mothers did not leave. B tells me:

> I always saw my mum and dad as very ill matched. She was, I think, fairly plain ... nothing out of the ordinary. He, I think, was probably a womaniser, quite attractive ... had something about him and that's the only reason I can see for her wanting to marry him ... I used to have a go at her and say, 'Why don't you leave him, why can't we go somewhere else?'

There was no choice over who should be the one to leave because, as she indignantly points out, '*The flat was in his name and my mum ... had no rights at all.*' The only place for a working-class woman with children to go was to her family, generally her mother. Her 60-year-old mother plus her three daughters aged 11 to 17 did move out for six months. She moved into her own mother's small council flat nearby where they all slept in one bedroom, '*I don't know what else she could have done*' (See also, Campbell, 1984, p.73) Judith Arcana writing about working-class mothers, noted: '... 'aware of their own disenfranchisement' they related to their daughter's situation' (1984, p.163).

They return to the father's home because 'Money is short'. From then on '*They never spoke as friends ... It was always very formal and uncomfortable, but there weren't any arguments*'.

R tells me,

> You'd never get her to say it ... because she's a very loyal person ... Had she been born in a different era, like the era we were born, she'd have been better educated she was born to better things ... I think ... she'd have married somebody connected with academia ... and have lived a more cultural life. I could see her marrying a doctor ... she's a very caring person.

She felt that her mother – one of thirteen children – was 'born to better things', a better life than a working-class man could offer her. The lack of educational opportunities for working-class people of her era had prevented her from achieving the middle-class life style to which her daughter felt she was more suited. Although people usually married within their class group, education could widen a working-class girl's opportunities by enabling economic independence or by increasing her chances of marriage to a non-working-class man.

R's views about her mother staying in her marriage are conflictual. She tells me, '*Certainly, had I been in her situation, I'd have walked out years earlier*' and recalls, in her early teens, suggesting to her mother that they leave her father. Her mother's response at the time was, '*Where else would we go?*' She also recalls talking her mother out of leaving when she was 15 for the same reason. '*[She] actually talked about leaving him and I, 'This is amazing to me', I actually stopped her and said ... 'Where were we going to go?*' In a more recent conversation with her mother the issue of women and 'where else is there to go' emerges again,

> Somebody we knew was periodically being beaten up by her husband and periodically went back to him ... and I was saying 'What a stupid woman! Why doesn't she take the kids and go. In this day and age she doesn't have to put up with that.' Mum was saying, 'It's not that easy. Where's she going to go?'

Her father's view at the time was that the women must have deserved what they got.

No matter what went on in our homes our mothers stayed put. Again, we must return to the notion of the matriarch in working-class families. What kind of power or status did you have when it was the man who had possession of the home and where you, as a woman, had no legal rights? What kind of power did you have when in order to be safe from a man behaving violently it was you who had to leave the home? What kind of power did you have when, economically, you were unable to provide for yourself or your children? What kind of power did you have when, in order to leave, you needed to find another man who would support you? Seen in this context, it was the working-class man who was all-powerful in the home. He alone had legal powers. And although much has changed, the changes are relative.

Mother/daughter relationships: identifying with mother

Carolyn Steedman (1986) challenged the myth of working-class mothers being utterly devoted to their children, which appears in many autobiographical and fictional accounts of working-class boyhood. The mother/daughter bonding relationships of the women in this study confirm its mystical nature. The 'devoted mother' is not a narrative that we often reconstructed. Our relationship with our mothers was often functional: rarely were we objects of affection, more mini-adults acting as mother's helper, confidant, companion, protector and, at times, protected.

Being 'a little girl'

My mother once said to me, 'I was never a little girl'. She cooked and cleaned for the family and when her father died she was also her mother's constant companion. Like our mothers and grandmothers, we had family responsibilities from a very young age (See Roberts, 1984) and we too were never little girls:

> I was never a little girl. I've got pictures that looks at me as a little girl ... I don't remember being young ... and I don't remember mucking about, life was deadly serious.

> I was my mother's 'little helper', running errands and doing domestic jobs. I was also her confidant and companion absorbing complaints about my sister in trouble, the burden of my ill brother, her dislike of my father's mother living with us, her discontent with my father for handing over his money and leaving her to worry about making ends meet. I learnt from an early age to parent myself.

Though one of the women does not make explicit her parenting role in her family from an early age, she supported and defended her mother when her father got drunk. She talked about locking her father and his male friends out when they brought him home drunk when she was 13. She recalls the men being frightened and saying, 'I wouldn't let my daughter do that'. Hardly the actions and of a little girl! Reading our transcripts it is hard to image any of us as little girls in the modern sense. I would argue that many working-class girls today live in economic and social conditions that do not allow them to be 'little girls'. There is little acknowledgement of this in academic texts on childhood.

Distant mothers

B recalls how, by 14, she was 'quite distant' from her mother, despite having been mother's little helper and companion. She remembers her father saying to her, '*If anything happens to her you'd jump in her grave*'. She tells me, '*Really, he'd completely misread it*'. What there is evidence of is mother/daughter collusion against fathers' undesirable behaviour. Her mother tries to defend her eldest daughter from father's aggressive behaviour, particularly during her teenage years when she was pleading with her mother to leave father. Her mother's ineffectiveness in defending her daughter may explain why the daughter rejected her emotionally. '*I did know she loved me but I didn't have much respect for her ... I saw her as a bit silly um a bit weak*'.

Another woman recalls being quite distant from her mother in childhood, saying: '*As I've gotten older she does fulfil that role [mothering]. Not when I was younger.*' She describes her relationship with her mother in the following way: '*She was always there ... but not ... as someone that you could sort of cuddle and kiss. I don't have memories of, sort of cuddling her or kissing her ... She never read me bed-time stories or ever did anything like that'*.

She was, she says, 'like a rock ... the dependable sensible one ... not affectionate', and adds, 'when you think about it, twelve kids, it's no bloody wonder she wouldn't of had time for it'. Our working-class mothers did not have the time to be attentive to their children, they had far too many responsibilities. Some of these responsibilities were delegated to girl children. Working-class boys were treated differently. J resentfully ironed her older brother's shirts, when she was a girl, at her mother's insistence. In K's home, it is she as a very young girl, not her older brother, who was expected to shop, help around the home and cook, a consequence of her mother's illness and early death. Being the daughter she was automatically expected to take her mother's place at the age of eleven.

Stressful childhoods

As Kohn (1971) has pointed out:

> Children in circumstances of poverty have to deal with problems that would floor many twice their age and ... attempts on their part to cope with these difficulties do not merely mirror the complexities of the adult life that surrounds them, but are rather a measure of the way in which the exigencies of general social life become their own and a dominant actor in the growth of their sense of self.

We were all living in families where high levels of physical and mental illness were the norm. Stressful childhoods were only to be expected given the material condition of our lives. Evidence of this stress is revealed in the women's stories. B talked about not wanting to wake up, wishing she were dead. Two others describe feelings of suicide. L remembers that at 11, '*I must have been so depressed. I remember this tin of zambuck. It was poisonous and I remember I took some ... attempted to commit suicide ...*'

Another woman felt similarly defeated at 16:

> After I did my 'O' levels I got really sort of very depressed ... really manic ... I tried to commit suicide by walking into the sea. Can you imagine? ... I can remember walking in the sea with me bloody coat on and my cousin ... starting a big yell and calling me back ... I remember thinking 'if I just keep on walking ...'

Depression lurks in the background of our lives.

These family insights, focusing as they do on the economic and emotional allegiances within working-class homes have been largely ignored in conventional historical and sociological analysis. Yet, they are central to an understanding of how working-class childhoods impact on educational opportunities and on the adult lives of working-class children. To sum up:

> [It] starts off as their problem [your parents'] and it spills over and becomes your problem.

Fathers as models for girls entering the work place

When we talked about our fathers, we talked about them as good providers – an idealisation which enabled them to be physically absent, display authority, opt out of home and child care responsibilities, to withdraw emotionally and so hide their emotional and physical dependency on women. These issues do not fit comfortably with the wider public discourse on father/daughter relationships, which fails to address the issue of such relationships in working-class homes. What of the daughter who grows up with a man who cannot be the idealised – middle-class – father who, according to Arcana, (1984), 'is supposed to protect his daughter, support her until she marries and oversee her training as a woman through the agency of his wife and whatever schooling he sees fit' (p.121).

This model of a father's role (an alien model to working-class girls) fails to take account of the oppressive situation of uneducated, working-class fathers in low-status jobs or unemployed, who could not provide their daughters with financial and emotional security as presented in the 'good father' discourses. In our stories we attribute to our fathers the role of provider, traditionally the lynch-pin of working-class male identity. In reality the majority of working-class men have not been able to provide adequately for their families, even if they work hard. At the same time we acknowledge society in general, with its promotion of the dependent family, continues to blame working-class men, individually, for this failure.

The public discourse also has it that fathers are the model for daughters entering and succeeding in the work place. What is not addressed is the fact that most working-class men do not model success for their daughters. Being a working-class male in itself meant being 'lower class', 'manual', or lowly non-manual, occupying jobs with low status and low pay. These jobs demanded long and often unsociable working hours – shift work, weekends and provided minimum holidays, little training and no career development. Frequently the jobs involved unpleasant, mundane and tiring work tasks which damaged both the physical and mental health of working-class male workers. One father developed asbestosis from working with asbestos, one had a breakdown, and two had serious drink problems. Working-class men's inability to cope with generally monotonous and dirty work and the financial hardship of taking adequate time off, led to high rates of illness, depression, withdrawal, aggression.

Furthermore, the nature of much of the work available reinforced working-class men's low self-esteem, indirectly labelling them as uneducated and, by implication, inferior. Employers of the time treated them accordingly. One cannot ignore connections between manual work, job insecurity and low self-esteem for working-class men. Talking about her father's breakdown, R describes this well,

> He was very concerned he was going to be thrown out of a job ... He had no skills, who would employ him? ... It was a financial thing because one of his strengths was he'd always been a provider.

Our fathers were always in very insecure positions in the role of the provider. The unstable employment markets, abundance of cheap labour and job-related illnesses worked against them fulfilling this role. At the same time, the hours they worked and the nature of their jobs in male-dominant work forces, left little time and energy for the family and did little to help develop their personal-interactional relationship skills, particularly with their wives and daughters.

Men, working as they were in such conditions, were often demanding at home. They made physical and emotional demands – his chair, his meals, his space, his word, his temper. The impact of this on daughters is reflected in the negative characteristics some daughters attributed to their fathers: 'mental cruelty', a 'verbal bully', a 'tyrant', a 'dictator', 'abusive', 'blinkered', 'uptight', 'strict', a 'bad-tempered ogre', 'a coward', 'weak', 'lazy', 'selfish'. All fathers were 'withdrawn', 'emotionally distant', 'kept things bottled up', but capable of 'cracking up', 'breaking down', 'falling apart', as some of us discovered.

Are these are the attributes of powerful men, masters in the home, or are they the attributes of powerless men, lacking self-esteem? As daughters we were expected to believe father was powerful and to excuse, if not understand, behaviours which camouflaged his powerlessness, his insecurities and his hidden dependency. As daughters we were aware that our mothers carried father, shouldered everything. It was to mother's defence most of us came, even in distant relationships.

Dependency is incompatible with masculinity. So containing emotions was tolerated and at times encouraged as the male thing to do, for working-class women also learn it is not manly to show vulnerability, to reveal an inability to cope with life. But working-class women's collusion left men free to behave in unreasonable ways and maintain the illusion of being a provider, thus benefiting from the privileges that went with this often false economic position.

Mothers as models for our future

In working-class families an understanding of the organisation of the households and the ties of money and responsibility that hold particular family members together is passed on through generations (Steedman, 1982). It is through this process, for instance, that working-class girls become their mothers' daughters.

We learnt from our mothers that women were solely responsible for looking after the home; making the money last, no matter how little there was, and for bearing, rearing, feeding, clothing and disciplining their children. In addition, they were expected to look after elderly relatives irrespective of whether they might be too much of a burden and to take on the children of relatives in times of trouble because there was no-one else to do so.

If economic necessity demanded – and the male permitted it – working-class women, we learnt, would be expected to work, part-time or full-time, in addition to being solely responsible for the children and the home. With no formal qualifications, they entered an exploitative labour market where their labour was seen as economically worthless. This was reflected in the low pay they received. Yet their purpose for working was for money, to supplement the male's inadequate provision.

All mothers are expected to put the family's needs before their own, to make personal sacrifices. But in working-class homes like ours, there was no money for paid domestic help, for nannies or child-care facilities, to place elderly relatives in private homes when the burden got too great, to pay for private health care irrespective of how seriously ill family members were, for private education where children could be boarded out, for restful, well-earned holidays, or for luxury items to reduce the work load. The fulfilment of these tasks demanded high levels of personal commitment, responsibility and duty from working-class women, and this has been described by some as evidence of working-class women's domestic power. Alongside overarching gender inequality in working-class homes, these huge obligations militate against the women being 'good' mothers. And they had the emotional responsibilities of good wives. Working-class women were expected to accept and understand or at least tolerate and certainly publicly defend, oppressed working-class men's negative strategies for personal survival: aggression, violence, withdrawal, excessive drinking. Mothers passed this information on to daughters while as the same time showing discontentment and resentfulness at having to deny their own needs in order to appease the man. Many responded to their oppression by 'risk-averse protests, non-confrontation, small acts of resistance' (Bourke, 1994, p.80).

To follow our working-class mothers, to assume their mantle, was to mirror women with no formal educational qualifications, poor job prospects, no personal income or inheritance and to be unable to support ourselves. Remaining single was not an easy choice. Being 'left on the shelf' was a working-class girl's greatest fear. Without a formal education, as in our mothers' era and my own childhood there were few real alternatives to marriage to a working-class man. Marriage, we learnt, brought with it not only economic dependence on a man, but minimum rights: for instance, no right to have possession of the home, no right to refuse to have ten children. Having children, an inevitability, 'tied you down' in a marriage, for 'where else could you go'?

Experience informed us that marriage was potential enslavement. Yet at the same time we learnt from our family, and from school , that marriage would be our salvation. That a man would and could support both the children we would naturally want and us. In this way we were being conditioned to be the next generation of women whose lives would consist of continuing poverty, insecurity, economic dependence and limited rights. To be a working-class woman was to be exploited, both in and outside the home.

The powerful nature of the conditioning is encapsulated in the belief that, 'you just get on with it'. 'You just got on with it, everybody was the same', said my mother about her life. These same words were uttered by a number of the women, including myself. 'He had that commitment that he put on to me that you get on with it' stated one. Talking about her parents' lack of time for her as a child, L tells me, 'You just get on with it.' This begs the question, 'What was it that we were to get on with?' 'Getting on with it' is about struggling for survival.

> As a [working-class] child, one didn't know what was going on but there was very much this sense of struggle for survival, no margin for happiness in any of its different forms. (Roberts, 1984, p.84)

For things to be different, society would have consciously had to change the material conditions of working-class people's lives. Working-class girls who want to avoid living a hard life are forced to move away from their class background.

Chapter 7

Parental and Peer Support for Education

Part 1: Parental Support

I don't know what their desires for me were.

A daughter's education, even for working-class parents who had a high regard for education, was, as K states, 'not that important'. Worries about unemployment, serious family illnesses and insufficient money took priority over education, especially a daughter's. Parental ambitions, where they existed, were seldom expressed.

Proud fathers: 'a difficult thing to acknowledge'

Four of the women felt their fathers were proud of their achievements, even if they didn't say so until the girls reached adulthood. Although they may have been proud, not all could tell their daughters so, though they boasted about their achievements to others, particularly people at work. The fathers often interpreted their daughters' success as an enhancement of their own social status.

> He'd got me up here on a pedestal ... boasting about me to his friends in terms of the prestigious job she's doing and the money she's earning.

B tells me her father never said a word about her going to grammar school and had no contact with the school. All she remembers was crying on her first day because she could not do the homework, and him shouting at her. So she was astonished when she met a work-mate of her father's who proceeded to tell her and her mother that her father was always talking about his daughters 'as though we were something special'. Embellishing the story, she adds, '[he] even had little school photographs on his desk'. Quickly, she corrects herself, 'Oh, he wouldn't have a desk.' What she regretted, she said, was that he never acknowledged her achievements to her, by saying, *'Haven't you done well ... it's great that you're getting good marks.'* Instead, his comments were negative. She relates this negativity to no longer being 'a little girl', going to grammar school and taking it 'too seriously', and maybe having 'developed or put on a posher accent'.

A similar thread ran through K's stories. She had not known until adulthood that her father was proud of her achievements.

> Didn't know he was that proud of me, I heard from someone else ... even with the MA ... I was actually able to show the certificate just about a month before he died. He hardly knew what time of day it was, but he was very clear about this and he said, 'I want you to have it framed' and he was so proud of this bloody certificate. I thought, 'Oh it all comes back to how proud he must have been before but not able to show it.'
>
> I think he was delighted I went to grammar school because I think he believed in things like that ... When I finally did ... get a job ... in the Bank of England and not just Westminster Bank or Barclay's ... he could go to work and boast about his daughter had gone to the Bank of England ... That was heights for my dad.

Her story reminded me of Evelyn Conlon's (1990) comment, '... the minute fathers die they tell us different. They speak their truth then. The power of the father, silent and all pervasive.'

Supportive fathers?

While K's father may not have revealed how proud he was of her achievements, there is evidence that he had ambitions for her. Although she doesn't '*remember him talking a lot about my education when I was at school'*, she recalls her father's reaction when she told him that her primary school teacher had said that she 'hadn't got a hope in hell of passing' the 11+. His response, she tells me, was, 'I'm going up there and sorting her out', although she didn't know 'whether it was a meeting or to have a row.' When she passed the 11+ she thinks he was delighted, that it was important to him she went to a 'decent' school.

She also recalls her father keeping details of his efforts to get her into a grammar school near their home, so she could look after her sick mother, a role working-class daughters were expected to take on irrespective of age. K tells me, '*There's this correspondence with my dad to kind of manipulate the education service. It was quite significant really because ... you know he had it all sussed.*' Her father, who was an aspiring blue collar worker, directly challenged decisions made in the education service. This was not something other fathers in this study – all manual workers – had done. It is possible that because he worked in a bank he had access to colleagues who could advise him on what to do.

K's mother died during her first year at grammar school and her father remarried and had another child. She says of her education, '*Can't imagine that was important*'. And evidently in the later years of her education her father was not so supportive. When K was asked to leave the grammar school during the fifth form, having truanted since the third year, it was her stepmother – not her father – who visited the school ... '*my stepmother ... saying there must be something we can do. Pleading on mybehalf kind of thing ... getting really upset.*' She explains: '*He was at work, couldn't get there in the day ... was quite heavy in the city and he had that job afterwards and that.*'

J's fathers took education very seriously and encouraged and actively supported his daughter.

> He was always into education, it was a big thing ... I was sort of like the first girl [in the family] that had passed her 11+ and he always used to take it very serious and try to help me with my homework, all this sort of thing ... I used to enjoy all that.

I was atonished when she told me that he took the day of work to take her to the grammar school on her first day. 'I can remember him taking me on the bus 'cause it was a long way to travel.'

R remembered being supported by both her parents who 'put education very highly' having been 'denied that chance'. For her father, it was 'a prestigious thing'. Evidence of his support appears in her story of failing the 11+ and him buying her a bike. When she was 16 his aspirations were strong enough for her to use them as a weapon against him: '*I had a lot of battles with dad. [I] said to him I wasn't going back to school because he was so difficult, I was going to save some money and move out.*'

Mother acted as arbitrator, telling her:

> [He is] 'obviously upset about the fact you're not going back to school'. Well of course I knew he would be, this was a weapon I had against him because, of course, he was very proud of the fact that I'd done very well.

In another father's support there is ambiguity which has to be seen in the context of the daughter's belief that she was sent off to boarding school on a scheme in East End of London for children who 'would benefit from being away from [home]'. There is some confusion when she recalls the circumstances. She tells me that her father, 'must have been earning good money, because he had to pay a certain amount for school fees. It wasn't very much', she adds. At the same time she was surprised first that he earned enough to pay fees, and second that he had been willing to pay. (She was the seventh of ten children.) She recalls: '*I never considered them rich. I never considered they had money ... had to have a means test ... I'm absolutely shocked they paid anything.*'

She also talks about getting pocket money at the school, adding that, 'I think my dad resented it', and remarks, 'I'd never had any [money] of my own before'.

The support was removed when she was 17.

> Suddenly my dad decided he wasn't ... paying any more money. They made me leave school ... and I had to get a job the day I left school ... I got this job filing bits in a bank ... and then that was all right because there was money so you weren't a burden.

While she was training as a teacher at a London college she was still living at home. She complained about her father's attitude, *'Couldn't do any work in the house ... dad was really nasty ... he'd make a noise just to make it difficult.'* She put this down to enviousness: '*He was clever ... frustrated intellectually ... he ... was doing what he considered a menial job ... I think he was jealous of us ... the opportunities.*' So while her father gained esteem: 'look at what I produced', he nontheless showed resentment.

Carolyn Steedman has commented on her parents' indifference to her education. 'What happened at school was my own business, no questions ever asked, no encouragement ever given' (1986, p.36). My father, like hers, showed little interest in my education or achievements. I cannot ever remember him saying anything to me about it until I was about 24, by which time I had a degree and was teaching. Out of the blue one day he said he thought I'd done the right thing. He never clarified what the 'right thing' was and I was so taken aback I did not ask. I interpreted his comment to mean that he had once thought I had *not* done the right thing in pursuing a formal education and a career. Neither of us referred to it again.

In my experience working-class fathers had little practical involvement in their daughters' education, or indeed with their daughters. The realities of being a working-class male and all that entailed, combined with fear and ignorance of schools, particularly secondary schools of which they knew nothing, would have contributed to their apparent lack of interest. But, as these case studies show, they were not indifferent and some fathers do support their daughters, something Lucey and Walkerdine's longitudinal study 'Transition to womanhood', also shows (1996).

Mothers who visit their disappointments on their daughters

One might have expected our working-class mothers to be supportive and proud of their daughters' educational achievements but this was not necessarily so. Supportive or not, our mothers were likely to be the parent who had most contact with the school, although this tended to be minimal. It was mothers who came to primary school, if only on our first day, and secondary school, if only when demanded by school. When J broke a school rule it was her mother who was contacted by the headmistress and when B (and her younger sister) 'were badly behaved', it was mother who was asked to go to the school. When a third was asked to leave the school it was her stepmother who dealt with the situation.

Only one mother was actively supportive. She made it clear that she valued education and wanted her daughter to benefit from opportunities she never had. There is evidence of her support and defence of her daughter at primary school, especially when R was accused of cheating in a class test. Her mother had just come out of hospital after a nervous breakdown, but she went to the school and 'demanded to see the head teacher'. And when the whole class was caned by the deputy head, she again came to the school, even though she had an eight till five job, because 'she was cross about it'.

This mother defended her daughter into adulthood. R tells me what of what happened when her mother met one of her former primary teachers, who had told her once that her daughter would not 'do well'.

> Years later mum saw this woman in the street and stopped her to say, 'Just thought you might like to know that [my daughter's] a teacher now' and took great pleasure in seeing the astonishment on this woman's face ... and then years later, 'Oh did I mention that [she's] now a deputy?'

She adds, 'Mum loathed this woman as much as I did.'

The other women were less sure of their mother's support. B offered examples of her mother sharing her school experiences: 'I can remember talking to my mum about Mrs Toni and how I hated her ... and she could remember her coming to the school [when she was a pupil]. She also remembers asking her mother 'what she suggested [she] did for the English half [of the 11+ paper]', and accepted her mother's suggestion. Yet when she passed her 11+, her mother said 'very little'. She recalls:

> That evening we went round to visit an aunt and a cousin. She told them, and I think that means she was probably pleased, but I think she probably tried to hide it from me. 'Cause, I didn't get, well certainly no praise or, it wasn't really mentioned a great deal.

Nevertheless, B is conscious that her mother pushed her daughters to 'get on', to get a good job and not repeat her own experience. She tells me:

> It seems as if she may of had the opportunity to get away but was too frightened to take it. Apparently her first job was in a solicitor's office in the City ... Her mother had given her a cold fish sandwich for lunch and when lunch-time came round my mum said that she was too ashamed to take this out and eat it ... She went home for lunch and told her mum that she 'didn't like it [the job]' ... [Her] Mum said, 'Oh if you don't like it don't go back' ... mum's never forgot that, 'cos then she would have got on.

Not recalling either being asked to leave or encouraged to stay, she left school at 17, but she tells me, '*I decided I would leave'cos of my mum leaving my dad*'. As with other women, she had to leave school before completing A-levels because fathers withdrew the money.

In my own family school was rated unimportant. It was somewhere we went because the law said we had to. On a practical level, my mother did not mind whether we went or not. Indeed, she condoned my sister's and brother's absence despite the visits from the school board man. That I wanted to go to school was tolerated until it began to have financial implications as I got older, when she became resentful.

Wanting more than you were entitled to

Working-class mothers may envy their daughter's opportunities.

> It was my mother's wish that I had stayed at secondary-modern school rather than transfer at thirteen to a comprehensive school. She led me to believe that her objection was purely economic. This move cost money which she did not have. Although I did transfer, it was still her wish that I left school at fifteen to go out to work, as did my brother and sister, for not only did I have to be financially supported, I was not bringing in money. As a child I was very aware that she wanted to be free of the burden that having children had brought. 'If it wasn't for you', she would say to us and mean it. In my teens she was quite open with me about her unwillingness to pay for something from which she would get no benefit. It would simply be the case that she gave and I took. In a sense, she was right.
>
> I recall vehemently arguing with her that I had a right to stay on in the sixth form and saying that if I had a daughter this is what I would want for her. I have no idea where this notion of having a right came from; presumably my observations of school peers. It was extremely difficult for me at the time to understand her aggressiveness and resentment. When I finally got into a teacher's training college at the age of twenty, I felt, once again, I had done wrong in my mother's eyes. Despite this resistance, which disappeared once I entered college, I was aware at the comprehensive school and at college, she would use her daughter's achievements for self-aggrandisement. Yet, to this day, she has never said anything to me about my academic achievements.

It is only now that I can put another level of meaning to my mother's resistance: envy. Though able enough to have gone to a grammar school she was prevented by poverty. Here was I wanting what she was not allowed to have and, what's more, my getting it depended upon her willingness to make further sacrifices in her life. What right had I to independence when she was trapped in dependency? What right had I to refuse the life she had had to live? It was as though I wanted more than my mother thought I was entitled to – something Valerie Walkerdine talks about (Walkerdine and Lucey, 1989). Looking back now I believe she could not willingly allow me these things, so great was her resentment and bitterness at what life had brought her. This belief is reinforced by my observations of how aggressive my mother was to career-women friends of mine, an aggression that did not surface with male equivalents.

We grew up in an era when education was considered more important for boys than for girls. One woman tells me her mother saw education as unimportant for girls: '*I mean the boys yes*', but girls '*You got on with it for the sake of it ... I just think she felt it was a bit of a waste of time.*' She then draws an interesting analogy between herself and the sister most like her mother, who '*was quite placid and easy-going and quite happy with her lot ... wasn't academic, she was into cooking and all that sort of thing ... Whereas, the rest of us, well I was academic*'. She adds that in her mother's eyes, '*we all wanted more than we were entitled to*'.

When talking about her own relationship with her mother, she tells me, '*She just sort of patronises me ... 'she's always been a little bit weird and ideas above her station' ... I can see this big hand gently patting me on the head.*' With her eldest sister, who went to secondary-modern school, took up a clerical post and eventually became successful in the business world, her mother was very uncomfortable: '*[In] one sense mum is quite frightened of her really ... because M's so strident. She admires her in one sense and in another sense she's sort of ...*'

This is an interesting perception – a mother who reacts differently to her own daughters, fearful but admiring of the successful one and most comfortable with the one whose life is most like hers. It raises an important issue: how comfortable were our mothers with daughters who would and did surpass them? As Arcana observed, 'we leave them *behind*; we go beyond the lives they have lived' (1984, p.154), seeking our identity and our power in non-manual work, not in manual work and/or the home.

The Wider Implications

The implications of being the first or one of the first girls to achieve educational success in a working-class family have to be understood in the context of the economic, social and emotional support that a family can provide. To allow working-class girls to take advantage of what was being offered at school, high economic, social and emotional costs were incurred. So commitment from our families was inevitably variable and ambiguous.

The economic costs

Parents' reactions to their daughters' education were tightly bound up with the family economy. Money was of major concern in all our families. The cost of school uniform, a massive expenditure for working-class families, was one point of tension. The fact that it was often our mothers who handled the family finances and bought our uniforms, may go some way to explaining why some mothers may have been less than enthusiastic about their daughters' education. B recalls her mother paying half the cost of her school uniform and her dad undertaking to pay the remaining half on a weekly basis to the school: '*I had to take in twelve and six a week or something like that ... We used to pay that to Mother A ... in the dining room.*'

The cost of the uniform for my comprehensive school was undoubtedly a serious source of contention with my mother, even with the help of the Provi (Provident Loan Cheques) and buying at the Co-op, the cheapest shop. The minimum number of items were bought and all were several sizes too big. They had to last.

Other women had similar experiences:

> It must of crippled her ... There was only one shop in Belfast ... I got everything about fifty sizes too big for me ... my gabardine coat was like that, round my ankles ... I suppose she [mum] was lucky ... I didn't shoot up or anything so it lasted.

L notes the one advantage in having to have a school uniform, '*I mean I had new clothes ... I don't remember having new clothes except the ones that were bought for me at school.*'

We had few clothes, rarely new, and now ironically our mothers were paying what were, to our families, large sums of money for new garments we detested – '*things for PE, with the divided legs: oh, vile bottle green hideous things. They were awful and you had to have brown shoes.*'

The problem of cost was exacerbated by the strictness of school rules. J talks about going to school in brown sandals and being stopped by a prefect who asked, '*whether they were my indoor shoes or my outdoor shoes and I only had one pair of shoes and I didn't know – my mum obviously didn't know.*' It was quite usual for working-class children to have only one pair of shoes.

K talks about the humiliation of having a uniform that was home-made, one mother's way of cutting the cost. She remembers her cardigan having a different dye number half-way up the back. Home-made jumpers and cardigans were the norm for working-class families, and the cardigans, like the shoes, separated us out. L recollects the demeaning experience of getting her uniform from the council. It was, she says, '*very humiliating when I think about it, because I had to go up to the Town Hall to get authorisation to buy these clothes and you had to buy them all from ... the Co-op.*'

Alison Fell wrote poignantly: 'You can tell the handful of working-class ones by the cheaper, rawer maroon of their Co-op blazers' (1985, p.20). As poorer families, our uniform identified us, the cheapness of the material, its home-made look, the fact that it was too big, the way it faded and frayed over time.

Financial demands and parental support affected other aspects of school life. One woman who had been sent to boarding school was aware that her parents could not support her financially in the way other parents could. She talks about, 'having to get [herself] to school at 11' – from the East End of London to a 'shire' county – because there was no money to pay for someone to travel with her. She also recalls not being able to come home for her first half-term.

> I wrote to my parents explaining that everyone went home for half term, they said they couldn't afford the fare. They didn't realise ... had no knowledge of boarding schools.

For others there was the issue of finding money for cookery and needle-work, a basic requirement in state schools. These caused a horrendous amount of tension in my home, whereas money for school trips, music lessons, extra tuition was unproblematic because the school did not expect 'poorer' families to pursue such luxuries. They were there for the better-off. Our sense of unfairness, of exclusion and envy again went unacknowledged.

From many parents' points of view, usually expressed through the mothers, working-class children were supposed to bring money into the home, not have it paid out. When we reached the legal age, many of us would be expected to do part-time work and at least to clothe ourselves. My mother insisted I took a Saturday job as soon as I was 15. The fact that I played netball for the school meant nothing to her. During my 'O' levels I worked on Saturdays and in the holidays. I started my 'A' levels working for two hours in a pub, five nights a week and by the time I sat them I was working full-time.

Other women also talk about having had to work. At 16, B '*can remember being pushed to get a Saturday job and I went to Woolworth in Oxford Street ... during the holidays and on Saturdays and Thursday evenings*'. J says: '*I always had a job. From when I was about 13 I worked in a local sweet shop and I worked in a local bakery ... and then I worked in a bookie's.*'

K mentions working in the holidays between doing 'O' levels and 'A' levels, looking after an old lady nearby and working in Woolworth. For some of us, having a part-time job was not enough for our families and we were compelled to leave school to work full-time. Parental support in working-class families needs to be considered in the context of having to pay back, as Carolyn Steedman noted. As J explains, '*You had to pay back some of the money that your parents had sort of spent ... I mean it was never said really but ... I was well aware of the fact.*'

Another tells me that when she got a job at 17, '*that was all right ... you weren't a burden*'. I too understood this notion of paying back and felt at the time that in my mother's eyes, I could never pay enough.

Other experiences were directly or indirectly economically significant, such as the demands placed on us in the home. Being at school did not exclude you from your domestic responsibilities: cleaning, childcare, running errands, looking after sick parents etc. And we had virtually no space or privacy. As B explains about school work: '*We all lived in the living room, that was where the TV was and I did my homework ... in the middle of a room with five other people all watching TV*'. I too recall this scenario. In addition to doing homework and revising for examinations under these conditions, we could rarely 'ask for help'. 'Parents hadn't got time to offer it you', states L. If they had, they would have found much of the curriculum was alien, as it was to us. In poor working-class families there were no back-up systems of support. We had to succeed on our own and first time around.

The emotional costs – 'too big for your boots'

By staying on at school after the minimum age in a community where everyone routinely left at 15, we had already begun to achieve some kind of inferred status. Our parents reacted differently to this situation, reflecting an individuality in working-class people that is seldom acknowledged in literature. For some parents their daughters' elevation, achieved through education, brought pleasure and pride whereas others, often the mothers, saw little value in it, particularly for girls. Working-class mothers' were socially conditioned to regard education as unimportant for women. Also, there was a genuine fear that education would alienate daughter from mother. Fathers, on the other hand, could gain status from having educated children.

Some parents experienced conflicting emotions of pride and resentment at our success. There we were taking public examinations that had value in the job market and destined to hold positions and earn incomes our parents could never hope to achieve and enjoy levels of security and independence they had been denied. In this, we had surpassed the head of the household at a relatively early age. Evidence that working-class parents have envied and felt threatened by their children's elevation, inflated or real, can be found in phrases commonly uttered during our childhood years:

> You're getting too big for your boots.
> You want pulling down a peg or two.
> Don't go getting any fancy ideas.
> Don't get above your station.
> Putting on airs and graces.

These put downs were explicitly aimed at keeping us in our place – at least within the family – as subordinate. The implicit message is that you were pretending to be what you were not, a fraud hence the emphasis on 'putting on', 'getting above', and the need for pulling down and exposing. Why? Because we dared to want more than some of our parents thought we were entitled to or deserved. Agnes Smedley, a working-class girl, described in *Daughter of Earth*, how her father indirectly put her down, 'You've got a datter that's been to eighth grade an' can't add' (1977, p.66). Intimidation, humiliation and belittling are illustrations of how threatened parents can be by their daughters' education and all that it implies. This area of conflict is rarely discussed in literature.

The anxiety and ambivalence which successful daughters raised in their parents were evident when they came to deal with school on our behalf. There were few examples in our stories of our parents' expecting or demanding of the schools that they do more for us. It would be fair to say that most did not know how to interact with or influence school. The one occasion when my parents came to a secondary school, for my interview for transferring from the secondary-modern to a comprehensive school, offers insight into how schools intimidated our parents, and us.

> Mr R, the headmaster, sporting a black gown – the significance of which was unknown to us – relaxed in his reclining, leather arm chair, positioned behind a large, oak desk in the centre of a very spacious room. We three – in stark contrast – were perched submissively on the edge on small, wooden school chairs, which were pinned against the wall facing him. We spoke when invited to, that is, in answer to his questions.

What power or status or knowledge could they as working-class parents, or we as working-class children, have brought to this situation? Parents like mine, who had not had a secondary school education, knew little of the workings of the education system, or how to challenge it and make it work in their children's interests. Neither did they have any confidence.

Schools, as one of the women points out, are bound up with, '*knowledge out there that they've got no access [to]*'. So much so, that our parents could not challenge or defend us from education's strongest myth: 'If you were able you will do well'; 'If you were not successful it was because you were not able enough'. Places in selective schools or streams were supposedly to be determined on the basis of merit, of ability alone. It is not accidental that working-class people, our parents, had no say in what counted as 'ability'.

Even when working-class children achieved academically, their parents' lack of 'knowledge out there', what Bourdieu calls 'cultural capital', meant they could offer little practical support in terms of directing you towards challenging career opportunities. Outside their own work experiences working-class people's knowledge of the employment market is very limited. More importantly, not only do working-class parents lack access to the appropriate social networks that smooth the way for middle-class students, many do not even know they exist.

The relationship between working-class parents and schools is a class relationship. Note the continuing degree of discomfort many working-class parents exhibit within the context of school and the differentiated authority relationship between working-class parents and teachers. For instance, in Dianne Reay's (1996) research working-class mothers perceive themselves as lacking educational expertise and confidence and are reluctant to approach teachers. Most parents strongly rely on teachers and hesitate to question their professional knowledge or to take up their time. Similar findings appear in the National Campaign for Learning Report (1998) which states that although women from poorer families understand the importance of a good education for their children, they have little confidence in their own ability to help their children and feel too intimidated by schools and teachers to ask for help. These behaviour patterns have earned them the labels: uninterested, unsupportive, uninvolved.

It is these constraints that continue to dictate working-class parents' involvement in their children's schooling (Smith and Nobel, 1995). The language of education still obstructs working-class parents talking about their children's education in any depth and blocks their interpretation of the information they are given, making them highly dependent upon teachers' judgement. They lack the knowledge to advise their children.

Though there have been government directives aimed to secure greater parental intervention by all parents these have done little to counteract the disadvantages working-class parents experience (Ball, Gerwirtz and

Bowe, 1994). The directives have failed to provide the educational knowledge working-class parents need, such as what schools could and should be doing for their children.

Part 2: Straddling Two Worlds

Working-class children who entered selective or comprehensive schools in the 1950s and 60s often found themselves being bussed out of working-class neighbourhoods. This isolated us geographically and socially not only from our family (brothers, sisters, cousins) but also the children with whom we grew up.

Social isolation from peers in the neighbourhood

Being schooled outside the local area and in institutions where street culture was considered highly undesirable, particularly for girls, made it problematic for us to continue to be members of local street groups. Yet interaction via street culture was a significant social aspect of our lives. As children we played in the street; as teenagers we hung around shop doorways or walls where we could sit and talk. K tells me 'I used to go out and play down the alleys and things with kids living nearby'. R recalls, '*We lived at the top of a big council estate ... and we all played in this cul-de-sac.*' L talks about street fights and 'tearing somebody's hair out'. B describes 'hanging about' with the 'Short Street Kids', local boys.

Our isolation from local peers increased as we got older. The woman who attended boarding school describes how at first she was able to fit back in during holidays: '*I'd have got friends at home in the street because I was a street urchin really*'. By seventeen she knew no one at home and felt quite lonely. The 'disjuncture' in having to move between the world of school and the world of home was apparent in her statement, '*I'd just got accustomed to being at school, a different way of life, and holidays would come and you'd go home. I didn't like going home.*'

Although not at boarding school, I travelled ten miles a day return trip to my comprehensive school. The daily journey was a process of geographical, social and psychological metamorphosis which cut me off from children I had grown up with.

This growing isolation increased through our middle and late teens. R talks about losing friends when she transferred from secondary-modern school to a grammar school sixth form. She was still at school and her friends had boyfriends. '*I stopped socialising with people ... I'd gone to the secondary [modern] school with because they were courting ... or married by that stage'*.

My friends in the community courted and married at relatively early ages, some at 16. Those of us who stayed on at school were seen as different and this often led to exclusion. Some girls tried to play down differences by covering up, disowning, or denying the impact of 'school'. B, who took school very seriously, typifies this in her attempts to mix with local working-class peers who had rejected school. Her connections with them came through her sister, who although at the same Catholic girls' grammar school , was less committed to the school. She says that '*It was Elaine who made friends with them ... she was much more liked by them and didn't do any work.*' She describes 'them':

> The Short Street Kids ... were ... I suppose a kind of bad bunch. Some of them were illiterate ... Short Street was a ... slum. Some of their parents were drunkards ... but ... there was something very adventurous about them and they used to play right down by the river in a wharf ... That's where we first took up smoking.

She talks about having to keep her educational achievements from 'them':

> [I] had to hide the fact that I used to come quite high up at school. I can remember saying I came last at school ... They were ... very anti doing well at school ... I think I may [have been] there on sufferance but, really, I only mixed with those and none of them were close friends.

She was well aware that her success in school would mean she would be ridiculed by this peer group. It was something that had to be hidden or played down if she was to be at least tolerated, if not accepted. B maps out how the Short Street kids differed from her within and across the gender divide.

> Dean who [swore] was illiterate, at a special school and Jimmy, who was mixed race ... was quite violent, I was frightened of him ... Although they were quite attractive boys they were a million miles away. I don't think I ever had a conversation with either of them.

> Lynda was about fourteen and had been going out with her boyfriend who was about seventeen ... for years ... They were really very very close and I could never understand that, cause I never had a boyfriend ... so I found them a real mystery.

She sees herself as being on the periphery, as there on sufferance, but there is a push-pull factor at play. The group was both appealing and unappealing. The boys were 'attractive', 'adventurous' but also 'illiterate', 'anti doing well in school', a 'bad bunch', 'quite violent'. She tells me they were disapproved of by her mother because they smoked, swore and had parents who were 'drunkards', although her own father had a similar problem. They were not boys she felt she could communicate with, indeed they were 'a million miles away'. Similarly, she cannot understand a girl having a long-term boy friend at 14.

Interestingly she sees herself as having been the misfit. School provided her with work which she used as a way of covering up her inability to make friends or attract boyfriends.

> I think I escaped in work ... I used to come and think well I'll do homework, go up and spend hours doing that ... I think I was the classic misfit, so I liked school work because it was an excuse not to have to go out and I could always say, 'Oh I've got loads of homework' ... and that covered up my not having a boyfriend, not having friends outside.

She attributed this to her own inadequacy, not the home/school divide. She coped by withdrawing, avoiding rejection and exclusion. She also dwells on the negative social implications of being obliged to wear school uniform, when 'no-one wore school uniform' at home. Wearing a uniform emphasised difference, as it was intended to. It worked against our attempts to appear the same as local peers, for which there were very good reasons. The inclusion in one social group – the school – not only led to the exclusion from another social group – local peers – but it also put us in a vulnerable position, a target for intimidation.

Travelling to and from school in the kind of school uniforms we were required to wear with their berets and boaters, led to our humiliation, particularly from working-class, teenage boys. Maureen Duffy (1983) recalled boys chanting at her, 'High Schoolite'. 'Snob' was the chant I was subjected to by groups of boys as I walked through the council estate. While I pretended not to hear, I found it frightening and unfair.

Having recently moved into the area I was actually a stranger to these youths and I doubt whether they even recognised that the school my uniform represented was comprehensive.

As someone who had been to secondary-modern school, attended almost exclusively by working-class students, I knew strict adherence to a uniform symbolised 'them' and 'us'. 'Them' were those included in selective education, 'us' were those excluded, mostly working-class students. Exclusion had connotations of inferiority, inclusion of superiority. That was the real issue. Ironically, for girls like me, the uniform was like a false skin. It hid from sight an overwhelming sense of inferiority rooted in social connotations of my working-class and family background.

J raises the issue of being separated out by a uniform in the eyes of local boys. Walking home after school, she says, '*You stuck out like a sore thumb ... They used to stand and watch you, jostling you or whatever ... but it was quite hair-raising ... You were never quite sure you were going to make it.*'

She is talking about class and gender based sectarian harassment. The potential harassers were working-class, male, Protestant teenagers. Interestingly, she tells me, it was a 19-year-old working-class male Protestant, who as a result of being shot had only one lung, who protected her and her friends, 'He took a fancy to Patricia ... he used to just smile but he used to sort of protect us'.

One could argue, certainly in the context of the neighbourhoods in which we lived, that it was our position as working-class girls (rather than just as girls) that created hostility from working-class boys we seldom even knew. The uniform which de-sexualised us and kept us in a state of girlhood in the eyes of these youths, also signalled a potential independence from them. An educated working-class girl was a threat to working-class masculinity, located as it was in the role of the provider, the protector, whose word was law. Working-class girls destined to be economically independent would have the choice of not becoming the working-class wives of the future. So our putting education first was seen as a form of rejection with which working-class boys had difficulty coming to terms. Why else would they torment and harass us? Like some of our parents, they were uncomfortable with working-class girls who wanted to move out of their allotted class-based gender role, so it was important to keep us in our place. Both family and school failed to acknowledge that such conflicts existed.

The relative failure of siblings and cousins

Categorised by 'ability'

The social distance between us and our neighbourhood peers could be discerned within families. Many of us grew up knowing relatively little about our brothers' and sisters' experiences or feelings about school, even though we lived with them. Educational practices had socially divided us through formalised tests and examinations, selective schooling, streaming, setting and year groups.

One woman experienced rejection by her nine brothers and sisters because she was the only one who was sent off to boarding school. This affected her deeply:

> What everybody had said was, 'You won't want to know us when you come home. Of course when I came home, I was just made fun of and laughed at ... I was just a snob, because ... I went to school with a strong cockney accent, broad ... the bane of my life, then I came home with a [middle-class] accent and everyone ignored me.

The two years I spent in a secondary-modern school taught me that streaming, like the 11+, created a them-and-us situation within families. Siblings or cousins in the same school were often socially divided because one was labelled able and placed in the top stream, and the other labelled less able and placed in a lower stream, as happened to my older sister and me. This social distancing increased when I transferred at 13 to a comprehensive school. We grew up knowing very little about each other, even though we slept in the same bed for eighteen years (another feature of working-class life of the time). She, like my younger brother, left school at 15 and took a low-paid, manual job while I stayed and entered the sixth form. That I was the more able one is open to debate.

The division of siblings and social distance is present in B's story. She and one of her sisters were at the same grammar school. This sister, a year younger, was in the stream below her though. She was not necessarily less able but simply took school less seriously. Being in different years and in different streams, even in a school of only three hundred pupils, resulted in the sisters having little contact. It was not until they took part-time work together that they became friends. Her other sister was five years younger and went to the local comprehensive, and her relationship with her old sister remained distant throughout their childhood. Despite their differing academic routes and levels of commitment, all three girls ended up in similar clerical jobs. Going to a selective school does not automatically guarantee better career opportunities for working-class girls.

Role models – a background of educational failure

Although we each had an older brother, sister, or some distant cousin who had gone to grammar school, they failed to stay within the education system long enough for it to change their lives. As J says of her brother and sisters, 'they only get so far' and then they 'drop out'. The usual time for dropping out was after taking 'O' or 'A' levels, before entering higher education.

R followed in her cousin's 'footsteps' and tells how, '*when I got to the grammar school E ... had been a star ... E was talked about with reverence*'. Though able and a star, E like so many such working-class pupils, dropped out of school after taking 'O' levels.

> I mean she was very bright but never did anything with it ... She was well into boys by this stage so she never actually ... I think she failed all her 'O' levels. Of course she later regretted this and then went on to try and educate herself, but of course got married quite young.
>
> She's comparable with my brother in the sense that they're both very talented but never used it. She was also very talented sports-wise. Peter was also very talented with his hands, craft-wise.

Of her brother, who also dropped out of grammar school, she says: '*The shining star has suddenly lost interest around the age of 13, 14 and started truanting.*'

She describes both her brother and her cousin as 'stars', 'leading lights', 'absolutely adored by everybody ... within the school system', yet both became disinterested. She felt that her brother opted out through boredom, but for her cousin it was 'boys'. Again we see girls having to choose between having a relationship with working-class boys or an education. It was not perceived as possible to have both. These are common, even stereotypical, explanations each containing elements of truth but also concealing over quite complex issues that relate to feelings of not fitting in.

K was separated from her older brother when he was sent by her parents to a private day school while she went to the local girls' grammar school. She says, '*He was obviously misplaced, for God's sake ... He just failed miserably*.' She too felt misplaced, and began truanting. About her working-class cousins who also failed in school, she says, they, '*quote, unquote failed in terms of a career, they haven't got any qualifications*'.

Only J did not experience a divide. The fourth girl and fifth child of twelve, she was the first girl to go to grammar school and to stay until 18. Her elder brother at grammar school and her older sisters at secondary-modern school left at 15 or 16. She tells me that '*even though we were in different schools we sort of believed in the same sort of things ... I didn't feel that different really*'.

She even talks about her and one of her sisters studying together for 'O' levels. Nevertheless, she is aware that although younger brothers and sisters followed her and some even went to university, they did not end up in jobs where a degree is required. She notes, 'We sort of got so far and then we didn't go any further in our family for some reason.' This elusive reason is what this book seeks to capture.

The same pattern is present in L's family, whose elder brother is 'outstandingly bright'. 'He excelled in his 'A' levels, he got a distinction or scholarship for everything.' She suggests his success is one reason that she has feelings of failure: 'perhaps it was not being [able] to compete.' Yet, this 'outstandingly bright' brother went on to a further education college, not university.

In our experience, it was normal for 'able' working-class children who were successful in the system to nevertheless drop out of school. This was very apparent in our families, and even among ourselves. Half of the women in this study and their 'able' brothers and sisters left school without taking 'A' levels, despite being in selective streams. The reasons we gave for this were to do with being 'misplaced', not taking school seriously, being bored, economic pressure, or the family tradition of 'only going so far'.

Friends in school: 'they dropped off'

The people we tended to make friends with at secondary school were, as might be expected, often from working-class backgrounds. Many of these friends left school at 15 or 16 taking on the jobs able working-class girls were directed towards: office work, nursing, banking, the police force. Some got pregnant and were single mums, some married as early as 17 or 18 and some had 'lots of kids'. This was normal. Significantly the longer you stayed on at school, the less likely you were to take these routes.

All my friends in the comprehensive school I went to were from working-class backgrounds. Those in the secondary-modern streams left at 15; those in the grammar streams, with a few exceptions, left at 16 after taking 'O' levels. P, who left at 15 to work in an office, had from the age of 11 when her mother died, assumed the housewife and mother role to her father and 2-year-old sister. L, S, and M, had all transferred with me from secondary-modern school, left at 16, the minimum age our parents had agreed to keep us at the school. L went to train as a nurse, S had a baby while in the fifth-form and left early. M went to work in an office. Only J completed 'A' levels. J's father was an electrician and her the family were well-off compared to mine and other friends' families. They had a small three-bedroomed house on a new housing estate, a telephone and a car, albeit an old one.

Several other women's accounts were similar. B mentions five friends, all from families with low incomes and who all left grammar school at the end of the fifth or lower sixth form. One who lived with her widowed mother in a council flat in Kentish Town took an office job at the same firm as her sister.

J confirms this pattern: '*Most of my friends were poor ... The working classes you all sort of got together ... but one-by-one you see they dropped off*'.

She gives examples. M and T transferred at 14 to a local secondary-modern. M 'didn't like the rules and they didn't understand her ... She sort of came from a very strong working-class background and she just hated it'. T, who 'lived in quite a poor arca', left school at 15, married at 18 and had 'lots of kids'. Other friends left school to go into banking, nursing, offices. Those who continued to the end of sixth form, she says, were those whose 'parents were sort of heavily into education'. By the end of the sixth form 'there was only C and I left'.

The same pattern is evident in R's story. She talks about her friends in the 'A' stream leaving her secondary-modern school, without doing the fifth-form. One joined the police force and another left at 16 and married at 17. K mentions two friends, one at a local secondary-modern school who left school at 15, and another at her grammar school. They were, she says, all 'from single-parent families'. The three truanted together.

Another problem was that our new friends at school rarely lived in the same neighbourhood as we did. As R who transferred at 16 to a grammar school eleven miles always from home, says, '*I couldn't actually socialise with most of these people after school. I usually just came straight home*'.

Distance, the absence of cars and the cost of bus fares restricted us from socialising with school friends after the school day. But distance was not the only reason for our social isolation. Taking school friends home was certainly something my mother and others discouraged. 'You never had your friends home', says L. In my case it would mean another mouth for my mother to feed. For R her father worked night shifts. This constraint was a source of great resentment for both of us. B said she hesitated to take friends home because she was ashamed of her home. She tells me, '*I was very very wary and I hated them coming there ... everywhere was so dirty ... There was no way you could even superficially tidy it up.*' Another woman was similarly critical of the dirtiness of her childhood home.

In one of the homes where there were twelve children things were different: friends were allowed in but under no circumstances could they go upstairs:

> Anyone was allowed in our house [but] ... they weren't allowed upstairs. My mother would never, ever, ever, let anybody upstairs. Well you can imagine, I mean there was beds everywhere and clothes everywhere and whatever ... The holiest of holies.

So there were many factors operating to make us feel cut off. Working-class school friends left school early, the significant geographical distances between our schools, not being able to take friends home and a growing separation from peers in the neighbourhood all contributed to our feelings of isolation.

Conclusion

While parental support was limited, peer support was wholly absent. Being formally educated was for us synonymous with being geographically and socially isolated, for we were educated out of the neighbourhood and away from working-class peers. For a number of us this segregation was to affect our relationships with friends and family, brothers, sisters, cousins, many of whom attended the local secondary-modern. Fitting in at home and in the community became more and more difficult as we got older. The longer we stayed on at school, the more excluded we were from old friends. B summed it up: 'No one was at school after 15.'

Separation, symbolised as it was by the daily wearing of a school uniform made us targets for verbal abuse and harassment from working-class boys we did not know, particularly as our minority status became more and more conspicuous. Working-class boys were threatened by educationally successful working-class girls' rejection of their traditional role; implicitly a rejection of them.

Dropping out at 15 or 16 was common among the women in this study and other able working-class girls (and boys) we knew. Was this simply to do with having boyfriends, as R suggested in the case of her cousin, a 'star' pupil? Having a boyfriend, getting married, not being left on the shelf, were crucial in our youth, not least because most girls could not hope to support themselves economically. The overall picture of boyfriends, pregnancies and early marriages suggest that for some working-class girls having a family of their own was paramount whereas for a few, qualifications were important. This dichotomy arises out of the lack of genuine options.

Wanting both boyfriends and qualifications was particularly problematic. Going to school and being seen on the bus in school uniform by a desired working-class youth already out of school was utterly humiliating for some of us. And having boyfriends and a life outside school worked against success in school. Prolonging childhood beyond fourteen or fifteen was uncommon where I lived. I was surrounded by girls who dressed up and made up to lure boys (a sensible thing to do when you could not support yourself economically). There was always the pull of wanting to do what other working-class girls of my age were doing, acting the grown up. I was in pubs at 15, at late night dances at 16, in night-clubs at 17. This was far more exciting than anything school offered. It was only the drive to become economically independent and a desire to prove myself that kept me hooked into the education system. K experienced some of these things. She tells me,

> I went out and had a good time ... Stayed out late ... went up West ... We'd be down the Marquee in Wardour Street, do outrageous things at such a young age. Fourteen and fifteen travelling back on the milk train and that's why I never went to school because it was much more exciting outside ... sitting up playing cards and going out with boys.

The pull of this more exciting life, which mitigated our isolation from local working-class peers, created huge conflict for those of us who stayed on at school. Working-class students have still to be assimilated into a culture where it is normal to stay on at school until 18.

Chapter 8

Schooling a Social Equaliser? Taking a Closer Look

The 1944 Education Act enabled the women in this book to be among the first generation of working-class children to attend secondary schools *en masse*. We were, it was argued, being offered equality of opportunity to a formal education and the benefits this brought. If this was true, why did the vast majority of working-class girls (and boys) leave school as soon as they could, at the minimum legal age?

While secondary education was both a right and a privilege it was also a legal imposition and an obligation, delivered by institutions which were never designed with working-class children in mind. Carolyn Steedman drew attention to this when she wrote, '... the transition from home to school is supposedly a non-problematic step' (1982, p.8). In fact, it is highly problematic for many working-class children. The conflicts that arise are a major factor in working-class children's continuing rejection of school.

This chapter focuses on the problematic nature of the push-pull of home/school assimilation and alienation. Another educated working-class woman, bell hooks, argues: '... working-class students drop out because of contradictions between the behaviour necessary to make it and those that allow them to be comfortable with friends and family' (1994, p.182). It is, she maintains, difficult to inhabit comfortably two confrontational worlds that are divided economically, socially and culturally.

Maureen Duffy, who presented herself as someone who smoothly assimilated into grammar school life, nevertheless talked about class and family alienation:

> the grammar school was the key to escape from poverty that at the same time brought with it alienation from the escapee's working-class background if not from the family roots themselves. (1983, p.vii)

Whilst assimilating into the school's class-culture brought the risk of alienation from home; not assimilating brought educational failure.

Our experience of school: setting the scene

Despite the rhetoric of the progressive 1960s, the women in this book all received what was thought of as a traditional education, even though our ages span twenty years, and the institutions we attended varied in terms of selective or non-selective status and religious denomination. As the youngest woman – in her early thirties – stated, *'Most of it was sitting behind desks in dead silence'*.

The stories we tell of our school experiences suggest that our relationship to the structure of our schools and to the teachers in them was a problematic one, not least because of the level of conformity demanded.

The experiences outlined below are those of women who, as girls, were all in selective streams, took school very seriously and wanted to gain qualifications.

> I adored that school probably as I always did very well, achieved a great deal.

> I loved school ...You took the mickey out of them and made their life a misery but you wanted to learn.

> I took school very seriously ... I wanted to do well.

Despite the desire to do well, success was a difficult thing for us to achieve. Discrimination is deeply embedded in institutional practices and while we were aware, on an experiential level, of being at odds with the school, any difficulties were taken to be our problem. As K states: '*Education, by definition, was good ... it was something you praised, you didn't have bad education*'.

Secrets: experiencing shame, learning in schools about class difference

To succeed in school we had to fit. To fit we had to change. bell hooks talks about avoiding 'feelings of estrangement' by changing 'speech patterns, points of reference' and dropping any habit that might reveal us as being from 'a non materially privileged background' (1994, p.181) and Maureen Duffy (1983) about working-class girls needing to surrender a culture of subordination. That we felt estranged and that we inhabited a culture of subordination, which school reinforced, was evident in our stories. We, like the educated working-class women discussed earlier, talked of being 'unable to handle it' 'misplaced' 'covering it up' 'trying to be what you weren't'.

Evidence of difference, of difficulty in fitting in at school, is manifest in a whole series of major and minor incidents and situations which caused discomfort. One woman, an East End girl sent to a boarding school in a 'shire' county, says, '*I loathed the school because I didn't fit and I can remember crying non-stop for a whole month*'.

Part of this distress was due to her and her family's ignorance of what others at the school took for granted – for instance, going home at half-term. The first half-term her parents had not allowed for this expense and she was invited home by one of the girls who lived on a farm. This – like her experience at the school – was '*really traumatic for me ... I just ... felt totally ashamed of my background, trying to be what you weren't. It's difficult*'.

K had also felt out of place. She says of her grammar school days that she had ...

> never been able to handle it ... [I just] got better at covering it up ... Just completely unfamiliar to me ... I just didn't like being at the school ... Remarkably quick though I learnt how to fail ... I didn't have the right voice and I had a home-made uniform ... You can't do that and succeed [laughs]. It doesn't work.

These extracts illustrate how class difference was learned through school. Both women compared themselves to other girls and came to feel 'misplaced', 'not fitting'. The differences they experienced were rooted in perceived economic, cultural and social inadequacies. These manifested themselves as feeling somehow lacking and having a sense of shame about one's background, voice, home-made uniform and so on. Survival depended on one's skills of 'trying to be what you weren't', 'covering it up'. If you were not from a privileged class-group 'adopting a demeanour similar to that of other students helped you to advance' (bell hooks, 1994, p.178). This could be traumatic but if you did not do it, you did not advance.

The pretence of belonging

Having one's home and school in separate geographical communities did have one advantage: we could keep up a pretence in school without risk of exposure from home. But this did not prevent or protect you from embarrassment. One woman remembers a girl in her grammar school saying to her, 'My mum said Bermondsey is an awful place' and feeling 'quite worried about that in case anybody picked up' that she lived in Bermondsey. 'There's no way I wanted to talk about that', she adds and suggests this might be where her 'secretive nature comes from.' Shame and a need to hide things about oneself for fear of being tormented or rejected by others was a feature of our lives.

Shame was also rooted in having to pretend. L, who went to boarding school, tells me:

> You're actually cut off from where you came from ... You were a young lady ... Sundays ... you donned your panama hat and white gloves and crocodiled to the church, imagine it [laughs] ... You didn't mix with the working-class in the surrounding village.

She was aware of being taken out of the working-class environment of home, cut off and placed in the boarding school environment. Boarding schools were alien to working-class culture and few working-class children went to one. Implicit in the school rules and codes of dress was a belief in the superiority of her peers at the school to which she now belonged – albeit temporarily – and the inferiority of the social group to which she would be returning.

The women's accounts are peppered with negative messages they were given about working-class people. To be included at school, or at least not excluded, we had to be silent and deceptive about who we really were, for we came from those dreadful places and were the very people to whom you were forbidden to speak. Having to be secretive and to cover up constantly reminded you that 'you did not really belong in the school'.

J's story is imbued with this same sense of not belonging. Although she had 'loved' school, she became very depressed when she entered the lower sixth form.

> There was some sort of like a common room for the lower and upper sixth ... and I don't know, I think it must have been because I'd always all along thought of this as the holiest of holies to people to go in there ... I can remember being very depressed.

Her awe of this building – the holiest of holies – and her reference to her depression suggests that entitlement to enter it possibly heightened her feelings of insecurity, of not being worthy.

Some things could be hidden but others could not, like the hand-knitted cardigans and having the 'right voice', accent and grammatical style. These were things the women remembered twenty or even forty years later. B recalls with horror when her ignorance of 'the proper past tense of verbs' was exposed. After saying: 'she learnt me how to do it', she recalls being told by a girl at the grammar school that, 'that's not the right word ... you say taught'. 'So there was all this', she goes on, revealing the immense pressure of constantly watching out, covering fundamental aspects of our identity such as the way we and our families and friends spoke. Lapses and ignorance brought exposure and humiliation. '*I really got teased bad because I had a cockney accent*', sums it up. I can still remember being smacked across the back of the head when I was 7 by a primary school teacher for not pronouncing 'h's' at the beginning of words. I learnt early that it was not all right to be your working-class self. Through the mechanisms of fear and humiliation we learned to be silent and ever-watchful. Silencing others is, as hooks remarks, 'the most oppressive aspect of middle-class life' (1994, p.180).

Curriculum

A sense of our inadequacies was conveyed to us in other ways, for instance how attitudes, values and beliefs are imposed via pedagogical strategies and subject material, something about which there has been little recent discussion.

> The selections teachers make in both overt and hidden curriculum demonstrate what is held in esteem and serves either to develop pupils' experience or to exclude them. (School Council, 1982, No. 19)

Messages signalling middle-class superiority were to be found in the curriculum from early on. Take reading schemes: I have vivid memories of *Happy Venture* infant reading books and my envy of and desire to be little Dora. Dora, blonde and petite, was pictured with Mother in the home, both of them immaculate and always doing things together. Father occasionally appeared dressed in a suit and carrying his briefcase, greeting Dora with a hug. The happy family, Mother, Father, Dick, Dora, Nip the cat and Fluff the dog, lived in a big house with an orchard. This was all in stark contrast to my own lived experience of a cramped urban slum, with a tired and ill working mother, and a father who came home from work covered in dirt. As outsiders looking in on the idealised middle-class home setting, how could we not see ourselves as people who were lacking?

Another closely related area of curriculum in which class bias emerged was story writing. I had always hated writing the stories that were required at primary school and even at 'O' level, about trips out or holidays. I hadn't been on holiday and outings were rare and unmemorable events. The significant events in my life were traumatic family illnesses, a father temporarily out of work, the burden of too many domestic responsibilities. Other activities like playing on the railway embankment, trespassing on derelict land, street fights, scrumping, all of them acts of defiance, could not be talked about in school. I could have written about my experience of being the only white child in a cinema showing an Indian film, or what I felt as an 8-year-old girl being taken to a wrestling match with a friend whose mother was white and father was Black, at a time when 'No Blacks' signs were commonly displayed in working-men's clubs. Somehow I knew these were not the topics being sought under the heading, 'Write about what you did at the weekend'.

The only time I can remember receiving a positive response to a piece of writing was on an occasion when I used the little adjectives book provided and strung together a glowing description of Autumn in a language I did not speak. This language form, presented as a universal norm, was not the language of those from working-class backgrounds – the true majority.

This class-based sense of inadequacy appeared in many curriculum areas and in many forms. For instance, in my secondary-modern school I can recall in the first year having to clean our shoes as part of our cookery lesson. As I only had one pair of shoes and these were badly worn down through use, I found this task extremely discomfiting. It brought to my attention my family's poverty and exposed it for public viewing. Then there was the expenditure required for cookery and sewing material that did not take into account our families' poverty. Money for things that would not be eaten, like rock cakes, and clothes that would not be worn, including the gingham cookery pinafore, was not forthcoming. The punishment at school for failure to comply was invariably public exposure.

At the same time, the housekeeping skills many of us acquired at an early age in our homes went unacknowledged. K remarks on how her practical skills were undervalued in grammar school:

> We had home economics ... and we made a cup of coffee and a slice of toast [laughs], piss off, I couldn't believe it that people lived in this situation where they'd never done this. Really bizarre but of course they hadn't.

Teachers, both through the curriculum but also through their overt and covert prejudice, subtly reinforced our sense of being different, of inadequacy. Talking about her sixth-form experience at a Catholic girls' grammar school where she, along with three other girls, had transferred on leaving an 11-16 Catholic secondary-modern school, R tells me that, '*We were always made to feel inferior to the rest of the girls ... [the] ones that made us feel inferior were on the whole the old biddies*'.

She makes specific reference to her form teacher, '*[she] never really liked us and actually referred to us on more than one occasion as 'the secondary element*'', and recalls them being blamed for 'odd little things', which certain staff had said, 'would not have happened two years ago', that is, before the secondary element were allowed in the school.

R identifies another problematic area for working-class girls: the implicit rules and codes of the school. Not knowing the 'rules of the game' had a noticeably detrimental effect on our chances of success. She gives an example:

> the rules of the game were ... as the other girls knew ... that you put your name down very quickly for the [A level] course you wanted ... [and] of course we hadn't ... the class was full. Interesting the ones they turned away were the secondary [modern] school ones.

B gives an example of how having to learn implicit rules handicapped her academic progress:

> there was all this talk about revision and I didn't know what revising was and girls used to take home great wads of books ... I really didn't know what they were doing and I came twenty-seventh I think out of a class of thirty ... Come that summer I knew what you had to do for exams and I think I came seventh then ... Once I figured out the rules ...

Who fitted in?

> There is an implicit consensus in our society as to where the various groups stand in the order of things. It is from within this consensual perspective children learn to notice group differences and how to evaluate them. (Davey, 1983)

> All those from the dominated class, signal their awareness of themselves as different, as peripheral, as the Other. (Stanworth, 1981, Intro)

Our sense of not fitting, of being different implies a real or imagined Other who did fit. There were, after all, those who did not wear home-made school uniform; whose language was not considered in need of correction; who were aware of implicit school rules and codes; for whom school knowledge appeared accessible; who could afford music lessons and school trips abroad; who were not the secondary element, and who were well received by teachers. To me these Others were those who were socially at ease in the school, confident, well-spoken and well-dressed. They may or may not have performed well academically, but they were not in the lower streams.

In my primary school, for instance, there was Joy. She was little Dora out of *Happy Venture*. I can visualise her now, a delicate girl with silky black hair, dressed in floral, cotton dresses with matching cardigans and ribbons. Joy was a model pupil, quiet, well-spoken, extremely polite and exceptionally neat. I adored her. Indeed, we sat together until her mother and the class teacher separated us. Although I was only 9, I sensed their fear lest I physically, mentally or culturally contaminate her. Joy went on to join her sister at the prestigious girls' grammar school: I joined mine at the local secondary-modern, just as the school had predicted.

Another of the women talked about having a friend with similar characteristics to Joy.

> My friend Catherine who had not only been an academic star (actually I don't think she'd done as well in her 'O' levels) ... I had her on this sort of pedestal. She was always terribly popular and pretty, her hair was never out of place, she was terribly fragile looking and she was wonderful at ... sport.

At my comprehensive school there was Vicky. She and I were in the same class. Observing Vicky gave me some insight into how class privileged certain students. Vicky was a doctor's daughter and although she was of Spanish origin and had lived abroad for a time, she spoke perfect Standard English in a very refined voice. The other thing I particular noted was the high quality fabric of her school uniform. It was these things which contributed towards making her special in teachers' eyes. In spite of being near the bottom of the class, Vicky was always treated with great respect and was clearly a favourite of many teachers. I recall that she entered the sixth form without the required number of 'O' levels – they changed the rule that year. She became head girl for reasons I did not understand at the time. Looking back however I can see that she and the Deputy Headmistress spoke the same language, had the same values and were socially and culturally at ease with one another. The same woman terrified me, such was the social and cultural gap between us. It was not because of her academic achievements that Vicky was rewarded but because she fitted the image the school wanted to portray, despite its comprehensive status. By putting girls like Joy, Catherine and Vicky on pedestals, we did not have to acknowledge our feelings of envy or our sense of injustice at the way we were treated by comparison.

One common attribute of the identified Other, referred to by all the women in the study, was wealth. L says of her boarding school, '*It was a school for people with money'*. K says of girls in her grammar school, '*They had big houses.*' B recalls, '*Lots of the girls were moneyed ... T's father was the astrologer in the* Daily Express *or something*'. J remembers that '*lots of pupils came from very rich backgrounds*' at her school and that there was a prep school attached to it. Compared with us these girls were wealthy, moneyed, rich.

Those who did particularly well at school, we perceived, were often from families that had money. Says J, '*They were the prefects. No one like me was ever made a prefect. No one like me was sort of chosen to be the star in the school productions'*.

K recalls how *they* were the ones in the top stream 'who did their three languages so they could be a doctor'. For B, *they* were the ones who had come to the school with specialised knowledge: 'lots had started to learn a foreign language'. For R they were the ones singled out for star treatment:

> A certain group in the sixth-form who were the teacher's [favourites] and all of them have actually been in school from the age of eleven. It was only a small number but the teachers had obviously decided they were destined for great things, like Oxford and Cambridge and they were obviously singled out for star treatment and everybody knew it ... There was very much a hierarchy [going to university]. We [the secondary element] came into the rest ... [University] wasn't for us. It was for these other groups.

In summary, our notion of the Other developed as we entered the secondary sector and came into contact with girls who came from seemingly rich backgrounds, who lived in big houses, had been to prep school and had started a foreign language. These were the girls for whom teachers had high expectations, who were far more likely to be prefects, head girls, stars in the school production, singled out for star treatment and destined for great things.

'Difference was structured into it': selection and streaming

> Difference was structured into it ... if you're not in the top stream you're stupid.
>
> If you're not in the twenty percent of that particular institution you're not valued in the same way.

Difference was structured by means of selection systems which had the effect of keeping most working-class children out of prestigious institutions. For instance, private school selection exams, the 11+ with its notions of fixed and hereditary general intelligence, streaming, setting. As Carolyn Steedman pointed out, 'ability groupings turn out in practice to make rough and comprehensible matches with social class divisions' (1982, p.6). That is, the hierarchy of ability corresponds with the hierarchy of class. Those in the lowest social positions, working-class children, find themselves in the poorest schools where achievement levels are likely to be low. This is in part due to powerful middle-class parental practices which ensure middle-class children get a privileged position in the state funded school system, irrespective of the educational needs of the mass of children whose need for support is greatest. This is seen in the subtle practise of social segregation by middle-class parents, operating through an implicit refusal to send their children to schools where there are 'too many' working-class children, that is, more than a tiny minority.

The women in this study took the 11+ and were sent to an allotted secondary-modern or grammar school. Two of us failed and were sent to secondary-modern schools. For me this was a devastating experience. Maureen Duffy captured my innermost thoughts at that time when she wrote:

> If I didn't pass I was stupid ... I was just a girl and life offered only things I despised, houses, children, security, housework ... I had to be different. (1983, p.99)

I was surprised when R, who had failed her 11+, told me she was not '*terribly sure what it was all about*', and that '*I can't even say it mattered to me ... it all sort of washed over me*'. Yet her father bought her a bike when she failed. She tells me, '*He must of thought that I was bothered by it.*' What is more, she also recalls, with some indignation, that those who passed their 11+ were publicly congratulated at school.

> It was the way they did it. In assembly in front of all the school they made the ones stand up who'd passed ... I mean can you imagine and everybody had to applaud them [she claps]. Of course the ones who hadn't there was no mention about where we were going.

One could conclude from these contradictory comments that failing did matter to her and that her denial was simply a form of self-defence.

Once at a state secondary school whether grammar, secondary-modern or comprehensive, it was common for students to be streamed, an even finer sifting process. We were both placed in 'A' streams within the first week of secondary-modern school, on the basis of one-hour mathematics and English tests, a common practice. It mattered what stream you were placed in initially because this was where you were mostly likely to stay throughout your school life. As R recalls,

> We were tested at the end of every year ... I've no memory of anybody moving from our stream down. Somebody did move in but only that once ... In effect you didn't really move out of your stream.

My own experience at secondary-modern and comprehensive school reaffirms this. When I entered a class for 13+ transfers at a comprehensive school, we were slotted in between the two top streams (the grammar) and two bottom streams (the secondary-modern). No-one moved up or down. If I think back now, the top two streams consisted mostly of those from the private housing estates while the bottom two consisted of the children from the nearby council estate. Through a product of the 1960s progressive thinking, the school's underlying ideology ensured the perpetuation of the elitism of the grammar school system, further symbolised by masters wearing gowns.

Streaming, whether at secondary-modern, comprehensive or grammar school, created social segregation by privileging those in the upper stream. This influenced your perception of yourself and of the 'Other'. R describes her experience of registering in a third year D stream class at her secondary-modern school:

> I really had no idea of what it was like in anywhere else apart from the 'A' stream until I became a fifth former ... Oh, I knew they existed, but I'd no idea of what it actually meant being in a 'D' stream class ... They were, I think, considered the terrors of the school... [I] picked up on the fact that ... some of them were illiterate ... I might of started thinking ... what syllabus are they doing 'cause it was obviously not the one I'd followed ... very different teaching must have gone on.

The 'A' stream by comparison were not 'terrors' or 'illiterate' and it was the heads of department who taught them.

B recalls of her grammar school, 'You rarely had anything to do with anyone in a lower stream ... we were very, very separate.' Being in a lower stream, in any institution, had negative implications and affected life chances. K, who also went to grammar school, reflects on this process,

> I was aware of streaming ... and not being in the top stream ... so I was stupid ... If you're not in the top stream don't matter what school you're in ... I didn't relate to the secondary [modern] school where all my other mates were ... I related to where I was in the structure.
>
> We all did Latin up to about the third year or something, but if you wasn't in that top stream and you hadn't done your five years of Latin so you could be a doctor ... There wasn't much else you could be except a doctor, you know what I mean [laughs].

Selection and streaming were socially divisive mechanisms that alienated the majority of working-class girls (and boys) and left them feeling they were somehow lacking, no matter where they were in the hierarchy. For instance, although I was in the 'A' stream I saw myself as a failure because I was in a secondary-modern school. At comprehensive school I continued to perceive myself as a failure because I was not in the top stream. K felt a failure at grammar school because she was not in the top stream. We blamed ourselves for not being clever enough, so taking on the implicit message of school that cleverness was something fixed and that their measurements of it were accurate. Our awareness of the effect of our economic, social and cultural background was to come much later: '*I look back and I look at the structure of that school, the people in there, the differences in their experiences and my experiences*', says one of the women with anguish.

Conflict: points of resistance

> It is when pupils feel unable to express themselves in school, or feel a wide gap between the values of home and those of school, that disenchantment and alienation are likely to set in. (Hughes, 1992, p.20)

Schools work on the assumption that any able student 'coming from a ... working-class background would willingly surrender all values and habits of being associated with this background' (bell hooks, 1994, p.182) and assimilate. If we assimilated we were rewarded, but 'if we chose to maintain those aspects of who we were, we were estranged, ... outsiders, interlopers, *undesirables*' (p.182). Acceptance meant assimilating middle-class values, so important for 'advancement', but it 'created a barrier, blocked the possibility of confrontation and conflict and warded off dissent' (p.178), confrontation and conflict which restricted, prevented or obliterated our chances of advancement.

Being accepted by the school meant conforming to what we came to perceive as ridiculous rules such as the specifics of school uniform. K comments on her refusal to wear a beret: '*You just wouldn't wear it ... just wouldn't do things like that*' and remembers making *'every kind of resistance to the most ridiculous kind of rules'*. Yet seemingly trivial offences were sevely punished. J, for example, was suspended in the fifth-form for changing her indoor shoes for outdoor shoes too early. What was this maintenance of strict dress code, the demand for rigid conformity and outright obedience about, if not social control? Rebellion was inevitable.

Despite our taking education very seriously, there was evidence of open conflict and resistance in our stories. A number of the women openly rebelled. One woman has memories of 'getting up to no good' and climbing out of a school toilet window and going along the roof, in a 'game we used to play'. K adopted a more extreme form of resistance: she forged letters until 'they found out.' She was truanting with another girl who lived near her and was also from a 'one-parent family'. Neither of them, she says, 'fitted in with anyone else'.

The school's punishment for this non-conformity was to ask her to leave school in the fifth form. The headmistress told her: 'This is a grammar school for girls' and that she was 'letting it down'.

> I can remember ... thinking this is really good, I hated the school so much I'm playing truant and there she is saying I don't have to come any more. Why hadn't I thought of this earlier [laughs] ... I get what I want after all... I don't know how much of it was just specifically that school or schooling ... It must have been painful ... It left such significant ... things at that age ... Yeah, because you go to a school ... connect with ... deviants, so that re-inforces the fact that, 'Oh god, you must be odd.'

Terms like 'deviant', 'odd', 'not fitting in' imply that she blames herself for not being able to cope in grammar school, a message that was reinforced by the Head. She had broken an implicit rule: 'grammar school girls' do not truant. Her behaviour is bad for the school's image and she had become a liability. Anyone not conforming must go. At no time was there any hint that the school had failed her. The school allowed her to go back to sit her 'O' level examinations. She believed this to be a punitive action, that they knew she would fail and they would be proved right. Reflecting on how this experience affected her, she says:

> I knew I didn't have the accepted factual knowledge that a lot of people had but I knew I wasn't stupid and I very quickly sussed out it was school I didn't like. I kind of latched on to that.

Despite now having a first degree and an MA, she is aware she lacks 'the accepted factual knowledge' acquired by those who succeeded through the conventional route – in the main, middle-class students. They are the norm against which she measures and finds herself wanting.

B was in the fifth form of grammar school when, she says, she 'started very slightly to rebel' doing no more than 'growing a very long fringe' and playing cards in the lunch hour, about which she says, *'I think maybe it would have been frowned on*'. That there were other incidents is evident because the school summoned her mother to be told that both she and her younger sister 'were badly behaved'. She observes tentatively, *'I suppose I just wasn't as biddable as I always had been.'*

Other women's rebelliousness also grew stronger as they got older. One in the lower sixth clashed with her RE 'A' level teacher, '*an old bitch ... aggressive, sarcastic, I hated her'*. She relates a particular incident,

> She sort of looked me up and down and ... All I wanted to do was hit her. I can remember I stood up and I had my fist raised ... and I was just about to punch her and then I thought, 'I don't fucking need this' and I just walked out and went straight to the head and told her that ... I wasn't doing it any more ... I'd had enough. She sort of calmed me down.

One is left wondering what was happening with this teacher that resulted in a pupil actually raising her fist to hit her? What message had been conveyed in the looking 'up and down'?

R confidently challenges teachers' behaviour when entering the sixth form – having transferred from secondary-modern to grammar school. She says of the formidable Miss Parol, '*I'd heard her spoken of in hushed tones ... around the school*' and recalls in her second week saying to this woman, '*You ought to be ashamed of yourself ... terrifying ...*' (a first-year class). '*Good grief*', she adds, '*this woman looked surprised ... I think nobody had actually said anything like that to her before*'.

Teacher attitudes

Teachers were usually our first sustained contact with anyone who occupied non-manual work roles. Most were women, since our primary schools were staffed largely by women and four of the girls attended single-sex secondary schools. It is of some significance that now we recall some of these teachers with emotionally charged words such as: 'loathed', 'hated', 'detested.' These negatives were a reaction to teachers we experienced as 'rigid', 'aggressive', 'sarcastic', 'vicious', 'arrogant', 'ignorant', 'distant', 'authoritarian', 'severe', 'dictatorial' and who evoked in us feelings of 'fear', 'terror', 'humiliation', 'resentment'. We perceived them as being 'old', 'ancient', 'looking about a hundred', 'wizened', 'been there for years', a 'hundred and ten if she was a day', and some of us spoke of them as 'old bitches', 'old bags', 'old biddies', 'women of a bygone era'. How old these women teachers actually were is not known.

One woman recalls an infant teacher as an '*old bitch, really vicious, she used to pull our ears ... and thump yer. She used to punch you on the back if you weren't listening and if you didn't have a hanky you used to get slapped*'.

Resistance started at an early age. '*I can remember ... we used to pass them [hankies] along the line.*' She laughs, but poignantly adds, '*You used to have your nails inspected so you did ... I suppose they thought they were saving the working-classes.*' Rules about having a hanky or clean nails, rigidly monitored by teachers, were again a matter of social control, in this case, forcing working-class children to be clean. This speaker remembers that she was allocated the responsibility and honour of washing her teacher's cup and saucer and recalls her humiliation at being publicly dismissed when she was caught 'picking her nose'.

R describes a primary school teacher as, 'ancient with grey hair in a bun ... so unsympathetic', and I also had an infant teacher like this. She appeared elderly, haggard, with straggly grey hair scraped back in a bun, and she bullied and humiliated you over seemingly trivial things. Her attitude was encapsulated in the words 15-year-old Annie Leitrim quoted her head saying: 'If their parents won't put any manners in them, then I will' (1979, p.122). It is significant that many such teachers came from the ranks of the upwardly mobile working- and lower middle-classes and despised the lower classes with whom they were often lumped.

Secondary school teachers were also criticised, particularly those who were very authoritarian. J says of her grammar school, '*I hated the PE teacher, an old bag. She didn't like me because I always used to answer her back and then she barred me from PE for the summer*'.

R describes her domestic science and needlework teachers at secondary-modern school as 'old biddies who were in a bygone era', and recalls with disdain 'being thrown out of needlework' for perching on the teacher's desk while queuing to see her. She laughs also as she remembers being in the sixth-form of a Convent grammar school where a pupil came in to the classroom and said: 'The principle would like to speak to that girl who ... actually ran past Signora'!

She tells me she had run over a bridge 'wide enough for three or four people to pass' not seeing the 'little woman', only 'a crocodile of children' as she went 'charging past'. Though she remembered a voice calling 'You girl stop', she had responded, 'Can't stop now, I'm late for a lesson' and she had thought no more about it. When she went to the principal 'feeling quite chirpy thinking this is going to be a tongue in cheek' she found she was 'furious' [again she laughs]. Like the other women she tells me, 'It is those attitudes I remember.'

If one dared to undermine teachers' implicit authority, for example, by answering them back, charging past them, sitting on their desks, breaking any of the unwritten rules, then the consequence was public humiliation: being looked up and down dismissively; a severe telling off; being barred from lessons. It was always expected that we would accept such punishments without demur.

Most of us are silenced by our acceptance of 'class values that teach us to maintain order at all costs' argued bell hooks (1994, p.179). Silence and obedience to authority are highly rewarded in schools, whereas 'loudness, anger, emotional outbursts are deemed 'unacceptable' ... vulgar disruptions of the classroom social order associated with being a member of the lower classes (p.178). Students who are unwilling to accept 'without question the assumptions and values of school' are quickly silenced or 'deemed trouble-makers' (p.179). As working-class students we were unable to defend ourselves openly and emotionally and express our thoughts and feelings, without putting our education in jeopardy.

Getting positive attention from teachers was equally difficult. R talks about wanting to be noticed and to have her success acknowledged throughout her primary school days. She remembers in infant class 'deliberately pretending to be asleep'. It was, she says, '*The only way I could get her [teacher] to notice me, which is quite interesting when you're only five or six*'. Her next infant teacher, she tells me, '*almost totally ignored me I think for the whole year ... I also have this feeling that she either didn't like me, or I certainly was not one of her favourites*'.

Rejection at such an early age made her determined. She says about a teacher at junior school, '*I got the impression that she thought I was not going to do very well at the end of the year's results ... Of course this made me determined that I was and that year I came third*'. This success made her re-evaluate herself:

> It made me realise that the gap between me and the children I considered bright, the untouchables, was not quite as vast as I thought it had been because now I appeared to be one of them.

R had observed that the children who were '*one of the hierarchy ... the top ones in the class ... the untouchables*' got more attention. When she joined this group, however, she found she got even less attention from teachers and blames herself for this. *'Perhaps I just wasn't a pleasant child'* [laughs]. Almost as an afterthought she adds that she '*didn't seem to have any problems getting on with other adults in the neighbourhood'*. Her problems lay with her teachers, not with working-class adults.

Nell Keddie in the 1970s talked about how teachers' denied that ability was associated with class whilst demonstrating the opposite in practice. The power of a teacher to undermine a child's success should not be underestimated as is illustrated in the continuation of R's story:

> In this school if you came first, second or third, you always got a prize ... considering this had only happened to me once before I thought this was wonderful .... I got no prize ... and when I asked her 'why?', she said, 'Oh I'm only giving first and second.'

She relates the teacher's negative response to the fact that she had challenged her:

> I never got on with this woman ... I suspect because I ... challenged things ... I don't think I would ever have been rude, but I think I might of on occasions said things like, 'that's not fair' [which] doesn't go down well with teachers.

Positively challenging a teacher was potentially dangerous for those who wanted to succeed.

I also remember having my achievements dismissed. When I got grade one for my commerce 'O' level examination, the class teacher made a point of telling me I 'should never have got it'. The reason was, I suspect, the fact that a working-class friend and I had complained to the Deputy Head when this teacher threatened to stop us taking our RSA typing exam. We had missed one of her lessons (claimed sickness) in order to revise for an 'O' level. In her eyes taking 'O' levels was not as important for the likes of us as a typing exam.

Such punitive acts have huge impact on our sense of self worth, not least because many of us linked our personal struggles in school to supposed defects in ourselves; a view which teachers, and the school's ethos, reinforced.

Were we successes or failures in school?

> Children of class IV and V are going to perform relatively badly compared with children of higher socio-economic groups. (Steedman, 1982, p.4)

One of the first things I became aware of when analysing the data was that we educated working-class women were not members of a special minority group of educationally successful working-class schoolgirls, as I had originally thought. Although more successful than many other working-class schoolgirls, we too were school failures. The difference was that our failure was less dramatic. Though we were all in grammar streams or equivalent classes in other secondary schools, not one of us was encouraged or thought able enough to apply for a place at a university. Given our current academic achievements now, one has to ask why. Five of the six women have first degrees and other equivalent qualifications, and three have masters' degrees.

Our definitions of success again derive from comparisons. At primary school level J spoke of being in the 'top group' and not one of the 'thickies'; R talked about joining the 'hierarchy', the 'untouchables'. Such comparisons became more pronounced at secondary school. L says, 'I was bright ... up against them', then wavers, remembering her brother saying the boarding school she was sent to was second-rate. K talks about feeling unsuccessful despite going to a grammar school. She measures herself against colleagues who, 'went on to the sixth-form ... have their three 'A' levels', whereas, 'I haven't kinda done that'.

In contrast R talks about feeling very successful at secondary-modern school. She too measured herself against 'the standards of other children' in the school. Though her abilities were not fully acknowledged at primary school or later in the grammar school sixth form, they were in the secondary-modern school where she spent the bulk of her secondary schooling. Significantly, she was the most academically successful of the women at school. And she is the only one of us who appeared to have developed any lasting sense of self-worth from her schooling.

While R found most of her primary teachers unsympathetic there was one teacher who had high expectations of her, a woman who lived in the same community and knew her family, including cousins who had done well at school. She tells me,

> My first day in the classroom, she ... informed me by the end of the year I was going to prove what I could do ... I was third overall of the class. Prior to that I'd always been twenty or thirty something and from that point on academically I didn't look back.

R attributes her success to the fact that she had 'got on with' this teacher. The teachers at her newly built secondary-modern school acknowledged her achievements. It did not seem to matter to her, as it did to me, that the school was not a grammar school. She tells me that '*I adored that school probably as I ... academically proceeded to do very well all the way through*' and that she was considered special by maths and English teachers and by the headmaster. R recalls her maths teacher's reaction to her test paper in her first week at the school,

> I finished it very quickly ... nobody else in the room had ... [he marked it whilst I was standing there] ... I'd got one mistake on the entire paper ... I then became, in his eyes, somebody who was very good at mathematics.

The head of department reinforced this perception of being good: '*I have a clear memory of him talking to me and actually him not being terribly interested whether anybody else in the class understood*'. Interestingly her view of herself as a good mathematician was maintained even though she failed 'O' level mathematics.

The Deputy Head also singled her out in English: '*It was our mock 'O' levels ... he'd marked them all ... he read out mine and said, 'Why is it that the youngest in the class ... seems to be able to do this and the rest of you aren't?*' She '*got on tremendously well with this man because he thought I was wonderful*'. R adds, '*I suppose I knew I was considered quite brainy*'. The head also reinforced her feeling of being successful.

> He decided that I had a very good speaking voice [laughs], so I became one of his stars ... We were something special to him because he could take us and show us off to other schools.

When she was in the fifth form he asked her, 'why did you fail your 11+?' R tells me:

> Just that statement in itself made me feel that I had great esteem in the eyes of teachers there ... I was made to feel I should have been a grammar school pupil and that obviously made me feel quite good.

She lays the blame for her 11+ failure on the last of her primary school teachers but '*I didn't feel like saying to him, 'Well actually I didn't get on well with the primary school teacher*'. This teacher had told her mother, that it 'wasn't really to be expected' that she would pass her 11+' [R whispers this as if she were the teacher secretly informing her mother].

Unlike at her primary school, key people in her secondary-modern school had high expectations of her, '*I knew I was considered quite brainy'; 'In his eyes [I was] somebody who was very good at maths'; 'I became one of his stars.*' This positive feedback fed her sense of worth, '*I should have been a grammar school pupil ... I left school feeling very successful*'.

There were also instances where she received negative feedback. For instance, she recalls that she 'wasn't any good' at science but relates her lack of success to low expectation, not lack of ability. '*I actually didn't get on terribly well ... I can remember doing my homework on the bus, obviously it [science] didn't hold very high expectations for me*'.

In the sixth-form of the grammar school to which she transferred she was labelled one of 'the secondary element' and less was expected of her. Just as in primary school, the school's low expectation of her was her driving force to success.

> I think the four of us who went there ... all passed our 'A' levels ... which actually I can't say of all the other girls who'd actually passed their 11+ and gone there. I suspect part of the reason is that we were battling against the odds ... they thought we weren't up to it ... didn't enjoy it.

This drive to 'prove oneself' is something the women in this study have in common, though at different levels.

The others offered little evidence of sustained feelings of success at either comprehensive, grammar or boarding school. References to success have had to be teased out of our texts.

Although in the top class at primary school a year early, I was not one of the few expected to pass the 11+. The only positive thing I can recall at this stage was the class teacher telling me that 'the head was pleased with my reading test results', which seemed to surprise him. I also recall that, in my last year when the special few got class prizes, the teacher discreetly invited me to choose a book from the classroom stock of old battered books. She never said, why. I assumed she felt sorry for me but perhaps I was a near miss.

I entered the 'A' stream of the local secondary-modern school in an inner-city slum area. Here I came third or fourth in the class, despite being twenty-eighth in English. At 13 I was one of a few to transfer to a new comprehensive school. I was delighted by this and left in the lower sixth with seven 'O' levels and an RSA Typing certificate. Despite being the only girl able to take geology 'O' level, one of the few to get maths 'O' level and representing the school and county in both netball and athletics, I did not feel successful or able. I always felt I didn't quite measure up. This feeling was reinforced by a number of factors. First, I was not at grammar school or in the top stream of the comprehensive. Second, I was not allowed to take English 'O' level until the sixth-form, and then, as expected, I failed it. Failing English, like failing the 11+ made me feel ashamed. Able people passed. Third, I was the last sixth-form girl in my house to be made a school prefect, a mark of my gross lack of confidence. Fourth, though my house master congratulated me on my 'O' level results, his handshake and genuine expression of delight exposed his low expectation of me – a very painful experience. Like some of the other women, I used these low expectations as my driving force forward. College and university brought success.

Though the other four women in this study passed their 11+, passing did not guarantee success. K tells me she has no memories of moments of success. Her primary school teacher's conviction that she would not pass the 11+ was to undermine totally her confidence when she did pass.

> It was a complete and utter shock when I passed ... I always throughout all me secondary school thought it was a fluke, that they'd got not exactly ... the scores wrong, but you know, it must have been a good day or something ... Well you do don't you because you believe it [laughs] ... for the whole of my life I have thought I was stupid.

The belief that it was 'a fluke' and that she was stupid was then reinforced by 'not being in the top stream' of grammar school. All she can remember is her truancy and its impact on her 'O' level results. '*I only got art, geography, English, stuff that you didn't need to ... or things that I knew I could write.*' Even now, she regards herself as lacking in subject-based knowledge, the kind transmitted in schools as fact.

Two women had positive images of themselves, at least in their early school years. J recalls a note her mother had kept, written by her teacher when she was about to change school at six. '*It goes on about how wonderful I was and what a clever girl and I would go far.*' At her new primary school she recalls, '*I must have been so bright [laughs] that they moved me into the next class and I was with my [older] sister.*' She says that '*It was easy for me ... I was one of the bright kids ... one of the chosen few ... I can remember when we passed the 11+ ... I was calm about it, joked beforehand*'.

Like B, she attributed her success to a teacher who knew her family and consequently held high expectations of her. '*My mum had gone to that school and the head of the school ... she had taught all my aunts ... We sort of had a tradition to live up to because they were all sort of good*'.

Her success, however, is confined to her primary school days. When talking about grammar school she refers to failure. She tells me she had 'loved school' until she started doing 'A' levels and had 'hated lower sixth' until she 'got really into studying' for her three 'A' levels. Despite doing well in RE she dropped this 'A' level after her clash with the teacher: '*I came first ... she nearly fainted ... and then I never did it, which was so stupid because it was interesting*'.

She failed geography 'A' level, despite studying it at night class alongside her father. She blames her teacher, 'a lovely little woman, really eccentric' but 'useless'. She did pass English 'A' level but '*by that stage it didn't matter because I'd been accepted at the College of Education*'.

B also went to the primary school her parents, grandparents and an older girl cousin who had passed the 11+ had attended. She also benefited from an attachment to a teacher who lived in the community and who had knowledge of family successes. For her, primary school was a time of 'always feeling able and being able to cope and enjoying what [she] did'. She recalls being 'a bit of a favourite', and offers evidence of this. For example, she was 'a staffroom monitor' and one of the first girls to be chosen by the headmistress to be 'taught to answer mass'. On passing the 11+ she was sent off to the headmistress's former school. 'All the girls with a high pass mark went there', she tells me.

This assured confidence that she gained in the primary school faded even though she was placed in the top stream of a two-stream grammar school. Talking about herself as a learner, she tells me, 'None of it really came naturally.' She attributes her success not to her ability but to her memory.

> I only ever learnt anything in a parrot fashion kind of way ... I never really thought very much for myself but my memory was very good at that time and it meant I could learn quite easily and do quite well ... I always had to work quite hard, had to revise ... I couldn't get away with not doing any work.

There is a powerful myth that in our society, if you are able school knowledge should come naturally. Interestingly, B did not judge a more privileged peer with the same harshness as she judged herself. '[She] had a photographic memory, she was way ahead, very, very bright'. Her peer's photographic memory meant that she was bright but her own 'very good memory' she associated with a lack of ability. This she substantiates by acknowledging that she had 'had to work quite hard'. This perception of herself as reliant on her memory left her with little confidence in her own ability. She tells me, '*I'm OK absorbing things that other people say and do and tell me, but I really can't come up with any new thoughts on anything*'.

L in the A stream in primary school, also had an attachment to a primary school teacher. '*I had the same teacher for four years, who I wrote to for a long time. She must have been the one that suggested I went away to school*'. But her memories of her success in primary school are ambiguous and she describes herself in conflicting ways:

> Quite submissive, hard working, bothered nobody ... I don't think I did very well, I think my natural intelligence got me by throughout school. I don't think I ever really put any effort into work.

Her strongest memory was of being sent away to boarding school. When she explains the borough's scheme to me, her explanation reflects her confusion:

> Where I lived ... they must have ran a scheme whereby they took children who would benefit from it ... I was told that, um, there were a set of places ... I used to say that I had this scholarship, school assisted places, but what was happening at this school it was people from homes that would benefit from being away from them ... I can see I must have been totally withdrawn.

L drew this conclusion from 'looking at the other kind of people that went to the school who were on assisted places'. She gives the example of another girl sent from her school whose mother 'was deaf and dumb'. L had been an elected mute at this age.

She had been very successful at the school, but explained that academic standards in the school were not very high. She '*felt it was a school for people with money and the academic standards just weren't very high, everything was within my reach*'.

Like several of the other women, she sees herself as bright and as 'against them'. She cites specific examples:

> I remember me and J took maths, nobody else in the whole school ... Did German when the rest of the form were doing extra maths, even did better in both areas ... things stuck in my head.

Like B she does not link her success to ability but to having 'an excellent memory'. She was, she says, lucky to have a photographic memory, which she also perceived to be a form of 'cheating'.

Although she said she had not failed anything in school, she did speak of failing 'O' level RE, and of having to give up geography. Of her RE exam she says, 'I deliberately failed ... a protest'. She tells me she was at a Catholic school which had accepted her on condition that she didn't let anyone know she was Jewish. L puts her failure in geography, down to lack of interest. 'Chucked out of geography because I got sixteen out of a hundred ... [It] didn't interest me.'

She also recalls being exceptional in staying on to take 'A' levels. 'I don't remember anybody else doing 'A' level with me ... perhaps C' and adds, 'I don't think I found the 'A' levels that I was doing easy. I think I struggled with that ...'

During our conversations about our school experiences, five of the women talked about lacking confidence and feeling a fraud. J tells me, 'I always appear to be very confident but I'm not really ... I do feel it very strong that I'm a fraud ... very strong sense of it.' L comments:

> It's basic insecurity and lack of confidence ... I think I probably feel threatened of being exposed ... found wanting ... It's about the values that you take on ... as opposed to valuing myself and my thoughts ... my experience is just the opposite ... unless I'm pretending somewhere along the line, that I'm not capable and don't acknowledge it.

Although achieving in the educational world, we continued to lack confidence in our own ability and to undervalue ourselves. Our assimilation in school and at college, as she observes, had required us to take on the values of others and at the same time to devalue those rooted in our home background, our language and culture. This left us with the belief that our real self is problematic and our false self a fraud.

Careers: we were to be office workers, teachers, nurses, nuns, good Catholic mothers

> The educational and occupational choices of those from the dominated class and sex implicitly take account of what is (or has been) typically possible for people with their ascribed position in the social structure. (Stanworth, 1981, Intro)

School taught me an early age that I belonged to a group of people who were perceived as inferior. The only way I knew of escaping this identity was to get qualifications. A second powerful driving force was the determination not to be economically dependent on anyone. I intuitively knew these things by the age of ten. Thwarted by the 11+ and being sent to a secondary-modern school offering no public examinations of value, transfer to a comprehensive school seemed to be the answer. However, any hopes that my career opportunities would genuinely open up once I was there were quickly shattered.

When option time came, seven months after I had joined the school and before the end of year examinations, the head of house pressured me, in the guise of professional advice, to choose commercial subjects. Commercial subjects, 'girls' subjects', were subjects 'marginalised within the curriculum' and 'discounted by the assessment system' (Jane Miller, 1992, p. 15) and as such, taken by pupils in the lower streams, the secondary-modern classes. Considering my poor performance in English his decision now seems somewhat bizarre. But with parents who had no knowledge base from which to advise me and for whom my future was of limited interest, I was in an extremely weak position to resist. With some resentment I compromised by taking commerce 'O' level and RSA Typing. I think it significant that Vicky the doctor's daughter – whose academic performance was far below mine – had received no such advice. It seemed inconceivable to me that she ever would. Commercial classes consisted only of girls from working-class backgrounds, all of whom, apart from myself and three friends (the only working-class girls in the 13+ transfer class) were in the bottom two streams.

Girls in selective schools and the top streams of the comprehensive were actively discouraged from taking commercial subjects. J says of her grammar school, '*We didn't do typing ... we never did any sort of commercial subjects' and B recalls that 'a very small number went into the commercial section ... shorthand and typing wasn't pushed at all.*' Nevertheless, she, her sister and closest friend, at her grammar school and L and K ended up in clerical jobs on leaving school before or during their 'A' levels. Selective education, with its rejection of commercial subjects on the basis of their perceived inferior status, had offered few achievable alternatives to these able working-class girls.

B remembers being guided towards careers that did not interest her. The school, she says, 'looked really for university, nurses ... teachers ... If you didn't do that you were pushed out really as office fodder.' The headmistress was always 'on the look out for nuns'. By her third year, she herself had decided she wanted to be a Carmelite nun, '*I think I was impressionable ... it probably seemed romantic*'. Other working-class school friends were similarly influenced. When she turned against the idea she found herself having to explain to a 'disappointed' head why she had changed her mind. She studied nine 'O' level subjects and then decided to '*give maths and physics and chemistry a miss*' and '*Again Mother Pat was quite upset, because she wanted me to go into nursing*' and had told her she would need physics. Not wanting to do nursing she opted for history, English and French 'A' levels. After two terms in the sixth form she left school because 'things were difficult at home.' Her mother left her father. Though she took a job in an insurance office, she had a desire to go to university. She tells me, '*I used to say I wanted to go to university ... I used to get philosophy books from the library and ... think I'd love to ... learn about it.*'

L commented that her 11-16 boarding school 'got in teachers' so that she could study for 'A' levels. At the end of her first year of French, German and economic history 'A' level, she had to leave unexpectedly because her father decided not to continue the payments. There were pressures on her to support herself financially so she took a filing job in a bank. She tells me she could have gone on to a local state grammar school and that she had wanted to finish her 'A' levels but that she *'couldn't cope ... couldn't face it meeting a whole ... lot of new people'*.

I also left school before completing 'A' levels. My parents no longer expected to support me. Although the school had directed me towards clerical jobs and the forces, I decided I was going to teachers' training college not because I wanted to teach but because I wanted the same opportunities as others. Exclusion had been such a strong feature of my school experience.

Only two women were able to stay on at school long enough to complete their 'A' levels. Both were directed towards primary school teaching. J recalls the lack of careers guidance by the school. You were *'either a teacher or a nurse ... for most of the girls that was your two choices ... The majority ... either went to the Catholic Training College or ... university'*. Moreover, 'the ethos of the school' was 'concerned with turning out good ... Catholic mothers'. Having dropped an 'A' level in which she was doing well, she lost the opportunity of applying to a university. Somewhat defensively she states, *'What was the point in me going to university, 'cos I wanted to be a teacher?'* Working-class girls were always grateful to be accepted into a teacher training college. Only in later years was she aware of the missed opportunity of a university place, *'I could kick myself that I didn't go.'*

R tells me that she had decided that she'd quite like to be a teacher, *'not that I can recall any other option being put my way'*. There was, she says, no careers structure in the school, and she was well aware that university was not perceived as appropriate for the 'secondary school element',

> University was the thing for aspiring to and the rest of you well, training college ... I don't think any attention was given to anybody who didn't want to go to either of those ... I can remember when it came round to filling in your form to apply to college or universities, it never entered my head to apply to university and nobody on the staff ever said, 'Oh why don't you apply to university.' Just never entered anybody's head because it wasn't for us ... it was for these other groups.

While most students took three 'A' levels, she took two which she passed. At a teacher's suggestion she, had dropped one subject, again without realising or being told that the option of university would be closed to her.

Fear of leaving home and being independent

> I could of left home and gone off somewhere but I didn't ever want to, so I didn't.
>
> Don't think I'd of been able to cope without my family.
>
> I wasn't very good at coping on my own.

Leaving school should have been the first step to independence but three of the women talk about their disbelief in their survival outside the family.

At 18 one woman went to teachers' training college (at the opposite end of the country to escape her father's domination). I lived in a flat – my parents having moved away – and worked as an unqualified teacher while finishing my 'A' levels. Another woman became pregnant at seventeen and then married. The three other women all felt they were not ready to leave home.

One woman who attended a Catholic, single-sex teacher training college lived at home. She tells me:

> I could of left home and gone off somewhere but I didn't ever want to ... I have a very strong family background ... totally cushioned by that ... None of us left home ... I used to hand over my grant to mum ... people think, 'Oh that's terrible', but I mean I knew when I was well off ... I never sort of had any problems with that ... I always felt quite safe.

Later in our conversation she acknowledges that '*I should of gone I think it's better if you do ... I suppose I was so comfortable at home, I didn't have any reason to leave*'. Living at home until you married was common in working-class families. Young women rarely had any choice but she did. Nevertheless, she stayed until she married at 24.

B also felt she needed family and friends around her for security and gives this as a reason for not pursuing her desire to go to university. '*I'd never been away from home and I don't think I'd of been able to cope without my family. I think I was so insecure.*' By 'family', she meant her sister. Had this sister chosen to go to university, she tells me, '*I think I'd have felt much happier about it*', but she 'just wouldn't have considered it, wouldn't have wanted it, whereas, I might'. The *desire* went, she says, 'quite soon after [I'd] started work ... perhaps when I found my first boyfriend'. We have seen that working-class females in formal education while in relationships with 'uneducated' working-class males often became discouraged, as Willy Russell dramatised in *Educating Rita*.

B told me that she and her sister had once thought of living on their own, but felt unable to. They '*did think of leaving and getting a flat with another girl ... If I'm honest I don't think we had it in us ... I think we were kind of tied, you know, very insecure*'. She lived at home until she married at 23.

> I always wanted to get married ... I was very much concerned with not being left on the shelf ... I wouldn't have known how to cope with that, although now I think it would have been the best thing that could have happened to me ... because then I would have to learn to live on my own for myself.

Being 'left on the shelf' or 'living on one's own' were common fears. The situation was exacerbated for the majority of working-class women by an inability to support themselves economically.

L left home to be married. Having been sent away to boarding school had left her feeling insecure and she had not wanted to leave home again.

> I was the one that went away but I felt I was deserted by being shoved away and I felt at that time I could cope least of all ... I had nothing to come back [to] and coping with boarding school isn't like living is it ... it's institutionalised.

She attended a teacher training college, but remained at home. In her last year her father had become so difficult that she lived in at college and when she qualified she moved into a flat. She tells me, '*I wasn't very good at coping on my own ... It was awful.*' So she went back home

> I never had the strength or the where-with-all to cope ... I realised that when I was at college because I hated it. I only went back [home] cause I couldn't cope ... I stayed until I was twenty-seven ... I did not have the 'what is it that you need to cope in life?' Sense of self.

These women stayed at home despite aggressive fathers and distant mothers. As one woman put it they 'learnt to survive in it'. It was not easy for any of the women in this study to break free. Emotional ties rather than economic and social dependency held us back.

Chapter 9
Conclusion

I have come to realise that the two parts of this book represent the two sides of my acquired identity, the middle-class woman and the working-class girl. These two identities stand apart. Part I of the book presents largely formal knowledge from the academic world, whereas Part II is based on the informal knowledge acquired through lived experiences. One source of knowledge could easily feed in to the other, both publicly and privately, were it not for the existence of a social hierarchy which privileges middle-class knowledge and cancels out working-class knowledge. This allows uncomfortable things such as white middle-class dominance and oppression to be avoided. The book places the two sources and forms of knowledge side by side as comparative perspectives, which occasionally overlap. Such disruption of the knowledge hierarchy is resisted by many academics, who deny or dismiss the validity of informal working-class knowledge, unless it is reworked within a traditional academic framework. The concept itself of class is largely absent from the mainstream academic agenda, as gender and educational texts reveal. This signifies where real class power lies.

Failing working-class girls stands alongside the accounts of other educated working-class women who strongly argue that social class 'continues to be an important part of social identity despite ... prevailing discourses which constitute it as irrelevant' (Reay, 1998, p.259). Being unaware of class difference does not mean that it doesn't exist. Classifying practices are 'enacted on a daily basis by many of those who do not think class is an issue' (Skeggs, 1997a, p.134). While the ways in which class is manifested have 'shifted and mutated', class 'continues to influence actions and attitudes across society (Reay, 1998, p.265). This prevails in the education market, whose growth in the 1990s has provoked further class and race segregation (Bagley, 1996). As illustrated in earlier chapters, exclusionary devices in education are widespread (Noden *et al*, 1997). By ignoring class and race interests, the education market has privileged white middle-class groupings, who are best skilled and resourced to exploit the market to their advantage (Gewirtz *et al,* 1995; Reay, 1996). Take for instance the 'current orthodoxy of individualistic self-realisation', which is simply a promotion of the 'almost universal acceptance of middle-class perspectives in society' (Reay, 1998a).

This book set out to highlight class as a learnt social position and confront the on-going identification of working-class people and particularly girls and women, as inferior 'Others' historically, socially and psychologically. The evidence is presented in Part I, examining mainstream academic disciplines and theoretical frameworks that describe and explain class and gender differences. It is affirmed in the autobiographical and biographical accounts of the lived experiences of working-class girls and women presented in the Introduction and Part II. The women's accounts offer differing versions of knowledge, insight and perspective to those in Part I.

This exposes the ways in which political and economic institutions and social structures explicitly or implicitly reinforce the belief that working-class people are lesser beings and deserve less. The process starts in childhood, when we internalise negative messages about ourselves, our family and community – based on shame. This oppression becomes individualised and we are conditioned to believe in our own inferiority.

The stories we have told of our school experience are not the fairy tale stories of a liberal 60s education, or tales of working-class heroines basking in the resplendence of high culture portrayed in Maureen Duffy's (1983) story. They are fragments of memories which offer a clue to the kinds of struggles able working-class girls, in varying degrees, experience within the education system. The women in this study were the subjects of a particular educational history when everyone, supposedly on the basis of their ability (defined as 'innate intelligence') competed for a limited number of privileged places in a few selective secondary schools. The advantages of the middle classes in this so-called provision of 'equality of opportunity' were denied or dismissed. The 'mass' failure of working-class children was attributed to their low ability. In a climate of educational theory and assumptions where 'social, linguistic and cultural deprivation' and 'compensatory education' discourses prevailed (Steedman, 1982), it was being the socially, culturally and economically disadvantaged that was the problem. Such discourses operate in middle-class interests. These are not terms we use to describe ourselves.

Success in school mattered to us. It was the only way to avoid the social and economic oppression – in the home and the work-force – endured by working-class women: our mothers and grandmothers. Rejecting our mother's life: her insecurity, dependency, poverty, illness, exploitation, by pursuing a formal education, 'without warning' presented us with dilemma, denial and treachery (Lynch and O'Neill, 1994; Reay, 1996). To succeed in school we had to 'fit'. This required us to abandon or keep secret a core aspect of our self: our working-class identity. At a superficial level this meant our accent, grammar, appearance; on a deeper level it meant the values and beliefs of our family and community. These things became shame-based.

If we became what the school wanted we could not be what family or local peers wanted. Our attempts to adopt and adapt met with disapproval. Educated daughters 'separating off', 'changing their values', 'wanting more than they were entitled to', caused within some families resentment and fear of loss. Peer rejection, particularly by boys, was another issue. Girls who aligned or appeared to align with school so as to pursue a career, severely undermined traditional working-class gender roles. We, for our part, found it difficult not to feel ashamed of aspects of our families and were fearfully dismissive of our peers betraying them in school through our silences or denial of their existence.

Being caught between these two often antagonistic forces that made different demands, left many of us feeling uncomfortable at home and at school; we did not belong. In neither place could we talk about the impact of the other. At the time the on-going damage to our sense of self, psychologically and emotionally, was never consciously acknowledged by the school, the family – or ourselves.

Academic achievement is difficult in a competitive system beset with barriers. We encountered a class-based and informed pedagogical process; a curriculum which excluded us; socially and culturally specific rules which were presented as taken-as-given ways of proceeding; teachers who had low expectations of us and who could dismiss or deny success; limited material and devalued cultural resources to call upon; parents who had no knowledge of how to make the system work for us or the confidence to challenge its unfairness.

Schooling has yet to be created by and for working-class communities. There is a major discrepancy between the institutions' criteria and the everyday 'lived' agendas of working-class people which needs to be kept in mind when addressing unequal educational outcomes. The on-going belief persists that schools have to work on us to change us, rather than to work with us as we are. How can a state education system insist that in order to receive full benefits, working-class children must be separated off and alienated from family and peers?

This partly accounts for the high levels of underachievement and high drop-out rates among working-class children who wanted what school had to offer. Though one might argue that girls (and boys) like those in this book were not able enough to gain the grades needed for a university, subsequently acquired academic qualifications and achievements show otherwise. Fitting in when you were socially and culturally misplaced was virtually impossible and the psychological cost of conformity too great. Even when striving to conform, underachievement is difficult to avoid when all acquired knowledge in working-class families was discounted and excluded from the school (and university) curriculum.

For those of us who overcame the obstacles and went on to higher education, the driving force had been less a desire 'to be a ...' than a determination 'not to be ...' trapped in poverty and dependency. Our knowledge of occupations was limited to those of the working class and schools simply directed us along the traditional avenues for upwardly mobile working-class girls: office workers, nurses, primary teachers. This is part of a mechanism for controlling the working-classes (Walkerdine, 1990).

A woman friend surprised me by talking about the ethos of her grammar school as being 'the development of intellectual potential, the value of intellect in itself'. It was, she said, 'not linked at all to work or money and people who did see it like that were sort of regarded as not aspiring to the Higher Good'. This, she suggested, is 'an indication of class'. I was left wondering how many educated working-class girls like myself saw education only as qualifications, a way of meeting a need to be legitimated by the system. Jackson and Marsden's description of the drift of working-class girls into teaching, not because of a desire to teach but as part of a drive to acquire further qualifications had a strong resonance for me. It was, the authors said, 'as if education had never nourished in them any other capacities except those needed to score high marks in academic examinations' (1968, p.179). Self-worth, the need to achieve and aquire academic qualifications through educational performance, can all become merged.

There are complex psychological implications for those of us presently living out unresolved conflicts from childhood, a part of the self that holds on to the working-class child's belief in its inherent inferiority. Being allocated 'middle-class status' in adulthood 'is not the same as inhabiting a middle-class identity' (Reay, 1998, p.264). Until recently this level of our experience has gone unnoticed; knowledge, embedded as it is in educated working-class women's peculiar isolation has remained untheorised. Educated working-class women are more confident about revealing their class background, and a growing body of research is emerging which highlights and legitimates the difficulties inherent in being working-class girls and academic women. Recognition of these tensions is a helpful step forward. However, the material conditions of working-class people's lives: health, housing, education and employment opportunities, have to change.

What does the future hold?

High levels of poverty and illness in working-class families persist. An unprecedented widening of income differences and the growth of relative poverty marks the closing decades of the twentieth century. Thousands still live in neighbourhoods in England where unemployment is two-thirds above average, under-age pregnancies are fifty per cent higher and a quarter more adults have poor basic skills. Poor health and life expectancy relate closely to the extent of income inequality (Wilkinson, 1996). The more deprived section of the population, in which women are over-represented, pay a heavy price for successive governments' failure to take seriously the social causes of disease and psychological problems. It is the women in our families who are expected to deal with these things. By April 2000 the government aims to lift one million children out of poverty. If they succeed, 3.6 million (of approximately 13.3 million) will still be left in poverty.

At the same time the government is allocating large sums to deprived areas, a marker of its recognition of social and educational inequalities. The blueprint is formal education, training and employment. An unprecedented array of initiatives has been introduced with the aim of reducing truancy and exclusions and raising educational standards – defined in terms of national test results – to ensure that councils and schools meet government-imposed targets. Though it remains unstated, we are talking about the educational failure and school rejection of working-class pupils, Black and white. The initiatives are additional to the current policies for raising standards, which focus largely on the mechanistic aspects of school input: honing the curriculum, identifying priorities, enforcing them through the publication of league table results and school inspections and the contentious practice of naming and shaming schools. By putting such emphasis on measured school outcomes, the policies have unintentionally exacerbated the class-based polarisation of schools and the failure of working pupils. Ignored are the social and psychological 'hows' and 'whys' of working-class children's failure.

Included in the new initiatives is 'Excellence in Cities', a £350 million package of proposals targeted at regenerating the most disadvantaged areas. For instance, up to fifty of the lowest-performing inner-city secondary schools, with their associated primary schools, are to become small educational action zones with allotted funding. These schools can disapply national pay and conditions regulations, the national curriculum, and national targets. The act of excluding the lowest performing schools will of itself drive up national standards, ensuring the government can meet its targets. Other supportive initiatives include Sure Start to support pre-school children, school based learning mentors for underachievers and single teenage mothers (again mostly working-class), learning centres, specialist and beacon schools. These initiatives have been clearly set out and communicated by the government but there is little information on the involvement of working-class people in the communities that these initiatives have been set up to serve.

Support for inner cities is aimed at a wider audience than working-class children, as evidenced by the setting up of 'world tests' targeting the top five to ten per cent of gifted pupils. We saw in Chapter 2 that middle-class children do significantly better than working-class children in formal 'tests' but the class-biased nature of these tests is ignored. It is envisaged that successful pupils will be able to attend university summer schools, master classes at local specialist schools or independent schools during the holidays, so disregarding the need for most able working-class pupils in poor families to work part-time and the discomfort any 'gifted child' might feel in such an environment. Or are these children to be left out? This initiative was not generated within a working-class community – another example of support that is always on the terms of Others.

Over three years a £2.3 billion Single Regeneration Budget and the new additional £800 million National Strategy for Neighbourhoods will target communities in deprived areas. The latter explicitly links improvements in social conditions to improvements in educational performance. The intention is to have maximum involvement of communities in tackling disaffection, unemployment, drugs and other social issues. Previous initiatives that have imposed without consultation with communities have failed. Yet the approach is still top-down, although community initiatives are encouraged. Current social and educational policies and practices largely exclude working-class people from policy-making decisions, even if implicitly. This in itself is a strong marker of continuing class inequality.

This book has demonstrated that it is not simply a case of 'deprived', 'disadvantaged' communities raising their educational standards by doing better on national tests. Such attitudes deny the existence of differing values, beliefs, ways of knowing and bodies of knowledge possessed by different groups of working-class people of various ethnic groups. A key requirement for raising standards in poorer areas is the involvement and support of working-class people. Governments and schools need to have working-class people on their side but are not adopting such an approach. Working-class people can rarely make decisions influencing educational practices within their own community and have no real say nationally. Consequently education has a long way to go before it can meet the differing needs of working-class people who meanwhile will continue, whether passively or aggressively, to drop out.

The book challenges the government on its attitudes to working-class people, and specifically towards the education of working-class girls and women. The social and psychological experiences of the people whose lives it is trying to change are still ignored and it is even implied that educational failure is not a problem for working-class girls. It is high time for attention to be paid to working-class girls in terms of examination performance, further education and work placements. Female work placements and further education training courses are being used as 'domestic apprenticeships', drawing upon domestic and caring skills learnt in the home (Skeggs, 1997). Such courses are training working-class girls to have 'realistic' – i.e. low – expectations for their futures (Buswell, 1992, p.94). The problems that underlie girls' educational failure and which manifest themselves in self-exclusion, anorexia, withdrawal, depression and early pregnancies, are forms of resistance and offer us an important perspective from which to review the education system.

The childhood experiences of educated working-class women, until now largely untapped, carry important messages for policy makers whose aim is to raise standards and reduce social exclusion. They reveal, through the generations, how class is acted out in daily interactions and what it means to be a working-class girl in the 1990s. With the decline of large manufacturing industries bringing the emasculation of traditional working-class men (Arnot, *et al*, 1999) and the growth in the service industry and increased female employment, working-class community life-styles are changing. These changes strongly affect the structure of working-class men and women's personal relationships in the home as well as the work-place. Any data collection needs to place working-class people's views on educational failure or success more centrally and involve them in how *their* children's failure can be overcome. Educated working-class women's accounts can provide important pointers for action.

Meanwhile we start the new millennium with a school system which remains very much 'classed'. The top seventy schools in the league tables are all private, many of them former grammar or direct-grant schools, and the divide between state and private education is stronger than at any time since 1945 (Adonis and Pollard, 1998). And the sharpening polarisation in income and wealth continues to correlate closely with the extreme social inequalities of examination outcomes year after year.

Notes

1. These ideas developed from a valuable exchange with Isobel Urquahart, Homerton College.
2. The inclusion of tokenistic material on Black women simply to add 'cross-cultural' spice has been avoided.
3. In focusing on working-class girls it is not my intention to deny or belittle the historical plight of working-class boys and men.
4. G. Whitty, S. Power, T. Edwards 'Destined for Success? Educational biographies of academically able pupils', reported in 'Blue-collar elite best off in private schools, *Times Eucational Supplement* (*TES)*, 27/3/98, p. 4
5. Former education officer of ILEA, 'Taking the terminology to task', *TES*, 22/3/96.
6. Sarah Cassidy, 'Middle-class boost to A-level results', *Times Educational Supplement (TES)*, 20/8/99, p. 4
7. Ian McCallum, former principal research officer, London Research Centre, reported in '5,000 pupils prove social class matters', *TES*, 25/9/98, p. 3
8. Educational Research Trust director, Report of the Social Market Foundation, An Anatomy of Failure: Standards in English Schools for 1997.
9. S. Demack, D. Drew, and M. Grimsley of Sheffield Hallam University reported in 'Learning gulf divides rich and poor pupils', *TES*, 2/4/99, p. 1
10. A. Gibson, Exeter Univ., S. Astjama, Plymouth Univ., American Research Assoc. Conference, April, 1999.
11. Jeremy Sutcliff, 'Who's out there on society's margins', *TES*, 13/11/98, p. 23
12. D. H. Moston, Brook High, Manchester, in a letter to the *TES*, 1994; P. Borchers in *TES*, 1999.
13. Mark Wightman, Durham University reported in 'Ofsted figures support failing schools poverty link', *TES*, 31/7/98, p.3
14. P. Borchers, 'Ofsted fails to grasp subtle issues of poverty', *TES*, 18/6/99, p. 19.
15. Government figures, *TES*, 9/8/96.
16. Maggie Woodrow's (European Access Network) 1998 commissioned report 'From Elitism to Inclusion', funded by CVCP and other Higher Education agencies. Reported in 'Working-class talent untapped', *TES*, 6/11/98, p. 9
17. Derek Fatchett, 'Our failed culture needs a good knock on the head', *Guardian*, 6/4/93
18. Higher Education Funding Council For England (HEFCE), 1998, 'Widening participation: specific funding proposals/programme for consultation 98/35; 98/39
19. Committee of Inquiry into Higher Education for Newham, 1993.

20. C. Howarth, P. Kenway, G. Palmer, and C. Street 'Monitoring poverty and social exclusion: Labour's inheritance' reported in 'Report lifts veil on poor ghettos' *TES*, 18/12/98, p. 7
21. Helen Epstein, 'Equality, fraternity, longevity', in The Editor, *Guardian*, 4/7/98, pp. 12-13

Bibliography

Abbott, P. and Sapsford, R., 1987, *Women and Social Class*, London: Tavistock

Abrahams, J., 1995, *Divide and School: gender and class dynamics in comprehensive education*, London: Falmer Press

Acker, S., 1973, 'Women and Social Stratification', *American Journal of Sociology*, 78, pp. 936-945

Acker, S., 1981, 'No-woman's-land: British Sociology of Education, 1960-1979', *Sociological Review*, 29(1), pp. 77-104

Acker, S., 1986, 'What do Feminists want from Education', in A. Hartnett and M. Naish (eds) *Education and Society Today*, Lewes: Falmer Press

Adams, C., 1982, *Ordinary Lives,* London: Virago

Adams, C., 1987, 'Gender, Race and Class: Essential Issues for Comprehensive Education', in C. Chitty, (ed.) *Redefining The Comprehensive Experience*, Bedford Way Papers, 32 London

Adonis, S. and Pollard, S., 1998, *A Class Act*, London: Penguin

Ainley, P., 1992, 'The Making of the Middle Class', *The Times Higher Education Supplement*, March 6, p. 17

Aldridge, J., 1993, 'The Textual Disembodiment of Knowledge in Research Account Writing', *Sociology*, 27(1), pp. 53-66

Alexander, S., 1976, 'Women's Work in Nineteenth Century London', in J. Mitchell and A. Oakley (eds) *The Rights and Wrongs of Women*, Harmondsworth: Penguin

Amos, V. and Parmar, P., 1987, 'Resistances and Responses: the experience of Black girls in Britain', in M. Arnot, M. and G. Weiner (eds), *Gender and the Politics of Schooling*, London: Hutchinson, pp. 211-222

Angelou, Maya, 1969, *I Know Why the Caged Bird Sings*, New York: Random House

Anon *Women Live*, Issue 2, Winter, 1987, p. 6

Anyon, J., 1980, 'Social Class and the Hidden Curriculum of Work', *Journal of Education*, 162, pp. 67-92

Anyon, J., 1983, 'Intersections of Gender and Class: Accommodation and Resistance by Working-Class and Affluent Females to Contradictory Sex-Role Ideologies', in S. Walker and L. Barton (eds), *Gender, Class and Education*, New York: Falmer Press

Appleton, W., 1981, *Fathers and Daughters: A Father's Powerful Influence on a Woman's Life*, London: Papermac

Arcana, J., 1984, *Our Mothers' Daughters*, London: The Women's Press

Aries, P., 1965, *Centuries of Childhood*, New York: Vintage

Arnot, M., 1983, 'A Cloud over Coeducation: an analysis of the forms of transmission of class and gender relations', in S. Walker and L. Barton (eds), *Gender, Class and Education*, Basingstoke: Falmer Press

Arnot, A., David, M and Weiner, G., 1999, *Closing the Gender Gap*, London: Polity

Arnot, M. and Weiner, G., (eds), 1987, *Gender and the Politics of Schooling*, London: Hutchinson

Ashendon, D., Connell, B., Dowsett, G., and Kessler, S., 1987, 'Teachers and working-class schooling', in D. Livingstone *et al.*, (eds), *Critical Pedagogy and Cultural Power*, London: Macmillan

Atkinson, P., 1990, *The Ethnographic Imagination*, London: Routledge

Attar, D., 1990, *Wasting Girls' Time: The History and Politics of Home Economics*, London: Methuen

Bagley, C., 1996, 'Black and White Unite of Fight? 'The racialised dimension of schooling and parental choice', *British Educational Research Journal*, 22(5) pp. 569- 580

Ball, S., 1981, *Beachside Comprehensive*, Cambridge: CUP

Ball, S., 1990, 'The Education Reform Act: Market Forces and Parental Choice', in A. Cashdan and J. Harris (eds), *Education in the 1990s*, Sheffield: Sheffield Hallam University, PAVIC

Ball, S., Gerwirtz, S. and Bowe, R., 1994, 'School Choice, Social Class and Distinction: The realisation of social advantage in education', *Markets in Secondary Education Project Paper*. Available from King's College, London

Barber, M., 1993, *National Commission on Education* (NCE), Briefing No. 16

Barker-Lunn, J., 1970, *Streaming in Primary School*, Windsor: NFER

Barnard, H. C., 1963, 'The Education of Girls and Women' in H. Barnard, *A History of English Education From 1760*, University of London Press

Barney Dews, C. and Leste Law, C., 1995, *This Fine Place So Far From Home: Voices of Academics From the Working Class*, Philadelphia: Temple University Press

Barrett, M., 1987, 'Gender and Class: Marxist feminist perspectives on education', in M. Arnot and G. Weiner (eds), *Gender and the Politics of Schooling*, London: Hutchinson

Barrett, M., 1980, *Women's Oppression Today: Problems in Marxist Feminist Analysis*, London: Verso

Barrett, M. and McIntosh, M., 1982, *The Anti-Social Family*, London: Verso

Barry, K., 1989, 'Biography and the Search for Women's Subjectivity', *Women's Studies International Forum*, 16, pp. 561-577

Basch, F., 1974, *Relative Creatures: Victorian Women in Society and the Novel 1837-67*, London: Allen Lane

Bates, I., 1990, 'No Bleeding Whining Minnies': Some Perspectives on the Role of YTS in Class and Gender Reproduction', *British Journal of Education and Work*, 3(2), pp. 91-110

Bates, I. and Riseborough, G., 1993, *Youth and Inequality*, Buckingham: Open University Press

Batsleer, J., Davis, T., O'Rourke, R. and Weedon, C., 1985, *Rewriting English*, New York: Methuen

Benn, R., and Burton, R., 1993, 'Women, Social Class and Access to Higher Education.' Paper presented at the British Sociology Association Annual Conference, University of Essex

Bentley, T., 1998, *Learning Beyond the Classroom*, London: Routlege

Bereiter, C. and Engelmann, S., 1966, *Teaching Disadvantaged Children in the Pre-school*, New Jersey: Prentice Hall

Bernstein, B., 1973, *Class, Codes, and Control, Vol. 1, Theoretical Studies towards a Sociology of Language*, London: Paladin

Bernstein, B., 1985, 'On Pedagogic Discourse', in J. Richardson (ed.) *Handbook of Theory and Research in Sociology of Education*, New York: Greenword Press

Bertaux, D., 1981, *Biography and Society*, London: Sage

Bhavnani, K. and Coulson, M., 1986 'Transforming Socialist Feminism: the challenge of racism', *Feminist Review* 23, pp. 81-92

Bhavnani, K. and Phoenix, A., (eds) 1994, *Shifting Identities Shifting Racism: A Feminism and Psychology Reader*, London: Sage

Billington, R., Strowbridge, S., Greensides, L. and Fitzsimons, A., 1991, *Culture and Society*, London: Macmillan

Bird, E., 1991, 'To Cook or to Conjugate: gender and class in the adult curriculum 1865-1990 in Bristol', in *Gender and Education*, 3(2), pp. 183-198

Blackman, L., 1996, 'The Dangerous Classes: Retelling the Psychiatric Story', *Feminism & Psychology*, 6(3), pp. 361-380

Board of Education, 1923, *Report of the Consultative Committee on differentiation of the curriculum for boys and girls respectively in secondary schools*, Second Impression, London: HMSO

Booth, C., (ed.) 1891, *Labour and Life of the People, Vol. II: London continued*, Williams and Norgate

Booth, J., 1885, *On the Female Education of the Industrial Classes*, Bell and Daldy, pp. 12-15

Bourdieu, P., 1973, 'Cultural Reproduction and Social Reproduction', in R. Brown, *Knowledge, Education and Cultural Change*, London: Tavistock

Bourdieu, P. and Passeron, J. C., 1977, *Reproduction in Education, Society and Culture*, London: Sage

Bourke, J., 1994, *Working-Class Cultures in Britain,* London: Routledge

Bowles, S., 1975, 'Unequal Education and the Reproduction of the Social Division of Labour', reprinted in R. Dale, G. Esland and M. MacDonald, (eds) 1976, *Schooling and Capitalism*, London: Routledge and Kegan Paul

Bowles, S. and Gintis, H., 1976, *Schooling in Capitalist America*, London, Routledge and Kegan Paul

Bradshaw, J., 1988, *The Family*, Florida: HCI

Brah, A., 1993, 'Re-Framing Europe: Engendered Racisms, Ethnicities, and Nationalisms', *Feminist Review*, 45, pp. 9-28

Brah, A., 1994, 'Time, Place and Others', *Sociology*, 28(3), pp. 805-813

Brand, C., 1996, *The g-Factor; General Intelligence and its Implications*, Chichester: Wiley

Braxton, J., 1989, *Black Women Writing Autobiography: A Tradition Within a Tradition*, Philadelphia: Temple University Press

Breen, R. and Whelan, C., 1995, 'Gender and Class Mobility: Evidence from the Republic of Ireland', *Sociology*, 29(1), pp. 1-22

Brewer, S., 1993, 'Theorising Race, Class and Gender: The New Scholarship of Black Feminist Intellectuals and Black Women's Labour', in S. James and A. Busia (eds) *Theorising Black Feminisms: The Visionary Pragmatism of Black Women*, London: Routledge

Brewer, S., 1996, 'The Political is Personal: Father-Daughter Relationships and Working-Class Consciousness', *Feminism & Psychology*, 6(3), pp. 401-410

Brodkey, L., 1987, *Academic Writing as Social Practice*, Philadelphia: Temple University Press

Brown, S and Riddel, S., (eds), 1992, *Class, Race and Gender in Schools,* Glasgow Scottish Council of Research in Education

Bryan, B., Dadzie, S. and Scafe, S., 1987, 'Learning to resist: Black women and education', in G. Weiner and M. Arnot (eds), *Gender Under Scrutiny*, London: Hutchinson

Bulletin of the Society for the Study of Labour History, 1966, No. 9, Spring

Bullock Report, 1975, *A Language for Life*, London: HMSO

Burgess, A., 1990. 'Co-education – the Disadvantages for School Girls', *Gender and Education*, 2(1), pp. 91-95

Burgher, M., 1979, 'Images of Self and Race', in R. Bell, B. Parker, and B. Guy-Sheftall (eds) *Sturdy Back Bridges*, New York: Anchor

Burgos, M., 1989, 'Life Stories, Narrative and the Search for the Self', *Life Stories/ Recito de vie*, No. 5

Burkitt, I., 1991, *Social Selves*, London: Sage

Burman, E., *et al,* (eds) 1996, *Challenging Women: Psychology's Exclusions, Feminist Possibilities*, Buckingham: Open University Press

Burton, C., 1985, *Subordination: Feminism and Social Theory*, Sydney: George Allen and Unwin

Buswell, C., 1992, 'Training Girls to be Low Paid Women', in C. Glendinning and J. Millar (eds) *Women and Poverty in Britain: the 1990s*, Hemel Hempstead, Harvester Wheatsheaf

Cameron, D., 1985, *Feminism and Linguistic Theory*, London: Macmillan

Campbell, B., 1984, *Wigan Pier Revisited*, London: Virago

Carby, H., 1987, 'Black Feminism and the Boundaries of Sisterhood', in M. Arnot and G. Weiner (eds), *Gender and the Politics of Schooling*, London: Hutchinson

Carey, J., 1992, *Intellectuals and the Masses: pride and prejudice among the literary intelligentsia 1880-1939*, London: Faber and Faber

Carr, W., 1991, 'Postmodernism and Educational Research', Paper presented at symposium, BERA Conference, Nottingham

Carrington, B. and Williamson, J., 1987, The Deficit Hypothesis Revisited (or Mary Mason, you're wide of the mark), *Education Studies*, 13, pp. 239-245

Carter, S. and Grosvenor, I., 1992, *The Apostles of Purity: Black Immigrants and Education Policy in Post-War Britain*, Birmingham: AFFOR

Casden, C., 1972, *Child, Language and Education*, New York: Holt, Rinehart and Winston

Channon, G. and Gilchrist, L., 1974, *What School Is For*, London: Methuen

Chernin, K., 1985, *The Hungry Self*, London: Virago

Childers, M. and hooks, b., 1990, 'A Conversation about Race and Class', in M. Hirsch and E. Fox Keller (eds) *Conflicts in feminism*, New York: Routledge

Chodorow, N., 1978, *The Reproduction of Mothering*, Berkeley: University of California Press

Clarke, J., Hall, S., Jefferson, T. and Roberts, B., (eds), 1979, 'Subcultures, Cultures and Class', in S. Hall and T. Jefferson, *Resistance Through Rituals*, London: Hutchinson

Clarke, J., Critcher, C. and Johnson, R., 1979, (eds) *Working Class Culture: Studies in history and theory*, London: Hutchinson

Clarricoates, K., 1981, 'The Importance of Being Ernest ... Emma ... Tom ... Jane', in R. Deem (ed.) *Schooling for Women's Work*, London: Routledge and Kegan Paul

Cole, M., (ed.), 1989, *The Social Contexts of Schooling*, London: Falmer Press

Cole, M. and Hill, D., 1995, 'Games of Despair and Rhetorics of Resistance: post-modernism, education and reaction', *Sociology of Education*,16(2), pp. 165-182

Coleman, J., 1975, *Review of Educational Research*, 45

Coleman, J., Campbell, E., Hobson, C., McParland, J., Mood, A., Weinfeld, F. and York, R., 1966, *Equality of Educational Opportunity*, Washington DC: Office of Education

Collet, C., 1891, 'Secondary Education – Girls', in C. Booth (ed.) *Labour and Life of the People, Vol. II, London continued,* Williams and Norgate

Collins, P., 1990, *Black Feminist Thought: Knowledge, Consciousness and the Politics of Empowerment,* London: Unwin Hyman

Collins, P., 1994, 'Shifting the Center: Race, Class and Feminist Theorising about Motherhood', in D. Bassin, M. Honey and M. Kaplan (eds) *Representation of Motherhood,* New Haven, CT: Yale University Press

Commission of Social Justice, 1993, *Social Justice in a Changing World*, London: IPRR

Commission of Social Justice, 1993, *The Justice Gap,* London: IPRR

Conlon, E., 1990, *Stars in the Daytime*, London: Women's Press

Connelly, F. M. and Clandinin, D. J, 1992, Paper prepared for the International Encyclopedia of Education, Oxford: Pergamon Press

Corrigan, P., 1979, *Schooling the Smash Street Kids*, London: Macmillan

Cotterill, P. and Letherby, G., 1993, 'Weaving Stories: Personal Auto/Biographies in Feminist Research', *Sociology*, 27(1), pp. 67-79

Coward, R., 1984, *Female Desire: Women's sexuality today*, London: Paladin

Crapanzano, V., 1992, *Herme's Dilemma and Hamlet's desire*, Cambridge Mass.: Havard University Press The Masking of Subversion in Ethnographic Description', in Crawford, J., Kippax, S., Onyx, J., Gault, U., Benton, P., 1992, *Emotions and Gender,* London: Sage

Crompton, R., 1993, *Class and Stratification*, Cambridge: Polity Press

Crompton, R. and Mann, M., 1986, *Gender and Stratification*, Cambridge: Polity Press

The Crowther Report 15-18, 1959, London: HMSO

Crozier, G., 1996, 'Empowering the Powerful: a discussion of the interrelation of government policies and consumerism with social class factors and the impact of this upon parent intervention in their children's schooling.' Paper, Bath College of Higher Education.

Curtis, A. and Blatchford, P., 1981, *Meeting the Needs of Socially Handicapped Children*, London: Nelson

Dance, D., 1979, 'Black Eve or Madonna? A Study in the Antithetical Views of the Mother in Black American Literature', in R. Bell, B. Parker and B. Guy-Sheftall (eds) *Sturdy Back Bridges*, New York: Anchor

Daniels, H. and Lee, J., 1989, Stories, Class and Classrooms: classic tales and popular myths, *Educational Studies*, 15 (1), pp. 3-130

Davey, A., 1983, *Learning to be Prejudiced,* London: E. Arnold

David, M., 1978, 'The Family-education Couple: towards an analysis of the William Tyndale Dispute,' in G. Littlejohn, *et al.*, *Power and the State*, London: Croom Helm, pp. 159-195

Davie, R., Butler, N. and Goldstein, H., 1972, *From Birth to Seven: a report of the National Child Development Study* (NCDS), London: Longman

Davin, A., 1987, 'Mind that you do as you are Told: Reading Books for Board School Girls, 1870-1902', in G. Weiner and M. Arnot (eds), *Gender Under Scrutiny,* London: Hutchinson

de Beauvior, S., 1953, *The Second Sex*, London: Jonathan Cape

Deem, R., 1978, *Women and Schooling*, London: Routledge and Kegan Paul

Deem, R., (ed.), 1981, *Schooling for Women's Work*, London: Routledge

Deem, R., (ed.), 1984, *Co-education Reconsidered*, Milton Keynes: Open University Press

Delphy, C., 1984, *Close to Home: A materialist analysis of women's oppression,* Amherst: University of Massachusetts Press

Delphy, C. and Leonard, D., 1992, *Familiar Exploitation*, Cambridge: Polity Press

Dens, C., 1997, 'Voices of Academics From the Working Class' [Review], *Work and Occupations*, Vol. 24(2), pp. 269-271

Dex, S., 1991, ed., *Life and Work History Analysis: Qualitative and Quantitative Developments*, London: Routledge

DFE, (Department for Education), 1992, *School Performance Tables: Public Examination Results*, London: DFE

DFE, 1992, *School Performance Tables: KS1 assessment*, London: DFE

DFE, 1994, *Statistical Bulletin*, 11/94, London: DFE

Dinnerstein, D., 1976, *The Mermaid and the Minotaur,* New York: Harper Colophon

Douglas, J. W. B., 1967, *The Home and the School*, St Albans, Herts: Panther

Douglas, J. W. B., Ross, J. M., Simpson, H. R., 1968, *All Our Future: A Longitudinal Study of Secondary Education*, London: Peter Davies

Dowling, C., 1982, *The Cinderella Complex*, London: Fontana

Dowling, C., 1989, *Perfect Women*, London: Fontana

Drew, D. and Gray, J., 1990, 'The Fifth Year Examination Achievements of Black Young People in England and Wales', *Educational Research*, Vol. 32, No. 3, pp. 107-117.

du Bois, D., 1983, 'Passionate Scholarship: Notes on Values, Knowing, Method in Feminist Social Science', in G. Bowles, R. D. Klein (eds) *Theories of Women's Studies*, London: Routledge and Kegan Paul

du Bois, D., 1994, 'Prospective Investigation of the Effects of Socioeconomic Disadvantage, Life Stress and Social Support on Early Adolescent Adjustment', *Journal of Abnormal Psychology*, 103(3), pp. 511-522

Duffy, M., 1983, *That's How It Was*, London: Virago

Dyhouse, C., 1981, *Girls Growing up in Late Victorian and Edwardian England*, London: Routledge and Kegan Paul

Edwards, E.G. and Roberts, I. J., 1980, 'British Higher Education: long-term trends in student enrolment', *Higher Education Review*, 12

Edwards, R., 1990, 'Access and Assets: the experience of mature mother-students in higher education', *Journal of Access Studies*, 5(2), pp. 188-202

Edwards, T., Fitz, J. and Whitty, G., 1989, *The State and Private Education: an evaluation of the Assisted Places Scheme*, Lewes: Falmer Press

Eichler, M., 1980, *The Double Standard: A Feminist Critique of Feminist Social Science*, New York: St Martin's Press

Eisenstein, Z., 1978, *Capitalist Patriarchy and the Case for Socialist Feminism*, New York: Monthly Review Press

Engels, F., 1969, *The Condition of the Working-class in England* (1845) reprinted by Panther Books Entwistle, H., 1978, Class, Culture and Education, London: Methuen

Ehrlich, C, 1979, 'Socialism, anarchism and feminism', in H. Ehrlich *et al*, (eds) *Reinventing Anarchy*, London: Routledge and Kegan Paul

Essen, J. and Wedge, P., 1983, *Continuities in Childhood Deprivation*, Aldershot: Gower

Evans, G, 1996, 'Putting Men and Women into Classes: An Assessment of the Cross-Sex Validity of the Goldthorpe Schema', *Sociology,* 30, pp. 209-34

Evans, M., 1991, *A Good School Life at a Girls' Grammar School in the 1950s*, London: The Women's Press

Evans, M., 1993, 'Reading Lives: How The Personal Might Be Social', *Sociology*, 27(1), pp. 5-13

Fairweather, E., 1984, 'The Man in the Orange Box', in U. Owen (ed.), *Fathers: Reflections by Daughters,* London: Virago

Fanon, F., 1967, *The Wretched of the Earth*, Harmondsworth: Penguin

Farrant, J., 1981, 'Trends in Admissions', in O. Fulton (ed.) *Access to Higher Education*, Guildford: SHRE

Fell, A., 1985, 'Rebel with a Cause' in L. Heron, *Truth, Dare or Promise*, London: Virago

Finch, J., 1984, 'It's Great To Have Someone to Talk To': The Ethics and Politics of Interviewing Women', in C. Bell and H. Roberts (eds) *Social Researching: Politics, Problems, Practice*, London: Routledge and Kegan Paul

Firestone, S., 1970, *The Dialectics of Sex*, New York: Morrow

Flude, M., 1976, 'Sociological Accounts of Differential Educational Attainment', in M. Flude and J. Ahier (eds) *Educability, Schools and Ideology,* London: Croom Helm, pp. 1-23

Foakes, G., 1976, *My Part of the River*, London: Futura

Foley, W., 1973, *A Child in the Forest,* London: BBC

Foster-Carter, O., 1987, 'Racial Bias in Children's Literature', in G. Weiner, and M. Arnot (eds), *Gender Under Scrutiny*, London: Hutchinson

Frankenberg, R., 1993, *The Social Construction of Whiteness: White Women, Race Matters*, London: Routledge

French, J., 1990, *The Education of Girls – A handbook for parents*, London: Cassell

Freud, S. (1901/64) 'The Psychopathology of Everyday Life', in J. Strachey (ed.) *The Standard Edition of the Complete Works of Sigmund Freud*, Vol. VI, London: Hogarth

Freud, S. (1905/77), 'Fragment of an Analysis of a Case of Hysteria ('Dora')', The Pelican Freud Library, Vol. 8, *Case Histories* 1, Penguin, pp. 27-164

Friday, N., 1977, *My Mother Myself*, London: Fontana

Friedan, B., 1965, *The Feminine Mystic,* New York: W.W. Norton

Friedman, N., 1967, 'Cultural Deprivation: a commentary in the sociology of knowledge', *Journal of Educational Thought*, 1(2), pp. 88-99

Frith, S., 1977, 'Socialisation and rational schooling: Elementary education in Leeds before 1870', in P. McCann (ed.) *Popular Education and Socialisation in the 19th Century,* London: Methuen

Fuller, M., 1980, 'Black Girls in a London comprehensive school', in R. Deem (ed.), *Schooling for Women's Work*, London: Routledge and Kegan Paul

Gelsthorpe, L., 1992, 'Response to Martyn Hammersely's paper 'On Feminist Methodology', *Sociology,* 26, (2), pp. 213-218

Gewirtz, S., Ball, S. J. and Bowe, R., 1995, *Markets, Choice and Equity in Education,* Buckingham: Open University Press

Gillborn, D. and Gipps, C., 1996, *Recent Research on the Achievements of Ethnic Minority Pupils*, Ofsted Reviews of Research, London: HMSO

Gilroy, P., 1994, *The Black Atlantic*, London: Verso

Glass, D., (ed.), 1954, *Social Mobility in Britain*, London: Routledge and Kegan Paul

Glastonbury, M., 1979, 'The Best Kept Secret: How Working Class Women Live and What They Know', *Women's Studies International Quarterly*, 2(2), pp. 171-181

Gluck, S. B., and Patai, D., (eds), 1991, *Women's Words: The Feminist Practice of Oral History*, London: Routledge

Goldthorpe, J., Llewellyn, C. and Payne, C., 1987, *Social Mobility and Class Structure in Modern Britain*, Oxford: Clarendon Press (2nd edn)

Goldthorpe, J. and Lockwood, D., 1968, *The Affluent Worker*, CUP

Goldthorpe, J., and Marshall, G., 1992, 'The promising future of class analysis: a response to recent critiques', *Sociology*, 26(3), pp. 381-400

Goldthorpe, J., and Payne, C., 1986, 'Trends in Intergenerational Class Mobility in England and Wales 1972-1983', *Sociology*, 20, pp. 1-24

Gomesall, M., 1988, 'Ideals and realities: The education of working class girls 1800-1870', *History of Education*, 17(1)

Goodson, I., (ed.) 1992, *Studying Teachers' Lives*, London: Routledge

Gorelicks, S., 1991, 'Contradictions of Feminist Methods', *Gender and Society*, 5, pp. 459-477

Gorham, D., 1978, 'The 'Maiden Tribute of Modern Babylon" Re-examined: Child Prostitution and the Idea of Childhood in Late Victorian England', *Victorian Studies*, 21(3), pp. 353-379

Grace, G., 1978, *Teachers, Ideology and Control*, London: Routledge and Kegan Paul

Graham, H., 1984, 'Surveying Through Stories', in C. Bell and H. Roberts (eds), *Social Researching: Politics, Problems, Practice*, London: Routledge and Kegan Paul

Grant, A. R., 1871, *School Managers' Series of Reading Books*, London: Weale

Griffin, C., 1985, *Typical Girls? Young women from school to the job market*, London: Routledge and Kegan Paul

Griffin, C., 1987, 'Young Women and the Transition from School to Un/employment: a cultural analysis', in G. Weiner and M. Arnot (eds), *Gender Under Scrutiny*, London: Hutchinson

Griffiths, M., 1994, 'Autobiography, Feminism and the Practice of Action Research', in *Educational Action Research*, 2(1), pp. 71-82

Griffiths, V, 1991, 'Doing Feminist Ethnography on Friendship', in J. Aldridge, V. Griffiths and A. Williams, 'Rethinking: Feminist Research Processes Reconsidered', *Feminist Praxis* 33, Department of Sociology, University of Manchester

Griggs, C., 1989, The Rise of Mass Schooling, in M. Cole (ed.) *The Social Context of Schooling,* London: Falmer Press

Griggs, C., 1989, 'The Rise, Fall and Rise Again of Selective Secondary Schooling', in M. Cole (ed.) *The Social Contexts of Schooling*, London: Falmer Press

Grumet, M., 1987, 'The Politics of Personal Knowledge', *Curriculum Inquiry,* 17(3), pp. 319-329

The Haddow Report, 1926, *The Education of the Adolescent*, London: HMSO

Haggis, J., 1990, 'The Feminist Research Process – Defining a Topic', in Stanley, L., (ed.) *Feminist Praxis*, London: Routledge

Hall, S., 1977, 'Education and the Crisis of the Urban School', in J. Raynor and E. Harris (eds), *Schooling in the City*, London: Ward Lock

Hall, S. and Jefferson, T., 1976, *Resistance through Ritual*, London: Hutchinson

Halsey, A. H., 1992, 'Opening Wide the Doors of Higher Education', *National Commission on Education Briefing*, No. 6, August

Halsey, A. H., 1993, 'Trends in Access and Equity in Higher Education', *Oxford Review of Education*, 19(2)

Halsey, A. H., Heath, A. F. and Ridge, J. M., 1980, *Origins and Destinations: Family, Class and Education in Modern Britain*, Oxford: Clarendon Press

Hamed, M., Burnett, R. and Reynold, A., 1988, *Students on CNAA's Part-time First Degree Course*, London: CNNA

Hammersley, M., 1992, 'On Feminist Methodology', *Sociology,* 26(2), pp. 187-206

Hammersley, M., 1994, 'On Feminist Methodology: A Response', *Sociology,* 28(1), pp. 293-300

Hampton, H., 1993, 'Behind the Looking Glass', *Educational Action Research Journal,* 1(2), pp. 257-273

Harding, S., ed., 1987, *Feminism and Methodology,* Milton Keynes: Open University Press

Hargreaves, D., 1967, *Social Relations in a Secondary School*, London: Routledge and Kegan Paul

Hargreaves, D., 1982, *The Challenge for the Comprehensive School: culture, curriculum and community,* London: Routledge and Kegan Paul

Harris, O., 1984, 'Heavenly Father', in U. Owen (ed.) *Fathers: Reflections by Daughters,* London: Virago

Harrison, B. and Lyons, E. S., 1993, 'A Note on Ethical Issues in the Use of Autobiography in Sociological Research', *Sociology,* 27(1), pp. 101-109

Harrison, J., 1973, 'The Political Economy of Housework', *Bulletin of the Conference of Socialist Economists*, 4, pp. 35-52

Hart, N., 1989, 'Gender and the Rise and Fall of Class Politics', *New Left Review*, 175, pp. 19-47

Hartley, D., 1985, *Understanding the Primary School*, Beckenham: Croom Helm

Hartmann, H., 1981, 'The Unhappy Marriage of Marxism and Feminism' in L. Sargent (ed.) *Women and Revolution*, Boston: South End

Haug, F., 1987, *Female Sexualisation: A Collective Work of Memory*, Tr. Erica Carter, London: Verso

Hayes, B. C. and Miller, R. L., 1995, 'The Silenced Voice: Female Social Mobility Patterns with Particular Reference to the British Isles', *Sociology*, 44(4)

Heath, S. B., 1983, *Ways with Words*, Cambridge: Cambridge University Press

Henriques, J., Holloway, W., Urwin, C., Venn, C. and Walkerdine, V., 1984, *Changing the Subject: Psychology, Social Regulation and Subjectivity*, London: Methuen

Herrnstein, R. and Murray, C., 1994, *The Bell Curve: intelligence and class structure in American life*, New York: Free Press

Hey, V., 1997, 'Northern Accent and Southern Comfort: Subjectivity and social class', in P. Mahony and C. Zmroczek (eds) *Class matters: Working-class women's perspectives on social class* pp. 140-151, London: Taylor Francis

Higginson, G., 1990, 'A Levels and the Future' in G. Parry and C. Wake, *Access and Alternative Futures for Higher Education*, London: Hodder and Stoughton, p. 77-79

Hillman, J. and Pearce, N., 1998, *Wasted Youth*, London: IPPR

Hirsch, D., 1994, *School, a Matter of Choice*, Paris: Centre for Educational Research and Development, Organisation for Economic Co-operation and Development (OECD)

Hobbs, M., 1973, *Born to Struggle*, London: Quartet Books

Hoggart, R., 1959, *The Use of Literacy*, Harmondsworth: Penguin

Holland, J., 1981, 'Social Class and Changes in Orientation to Meaning', *Sociology,* 15(1)

Holland, J. and Skours, G., 1977, 'Study of children's views of aspects of the social division of labour: children's aspirations and expectations with respect to work', *Social Research Unit/Social Science Research Council Report*, No. 3

Holland, R., 1993, Double Exposure: Exploring the Social and Political Relations of Ethnographic Research, paper presented at the British Sociological Association Conference, University of Essex

Holloway, W., 1989, *Subjectivity and Method in Psychology*, London: Sage

Holton, R. and Turner, B., 1994, 'Debate and Psuedo-Debate in Class Analysis: Some Unpromising Aspects of Goldthorpe and Marshall's Defence', *Sociology*, 28(3), pp. 799-804

hooks, b., 1984, *Feminist Theory from Margin to Center*, Boston: South End Press

hooks, b., 1991, *Everywoman Magazine*, May

hooks, b., 1994, *Teaching to Transgress: Education as the Practice of Freedom*, London: Routledge

Horn, P., 1988, 'The Employment of Working-Class Girls 1870-1914', *History of Education*, 17(1)

Howarth, C., Kenway, P., Palmer, G., Street, C., 1998, *Monitoring poverty and social exclusion*, London: New Policy Institute

Howieson, C., 1991, *The Guidance Project – Final Report,* University of Edinburgh

Hughes, D., 1992, 'Social Class and Educational Disadvantage: Are the Schools to Blame?' in S. Brown and S. Riddell, *A New Agenda for Policy and Practice in Scottish Education*, Practitioner Mini Paper 12, SCRE in association with the Educational Institute of Scotland

Humphrey, R., 1993, 'Life Stories and Social Careers: Ageing and Social Life in An Ex-Mining Town', *Sociology*, 27(1), February, pp. 166-178

Hunt, D., 1970, *Parents and Children in History*, New York: Basic Books

Hunt, F., 1984, 'Social Class and the Grading of Schools. Realities in Girls' Secondary Education 1880-1940', in *History of Education Society, The Education of Girls and Women*, Conferences Papers, December, pp. 27-46

IPPR, (Institute of Public Policy Research), 1993, *Social Justice in a Changing World,* The Commission of Social Justice

IPPR, 1993, *The Justice Gap*, The Commission of Social Justice

Jackson, B. and Marsden, D., 1968, *Education and the Working-Class*, Harmondsworth: Penguin

Jarrold, 1871, *New Code Reading Book V*, London: Jarrold and Sons

Jenks, C., 1972, *Inequality: A Reassessment of the Affects of Family and Schooling in American*, New York: Harper and Row

Jones, D. and Barrett, H., 1993, 'Class and Hatred', in V. Varma (ed.) *How and Why Children Hate*, London: Jessica Kingsley

Johnson, M., 1999, *Failing School Failing City*, Jon Carpenter

Johnson, R., 1976, 'Notes on the Schooling of the English Working-class', in R. Dale, G. Esland, M McDonald (eds) *Schooling and Capitalism*, London: Routledge and Kegan Paul

Johnson, R., 1979, 'Culture and the Historians', in J. Clarke, C. Critcher and R. Johnson, *Working-Class Culture*, London: Hutchinson

Joseph, G. and Lewis, J., 1981, *Common Differences: Conflicts in black and white perspectives,* New York: Anchor

Keddie, N., 1971, 'Classroom Knowledge', in M. Young (ed.) *Knowledge and Control,* London: Collier Macmillan

Kellmer Pringle, M., 1980, *The Needs of Children,* London: Hutchinson

Kenway, J., 1990, 'Privileged Girls, Private Schools and the Culture of Success', in J. Kenway and S. Willis (eds) *Hearts and Minds: self-esteem and the schooling of girls,* London: Falmer Press

Kessler, S., Ashenden, D., Connell, B. and Dowsett, G., 1987, 'Gender relations in secondary schooling', *Sociology of Education*, 58, pp. 34-48

King, R., 1978, *All Things Bright and Beautiful,* Chichester: Wiley

Kitzinger, C., 1991, 'Feminism, Psychology and the Paradox of Power', *Feminism and Psychology,* 1, pp. 111-129

Klein, R. D., 1983, 'How do we do what we want to do?: thoughts about feminist methodology', in G. Bowles and R. D. Klein (eds) *Theories of Women's Studies,* London: Routledge and Kegan Paul

Kohn, M., 1971, 'Social Class and Parent-Child Relationships', in M. Anderson, *Sociology of the Family*, Harmondsworth: Penguin

Kramer-Dahl, A., 1995, 'Reading and Writing Against the Grain of Academic Discourse, *Discourse*, 16(1), pp. 21-38

Kumar, V., 1993, *Poverty and Inequality in the UK: The Effects on Children*, London: National Children's Bureau (NCB)

Labov, W., 1972, 'The Logic of Non-Standard English in A. Giglioli, ed., *Language and Social Context*, Harmondsworth: Penguin

Lacan, J., 1977, *Ecrits: A Selection*, London: Tavistock

Lacey, C., 1970, *Hightown Grammar: The School as a Social System*, Manchester: Manchester University Press

Lampard, R., 1995, 'Parents' Occupations and Their Children's Occupational Attainment: A Contribution to the Debate on the Class Assignment of Families, *Sociology,* 29, pp. 715-738

Lather, P., 1991, *Getting Smart: feminist research and pedagogy with/in the postmodern*, New York/London: Routledge

Lee, J., 1980, 'Teacher Ideology and the Realisation of Pedagogy: A study in a Progressive Inner-City Infant School', MA dissertation. London: King's College

Lee, J., 1984, 'Contradictions and Constraints in an Inner City Infant School', in G. Grace (ed.) *Education and the City*, London: Routledge and Kegan Paul

Lee, J., 1987, 'Pride and Prejudice: Teachers, Class and an Inner City Infants School', in M. Lawn and G. Grace (eds) *Teachers: The Culture and Politics of Work*, Lewes: Falmer Press

Lee, J., 1989, 'Social Class and Schooling', in M. Cole (ed.) *The Social Context of Schooling*, London: Falmer Press

Leeds University, 1992, *Report of the ENCA Project*, SEAC

Leeds University/NUT, 1993, *Assessment and Testing of Six and Seven Year Olds*, London: NUT

Leitrim A., 1979, 'Me and My History', in P. Ashton, M. Simons, D. Denaro, M. Raleigh (eds) *Our Lives: Young People's Autobiographies,* London: ILEA English Centre

Livingstone, D., 1983, *Class, Ideologies and Educational Futures*, Falmer Press

Llewellyn, M, 1981, 'Studying Girls at School: The Implications of Confusion', in R. Deem, (ed.) *Schooling for Women's Work*, Routledge and Kegan Paul

Lowe, R., 1867, 'Primary and Classical Education', 1, in B. Simon, 1960, *Studies in the History of Education 1780-1870*, London: Lawrence and Wishart

Lucas, S. and Ward, P., 1985, 'Mature Students at Lancaster University', *Adult Education*, 58(2), pp. 151-157

Lucey, H. and Walkerdine, V., 1996, 'Transition to Womanhood: construction of success and failure for middle and working class young women', paper presented at the British Youth Research: the New Agenda conference, Glasgow University

Luke, C. and Gore, J., ed., 1992, *Feminism and Critical Pedagogy,* London: Routledge

Luttrell, W., 1992, 'Working-Class Women's Ways of Knowing: Effects of Gender, Race and Class', in J. Wrigley (ed.) *Education and Gender Equality,* London: Falmer Press

Lynch, K. and O'Neill, C., 1994, 'The Colonisation of Social Class in Education', *British Journal of Sociology of Education*, 15(3), pp. 307-324

Macintosh, M., 1992, 'Bringing about Change in the Culture of a School', in S. Brown and S. Riddell, S., *Class, Race and Gender in Schools*, SCRE

MaClure, J. S., (ed.), 1986, *Educational Documents England and Wales 1816-1963*, London: Methuen

MaClure, M., 1995, Postmodernism: A Postcript', *Educational Action Research Journal*, 3(1), pp. 105-116

McCabe, T, 1981, in A. McRobbie and T. McCabe (eds), *Feminism for Girls: An Adventure Story,* London: Routledge and Kegan Paul

McCallum, I., 1993, 'Testing Seven year olds – Performance and Context', *Projecting school rolls and assessing performance*, London: London Research Centre

McCulloch, G., 1998, *Failing the Ordinary Child,* Philadelphia: Open University Press

McLaren, A. T., 1996, 'Coercive Invitations: how young women in school make sense of mothering and waged labour', *British Journal of Sociology of Education*, 17(3), pp. 279-298

McMahon, M., 1987, *Telling Tales Out Of School – The ABCs of Repression in Education*, MA Thesis, University of Toronto

McMahon, M., 1991, 'Nursing Histories - Reviving Life in Abandoned Selves', *Feminist Review*, 37, pp. 23-37

McMillan, M., 1912, *Labour Leader,* 11, July

McRobbie, A. and Garber, J., 1976, 'Girls and Subcultures', in S. Hall and T. Jefferson (eds), *Resistance through Rituals,* London: Hutchinson

McRobbie, A., 1978, 'Working-class Girls and the Culture of Femininity', in Women's Studies Group, CCCS (ed.), *Women Take Issue*, London: Hutchinson

Mahony, P. and Zmroczek, C., (eds) *Class Matters: 'working-class' women's perspectives on social class,* London: Taylor and Francis

Maitland, S., 1984, 'Two for the Price of One', in U. Owen (ed.), *Fathers: Reflections by Daughters*, London: Virago

Mann, C., 1996, 'Finding a Favourable Front: the contribution of the family to working class girls' achievement', Ph.D diss., University of Cambridge

Marshall, J., 1986, 'Exploring the Experiences of Women Managers: Towards Rigour in Qualitative Methods', in S. Wilkinson (ed.), *Feminist Social Psychology*, Milton Keynes and Philidelphia: Open University Press

Marshall, J., 1990, 'Open Letter to Shulamit Reinhaiz', *Collaborative Inquiry*, 3, pp. 2-4

Mason, M., 1986, The Deficit Hypothesis Revisited, *Educational Studies*, 12, pp. 279-289

Mayhew, H., 1851, *London Labour and the London Poor*, 1, George Woodfall

Maynard, M., 1995, 'Feminism and the Possibilities of a Postmodern Research Practice', *British Journal of Sociology of Education*, 14(3), pp. 327-331 [Extended Review]

Mead, G., 1934, *Mind, Self and Society*, University of Chicago Press

Metcalf, H., 1993, *Non-Traditional Students' Experience of Higher Education*, April, CVCP

Michaels, S., 1981, 'Sharing Time' Children's narrative styles and differential access to literacy', *Language in Society*, 10, pp. 423-442

Middleton, S., 1984, 'The Sociology of Women's Education as a Field of Academic Study', *Discourse,* 5(1), pp. 43-62

Middleton, S., 1987, 'The Sociology of Women's Education as a Field of Academic Study', in M. Arnot and G. Weiner (eds), *Gender and the Politics of Schooling,* London: Hutchinson

Middleton, S., 1987, 'Streaming' and the Politics of Female Sexuality: Case studies in the schooling of girls', in G. Weiner and M. Arnot (eds), *Gender Under Scrutiny*, London: Hutchinson

Miller, A., 1987, *For Your Own Good*, London: Virago

Miller, J., 1990, *Seduction: Studies in Reading and Culture*, London: Virago

Miller, J., 1992, *More Has Meant Women: The Feminisation of Schooling*, Institute of Education and London: Tufnell Press

Miller, J., 1996, *Schooling for Women*, London: Virago

Miller, N., 1991, *Getting Personal: feminist occasions and other autobiographical acts,* London: Routledge

Millett, K, 1969, *Sexual Politics*, New York: Avon Books

Mills, C. Wright, 1959, *The Sociological Imagination*, Harmondsworth: Penguin

Mirza, H., 1997 (ed) *Black British Feminism: a reader*, London: Routledge

Mischler, E., 1990, 'Validation in Inquiry-guided Research: the role of exemplars in narrative studies', *Havard Educational Review*, 60(4), pp. 414-442

Mitchell, H., 1977, *The Hard Way Up,* London: Virago

Mitchell, J., 1975, *Psychoanalysis and Feminism*, Harmonsworth: Pelican

Mitchell, J. and Rose, J., (eds), 1982, *Feminine Sexuality: Jacques Lacan and the Ecole Freudienne*, London: Macmillian

Mitchell, J., 1984, *The Longest Revolution*, London: Virago

Modood, T., 1993, The Number of Ethnic Minority Students in British Higher Education: Some Grounds for Optimism', *Oxford Review of Education*, 19(2), pp. 167-182

Modood, T. and Shiner, M., 1994, *Ethnic Minorities and Higher Education*, London: PSI/UCAS

Moers, E., 1979, *Literary Women*, London: The Women's Press

Moraga, C. and Anzaldua, G., (eds), 1981, *This Bridge Called My Back: Writings by Radical Women of Color*, Mass: Persephone Press

Morgan, D.H.J., 1975, *Social Theory and the Family*, London: Routledge and Kegan Paul

Morrison, T., 1987, *Beloved*, London: Chatto and Windus

Mortimore, J. and Blackstone, T., 1982, *Disadvantage and Education*, London: Heinemann

Mortimore, P. and Mortimore, J., 1986, 'Education and Social Class', in R. Rogers (ed.), *Education and Social Class*, Lewes: Falmer Press

Mortimore, P., Sammons, P., Stoll, L., Lewis, L. and Ecob, R, 1986, *The Junior School Project* (4 volumes), London: Research and Statistics Branch, Inner London Education Authority

Mosteller, F. and Moynihan, D., (eds) 1972, *On Equality of Educational Opportunity*, New York: Random House

Muller, W., Luttinger, P., Konig, W. and Karle, W., 1989, 'Class and Education in Industrial Nations', *International Journal of Sociology*, 19(3), pp. 3-39

Munro, P., 1991, 'Multiple 'I's': dilemmas of life history research. Paper prepared for American Educational Research Association Conference, Chicago, April 3-7, pp. 1-21

National Commission on Education, 1993, *Learning to Succeed: A Radical Look at Education Today and a Strategy for the Future*, London: Heinemann

National Curriculum Council (NCC), 1993, *The National Curriculum at Key Stages 1 and 2*, 7th Jan

Newsom Committee, 1963, *Half Our Future*, London: HMSO

Newson, J . and Newson, E., 1977, *Seven Years Old in the Home Environment*, London: Allen and Unwin

Noden,, P., West, A., David, M. and Edge, A., 1997, 'Choices and Destinations at Transfer to Secondary School'. Paper presented to the Market Forces Seminar, King's College, London

NUT (National Union of Teachers), 1987, *The Education Reform Bill: A Union Commentary*, London: NUT 1870-1970, NUT

NUT, 1993, *The Teacher*, Dec. Issue

NUT and University of Leeds, 1993, *Testing and Assessing Six and Seven Year Olds: The Evaluation of the 1992 Key Stage 1 National Curriculum Assessment*, London: NUT

Oakley, A., 1981, 'Interviewing Women: A Contradiction in Terms', in H. Roberts, (ed.) *Doing Feminist Research*, London: Routledge and Kegan Paul

Oakley, A., 1984, *Taking It Like a Woman*, London: Cape

Office for Standards in Education (Ofsted), 1993, *Curriculum Organisation and Classroom Practice in Primary Schools: a follow-up report,* London: HMSO

Office for Standards in Education (Ofsted), 1993, *Access and Achievement in Urban Education*, London: HMSO

Oppenheim, C., 1993, *Poverty: The Facts*, London: CPAG (Child Poverty Action Group)

Osborn, A. F., Butler, N. R., Morris, A. C., 1984, *The Social Life of Britain's Five Year Olds*, London: Routledge and Kegan Paul

Osborn, A. F. and Milbank, J. E., 1987, *The Effects of Early Education*, Oxford: Clarendon Press

Owen, U., 1983, (ed.) *Fathers: reflections by daughters*, London: Virago

Ozolins, U., 1982, 'Lawton's 'Refutation' of a Working Class Curriculum', in T. Horton and P. Raggatt, *Challenge and Change in the Curriculum*, London: Hodder and Stoughton

Paechter, C. and Weiner, G., 1996, 'Editorial', Special Issue: Post-modernism and Post-structuralism in Educational Research', *British Educational Research Journal,* 22(3), pp. 267-272

Pahl, R., 1989, 'Is the Emperor Naked? *International Journal of Urban and Regional Research*, 13(4), pp. 711-20

Pakulski, J. and Walters, M., 1996, 'The Reshaping and Dissolutin of Social Class in Advanced Society', *Theory and Society*, Vol. 25, pp. 667-91

Paterson, L., 1992, 'Social Class in Scottish Education', in S. Brown and S. Riddell, (eds), *Class, Race and Gender in School*, SCRE

Payne, I., 1983, 'A working-class girl in a grammar school', in J. Purvis and M. Hale (eds) *Achievement and Inequality in Education*, London: Routledge and Kegan Paul, pp. 142-158

Personal Narratives Group, 1989, *Interpreting women's lives*, Bloomington: Indiana University Press

Phillimore, P., Beattie, A. and Townsend, P., 1994, 'Widening Inequality of Health in Northern England 1981-1991, *British Medical Journal*, 308

Phillips, A., 1987, *Divided Loyalties*, London: Virago

Phillips, A., 1992, 'Classing the Women and Gendering the Class', in L. McDowell and R. Pringle (eds) *Defining Women: Social Institutions and Gender Divisions*, Cambridge: Polity Press

Phoenix, A., 1987, 'Theories of gender and black families', in G. Weiner and M. Arnot (eds), *Gender Under Scrutiny*, London: Hutchinson, pp. 50-63

Phoenix, A. and Tizard, B., 1996, 'Thinking Through Class: The Place of Social Class in the Lives of Young Londoners', *Feminism and Psychology*, 6(3), pp. 427-440

Piaget, J., 1926, *The Language and Thought of the Child*, London: Kegan Paul, Trench and Trubner

Pile, S. and Thrift, N., 1995, 'Mapping the Subject', in S. Pile and N. Thrift (eds) *Mapping the Subject: Geographies of Cultural Transformation*, London: Routledge

Pilling, D. and Pringle, M., 1978, *Controversial Issues in Child Development*, London: Paul Elek

Plowden Committee, 1967, *Children and Their Primary Schools*, London: HMSO

Plummer, G., Newman, K., and Winter, R., 1993, 'Exchanging Letters – A Format For Collbaborative Action Research', in G. Plummer and G. Edwards (eds) *Dimensions of Action Research: People, Practice and Power*, Bournemouth: Hyde Publications

Plummer, G., 1997, What has education done for working-class women and girls?, Unpublished Ph.D, Institute of Education, University of London

Plummer, G. 1999, 'Dilemma: Maintaining one's working-class female identity whilst writing for a research community, *Changing English*, 6(2), pp. 155-167.

Pollard, A., 1985, *The Social World of the Primary School,* London: Holt Education

Popkewitz, T., 1988, 'What's in a research project; some thoughts on the intersection of history, social structure and biography', *Curriculum Inquiry*, 18(4), pp. 379-400

Porter, S., 1993, 'Critical Realist Ethnography', *Sociology*, 27(4), pp. 591-609

Policy Studies Institute, 1993, *British Ethnic Minorities*, London, p. 51

Powell, M., 1968, *Below Stairs*, London: P. Davies

Powell, R., and Clarke, J., 1976, 'A Note of Marginality', in S. Hall, and T. Jefferson (eds), *Resistance through Ritual*, London: Hutchinson

Prandy, K. and Blackburn, R. M., 1997, 'Putting Men and Women into Classes: But is that where they belong? a comment on Evans', *Sociology*, 31, pp. 143-152

Prandy, K. and Bottero, W., 1995, *The Social Analysis of Stratification and Mobility,* University of Cambridge: Sociological Research Group (Working Paper Series No. 18)

Purcell, K., 1988, *Gendered Jobs: Factory Fates*, Oxford University Press

Purvis, J., 1980, 'Working-class women and adult education in nineteenth-century Britain', *History of Education*, 9(3), pp. 193-212

Purvis, J., 1981, 'The Double Burden of Class and Gender in the Schooling of Working-Class Girls in Nineteenth-Century England, 1800-1870', in L. Barton and S. Walker (eds), *Schools, Teachers and Teaching*, Lewes: Falmer Press

Purvis, J., 1987a, 'Social class, education and ideals of femininity in the nineteenth-century', in M. Arnot and G. Weiner (eds), *Gender and the Politics of Schooling*, London: Hutchinson

Purvis, J., 1987b, 'Understanding Personal Accounts', in G. Weiner and M. Arnot, M., (eds), *Gender Under Scrutiny*, London: Hutchinson

Purvis, J., 1989, *Hard Lesson. The Lives and Education of Working-Class Women in Nineteenth-Century England*, London: Polity Press

Ramazanoglu, C., 1992, 'On Feminist Methodology: Male Reason Versus Female Empowerment', *Sociology,* 26(2), pp. 207-212

Rapport, N., 1993, [Review] E. Tonk's, Narrating Our Pasts: The Social Construction Of Oral History, Cambridge: Cambridge University Press, *Sociology* 27(1), pp. 196-197

Reay, D., 1996, 'Dealing with Difficult Differences: Reflexivity and Social Class in Feminist Research', *Feminism & Psychology,* 6(3), pp. 443-456

Reay, D., 1996, 'Contextualising Choice: social power and parental involvement', *British Educational Research Journal*, 22(5), pp. 581-96

Reay, D.,1996, 'Insider Perspectives or Stealing the Words out of Women's Mouths', *Feminist Review*, Summer, 53, pp. 57-73

Reay, D., 1997., Feminist Theory, Habitus and Social Class: Disrupting notions of classlessness, *Women's Studies International Forum* 20(2), pp. 255-233

Reay, D., 1998, 'Rethinking Social Class: Qualitative Perspectives on Class and Gender, in *Sociology*, 32(2), pp. 259-275

Reay, D., 1998a, 'Surviving in Dangerous Places: Working-Class Women, Women's Studies and Higher Eduction', in *Women's Studies International Forum*, 2(1), pp. 11-19

Redpath, B. and Robus, N., 1989, *Mature Students' Incomings and Outgoings*, London: HMSO

Reid, I., 1989, *Social Class Differences in Britain*, London: Fontana Press

Reinfelder, M., 1997, 'Switching Cultures' in P. Mahoney and C. Zmroczek, (eds) *Class Matters: Working-class women's perspectives on social class*, London: Taylor and Francis

Ribbens, J., 1993, 'Facts or Fictions?', *Sociology*, 27(1), pp. 81-92

Rich, A., 1977, *Of Woman Born*, New York: Bantam

Richardson, L., 1990, *Writing Strategies: reaching diverse audiences*, Newbury Park: Sage

Riessman, C. K., 1993, *Narrative Analysis*, Newbury Park: Sage

Riley, D., 1983, *War in the Nursery*, London: Virago

Rist, R., 1970, 'Student Social Class and Teacher Expectations: the self-fulfilling prophecy in ghetto education', *Harvard Education Review* 40, pp. 411-451

Roberts, E., 1984, *A Woman's Place: An Oral History of Working-Class Women 1890-1940*, Oxford:Basil Blackwell

Roberts, H., 1981, ed., *Doing Feminist Research,* London: Routledge and Kegan Paul

Roberts, H., and Barker, R, 1989, 'What are People doing when they Grade Women's Work', *British Journal of Sociology,* 40(1), pp. 130-146

Roberts, H. and Barker, R., 1990, *The Social Classification of Women's Work* (SCOWW), London: City University, Statistics Research Unit

Robins Report, 1963, *Higher Education*, HMSO

Rogers, R., 1986, (ed.) *Education and Social Class*, Lewes: Falmer Press

Rosen, H., 1972, *Language and Class*, London: Falling Wall Press

Rosen, H, 1986, 'Language and the Education of the Working Class', in R. Rogers (ed.) *Education and Social Class*, Lewes: Falmer Press

Rosenwald, G. C. and Ochberg, R. L., (eds), 1992, *Storied Lives: the cultural politics of self understanding*, New Haven: Yale University Press

Rowe, D., 1988, *The Successful Self*, London: Fontana

Rowe, R., 1881, *Life in the London Streets*, London: Nimmo and Bain

Rubin, L., 1978, *Worlds of Pain: Life in the Working-Class Family*, New York: Basic Books

Ruskin, J., '*The Art of England', The Library Edition of the Works of John Ruskin*, vol. 33, 1908, pp. 327-49, London: Allen and Unwin

Rutter, M., Maugham, B., Mortimore, P. and Ousten, J., 1979, *Fifteen Thousand Hours: Secondary Schools and Their Effects on Children*, London: Open Books

Rutter, M., 1972, *Maternal Deprivation Reassessed,* Harmondsworth: Penguin

Sammons, P., 1995, 'Gender, Ethnic and Socio-economic Differences in Attainment and Progress', *British Educational Research Journal*, 21(4), pp. 465-485

Saunderson, K., 1988, 'Women's Lives: Social Class and the Oral Historian, *Life Stories/ Recito de vie*, No. 4, pp. 27-34

Sayers, J., 1986, 'Sexual Identity and Difference: Psychoanalytic Perspectives', in S. Wilkinson (ed.) *Feminist Social Psychology*, OUP

Scannell, D., 1974, *Mother Knew Best,* London: Macmillan

Scott, P., 1990, 'Post-binary Access and Learning' in Parry, G. and Wake, C.,*Access and Alternative Futures for Higher Education*, London: Hodder and Stoughton, p. 16-42

Seabrook, J., 1982, *Working Class Childhood*, London: Gollancz

Segal, L., 1987, *Is The Future Female? Troubled Thoughts on Contemporary Feminism*, London: Virago

Sharp, R. and Green, A., 1975, *Education and Social Control*, London: Routledge and Kegan Paul

Sharp, R., 1989, 'Independent Working Class Education: A Repressed Historical Alternative, *Discourse*, 10(1), pp. 1-26

Sharpe, S., 1976 and 1994, *Just Like a Girl: How Girls Learn to be Women from the Seventies to the Nineties,* first and second edition, London: Penguin

Shaw, J., 1981, 'Education and the Individual: schooling for girls, or mixed schooling: A mixed blessing', in R. Deem (ed.), *Schooling for Women's Work*, London: Routledge

Silver, H., 1965, *The Concept of Popular Education*, London: MacGibbon and Kee

Silver, H., 1974, *The Education of the Poor. The History of a National School 1824-1974,* London: Routledge and Kegan Paul

Sime, N., Pattie, C. and Gray, J., 1990, *What Now? The Transition from School to the Labour Market Amongst 16 to 19 Year Olds,* England and Wales Youth Cohort Study, Research and Development No. 62, Youth Cohort Series, No. 14, Sheffield University Division of Education

Simon, B., 1974, *The Two Nations and the Educational Structure 1780-1870,* London: Lawrence and Wishart

Simon, B., 1988, *Bending the Rules: the Baker Reform of Education*, London: Lawrence and Wishart

Simon, B., 1993, 'A Return to Streaming', *Forum,* 35(2), pp. 36-37

Skeggs, B., 1995, *Feminist Cultural Theory: Process and Production*, Manchester: Manchester University Press

Skeggs, B, 1997, *Formations of Class and Gender*, London: Sage

Skeggs, B.,1997a, 'Classifying Practices: 'Representations, Capitals and Recognitions', in P. Mahony and C. Zmroczek (eds.) *Class matters: Working-class women's perspectives on social class*, pp. 123-206, London: Taylor and Francis

Sloggett, A. and Joshi, H., 1994, 'High Mortality in Deprived Areas: community or personal disadvantage', *British Medical Journal,* 309, pp. 1470-1474

Sluckin, W., Herbert, M. and Sluckin, A., 1983, *Maternal Bonding*, Oxford: Basil Blackwell

Smedley, A., 1977, *Daughter of Earth*, London: Virago

Smith, B., (ed.) 1983, *Home Girls: A Black Feminist Anthology*, New York: Kitchen Table, Women of Color Press

Smith, T. and Noble, M., 1995, *Education Divides: Poverty and Schooling in the 1990s,* London: CPAG

Smithers, A. and Robinson, P., 1989, *Increasing Participation in Higher Education*, British Petroleum Educational Service

Snow, C., 1983, 'Literacy and Language; results during the pre-school years', *Havard Educational Review*, 53(2)

Solomos, J. and Back, L., 1994, 'Conceptualising Racisms: social theory, politics and research', *Sociology,* 28(1), pp. 143-161

Spelman, 1990, *Inessential Women,* London: The Women's Press

Spender, D., 1980, *Man Made Language*, London: Routledge and Kegan Paul

Spender, D., 1980, *Learning to Loose; Sexism and Education*, London: The Women's Press

Stacey, J., 1988, 'Can there be a Feminist Ethnography?' *Women's Studies International Forum*, 11(1), pp. 21-27

Stanley, J., 1989, *Marks on the Memory – Experiencing School*, Milton Keynes: Open University Press

Stanley, L., 1990, *Feminist Praxis: Research, Theory and Epistemology in Feminist Sociology*, London: Routledge

Stanley, L., 1992, *The Auto/Biographical I*, Manchester: Manchester University Press

Stanley, L., 1993, 'On Auto/Biography in Sociology', *Sociology*, 27(1), pp. 41-52

Stanley, L. and Wise, S., 1983, *Breaking Out: Feminist Consciousness and Feminist Research*, London: Routledge and Kegan Paul

Stanworth, M., 1981, *Gender and Schooling: A Study of Sexual Divisions in the Classroom*, London: Women's Research and Resources Centre

Stanworth, M., 1984, 'Women and Class Analysis: A Reply to John Goldthorpe', *Sociology,* 18(2) pp. 159-170

Steedman, C., 1982, *The Tidy House,* London: Virago

Steedman, C., 1985, 'The Mother Made Conscious: The Historical Development of a Primary School Pedagogy', *History Workshop Journal,* 20, Autumn

Steedman, C., 1986, *Landscape for a Good Woman: A Study of Two Lives*, London: Virago

Steedman, C., 1987, 'Prisonhouses', in M. Lawn and G. Grace (eds), *Teachers: The Culture and Politics of Work*, Lewes: Falmer Press

Steedman, C., 1990, *Childhood, Culture and Class in Britain: Margaret McMillan 1860-1931,* London: Virago

Storey, J., 1987, *Women Live*, Winter

Strickland, S., 1994, 'Feminism, Postmodernism and Difference', in K. Lennon and M. Whitford (eds), *Knowing the Difference: Feminist Perspectives in Epistemology,* London: Routledge

Taking Liberties Collective, 1989, *Learning the Hard Way: Women's Oppression in Men's Education*, London: Macmillan

Taylor, P., 1979, 'Daughters and Mothers – Maids and Mistresses: domestic service between the wars', in J. Clarke, C. Critcher, R. Johnson (eds), *Working Class Culture* London: Hutchinson

Temple, P., 1978, 'Experiences of Literacy in Working-class Life, in E. Grugeon and P. Walden (eds), *Literacy and Learning*, London: Ward Lock/OUP

Thomas, D., 1992, 'Putting Nature to the Rack: Narrative Studies as Research', paper presented at the Teachers' Stories of Life and Work Conference, University of |Liverpool, April 9-11th

Thompson, E.P., 1963, *The Making of the English Working Class*, London: Gollancz

Thompson, F., 1973, *Lark Rise to Candleford,* Harmondsworth: Penguin,

Thorton Dill, B., 1983, 'Race, Class and Gender: Prospects for an All-Inclusive Sisterhood', reprinted in L. Stone, (ed.) *The Education Feminism Reader*, London: Routledge

Tight, M., 1991, *Higher Education: a part-time perspective*, Milton Keynes: Open University Press

Tizard, B. and Hughes, M., 1984, *Young Children Learning: Talking and Thinking at Home and at School*, London: Fontana

Tizard, B., 1986, 'On Mothering', *Thomas Coram Working Papers,* No. 1, London

Tizard, B., Blatchford, P., Burke, J., Farquhar, C. and Plewis, I., 1988, *Young Children at School in the Inner City*, London: ILEA

Tokarczyk, M. and Fay, E., (eds), 1995, *Working Class Women in the Academy: Labourers in the knowledge factory,* Amherst: University of Massachusetts Press

Tomlinson, S., 1982, *A Sociology of Special Education*, London: Routledge and Kegan Paul

Toomey, D., 1989, 'Linking Class and Gender Inequality: the family and schooling', *British Journal of Sociology of Education*, 10(4), pp. 389-402

Townsend, P. and Davidson, N., (ed.), 1982, *Inequalities in Health: The Black Report,* Harmondsworth: Pelican

Trevithick, P., 1988, 'Unconsciousness Raising with Working-Class Women', in S. Krzowski and P. Land (eds), *In Our Experience*, London: The Women's Press

Tuckett, A., 1990, 'A Higher Education System Fit for Adult Learners' in G. Parry and C. Wake, *Access and Alternative Futures for Higher Education*, London: Hodder and Stoughton, pp. 113-133,

UCCA Statistical Supplement 1991-92, 1993, UCCA

Ussher, J., 1990, *Women's Madness: Misogyny or Mental Illness*, Hertfordshire: Harvester Wheatsheaf

Ussher, J., 1996, 'Masks of Middle-Class Belonging: Speaking of the Silent, Working-Class Past', *Feminism and Psychology*, 6(3), pp. 463-470

Wade, B, 1982, *Language and Perspectives: papers from the* Educational Review, London: Heinemann

Walkerdine, V., 1985, 'On the Regulation of Speaking and Silence: Subjectivity, Class and Gender in Contemporary Schooling', in C. Steedman, C. Urwin and V. Walkerdine, *Language, Gender and Childhood*, London: Routledge and Kegan Paul

Walkerdine, V., 1995, 'Subject to Change Without Notice. Psychology, Postmodernity and the Popular', in S. Pile and N. Thrift (eds), *Mapping the Subject: Geographies of Cultural Transformation,* London: Routledge

Walkerdine, V., 1990, *Schoolgirl Fictions*, London: Verso

Walkerdine, V., 1996, 'Subjectivity and Social Class: New Directions for Feminist

Walkerdine, V. and Lucey, H., 1989, *Democracy in the Kitchen,* London: Virago

Psychology', *Feminism and Psychology*, 6(3)

Wallace, C., 1987, 'From girls and boys to women and men: the social reproduction of gender', in M. Arnot and G. Weiner (eds) *Gender and the Politics of Schooling*, London: Hutchinson

Walvin, J., 1982, *A Child's World: A Social History of English Childhood 1800-1914,* Harmondsworth: Penguin

Warren, E., 1988, *Gender Issues in Field Research*, Beverley Hills: Sage

Webb, C., 1992, 'The Use of the First Person in Academic Writing: Objectivity, Language and Gatekeeping', *Journal of Advanced Nursing*, 17(6), pp. 747-752

Weil, S., W., 1986, 'Access Students: Non-Traditional Learners within Traditional Educational Institutions', *Studies in Higher Education*, 1(3) pp. 219-235

Weis, L., 1990, *Working Class without Work: high school students in a de-industrialising economy,* New York: Routledge

Wells, G., 1981, *Learning through Interaction,* Cambridge: Cambridge University Press

Wells, G. and Nicholls, J., (eds), 1985, *Language and Learning: An International Perspective*, Lewes: Falmer Press

Wells, G., 1987, *The Meaning Makers*, London: Hodder and Stoughton

Westergaard, J. and Little, A., 1964, 'Trends in social class differentials in educational opportunity', *Sociology,* XIV

Wilby, P., 1977, 'Eduction; and Equality', *New Statesman*, 16th October

Wilkins, R., 1993, 'Taking it Personally: A Note on Emotions and Autobiography', in *Sociology*, 27(1), pp. 93-100

Wilkinson, R., 1994, *Unfair Shares*, Barkingside: Barnardos

Wilkinson, R., 1994, 'Divided We Fall – The poor pay the price of increased social inequality with their health', *British Medical Journal*, 308, pp. 1113-1114

Wilkinson, R., 1996, *Unhealthy societies*, London: Routledge

Wilkinson, S., 1986, 'Sighting Possibilities: Diversity and Commonality in Feminist Research', in S. Wilkinson (ed.), *Feminist Social Psychology,* Milton Keynes: Open University Press

Williams, A., 1990, 'Reflections on the Making of an Ethnographic Text', *Studies in Sexual Politics*, 29, Dept. of Sociology, Manchester: University of Manchester

Williams, A., 1993, 'Diversity and Agreement in Feminist Ethnography', *Sociology,* 27(4) pp. 575-589

Williams, J., 1987, 'The Construction of Women and Black Students as Educational Problems: re-evaluating policy on gender and 'race'', in M. Arnot and G. Weiner (eds), *Gender and the Politics of Schooling*, London: Hutchinson

Williams, R., 1961, *Culture and Society*, 1780-1950, Penguin

Willis, P., 1977, *Learning to Labour: How Working-Class Kids get Working-Class Jobs,* Farnborough: Saxon House

Willms, J. and Echols, F., 1992, 'Alert and Inert Clients: The Scottish Experience of Parental Choice of Schools', *Economics of Education Review*, 11(4), pp. 339-50

Winter, R., 1994, 'The Relevance for Action Research of Feminist Theories of Educational Development', in *Educational Action Research,* 2(3), pp. 423-426

Wolpe, A., 1978, 'Education and the sexual division of labour', in A. Kuhn and A. Wolpe (eds), *Feminism and Materialism,* London: Routledge and Kegan Paul, pp. 290-328

Woodward, K., 1983, *Jipping Street*, London: Virago

Wright, E., 1992, *Feminism and Psychoanalysis*, Oxford: Blackwell

Young, M. and Willmott, P., 1957, *Family and Class in a London Suburb*, London: Routledge and Kegan Paul

INDEX

ability viii, 17, 21, 22, 23, 33, 75, 148, 153-154, 171, 179, 184-7, 194, 195, 200
academic success vii, ix, xii, xiv, 76, 95
assessment 23, 24, 25, 31, 36, 187
assimilation 161, 162, 174, 186
attitudes to working-class 1, 6-7, 10, 31, 32, 47
autobiography xv, 42, 88, 90
  text 98-192

belonging xi, 7, 60, 66, 114, 164-165
Black
  pupils 27, 28, 30, 33, 39, 80, 82, 83, 198
  women 63, 70, 86
boyfriends 152-153
boys, working-class vii, 20, 26, 39, 71, 72, 73, 142

careers advice 148, 187-190
certificates *see qualifications*
class and classifications 193
  definitions 66, 67, 69, 89
  indicators 98-104
  parameters 65-67
classism xv, 47, 51, 54
  see also oppression, class
commerce 76, 187-188
comprehensive school 17, 22, 23, 25, 38, 172, 173, 187, 188
conflict ix, xvi, 58, 61, 71, 86, 91, 96, 106, 115, 126, 146, 147, 153, 159, 161, 173-176, 197
cultural
  capital 149
  deprivation 19, 27, 28
  see also deprivation
  practices 4, 71, 72, 73, 74, 101, 195, 196
  street culture 98, 149

curriculum 146, 165-168, 196
  class difference 3, 10-13, 15, 35
  national 23, 24, 36

Dearing inquiry
  see higher education
dependency 77
  fear of independence 190-193, 196
  female 122, 123, 141
  male 108-109, 130, 131
depression vii, 103, 129, 130
deprivation 2, 16, 28, 32, 89, 91, 198, 199 *see also cultural deprivation*
developmental psychology xv, 46, 49-51,
  centrality 62
difference
  as inferior 20, 48, 69, 83
  class vii, xiii, xv, 2, 23, 26, 29, 36, 37, 38, 44, 57, 70, 83, 92-93, 97, 98, 101
  school 163-164, 168-170, 193, 198
domestic viii, 4-5, 11, 12, 13, 14, 57, 58, 74, 75, 107, 120, 132, 133
  ideology 1, 2-4, 11, 16

Education Acts 1870, 9-10
  1902, 13
  1944, 14-15
educational, achievement vii, 16, 95, 139, 150, 198
  as an equaliser 10, 20, 21, 76, 161-192
  economic and emotional costs 93, 143-149, 196
  failure vii, 19, 21, 24-27, 28, 153-156, 162, 173, 179-186, 198, 200
  see also failure
  success vii, viii, ix, xi, xiii, xvi, 77
employment 16, 75, 77, 117, 131
  changing patterns 69
envy 53, 141, 145, 166, 169
ethnic group 24, 27, 34, 35, 39, 50, 57, 87, 200

examination
results ix, 23, 24, 25, 36, 37, 197, 200
systems ix, 22, 146, 153, 171
Excellence in Cities 37, 198
see also Labour Government
Excellence in Schools 36
see also Labour Government

failure, working-class xiii, 22, 23, 27, 30, 33, 36, 43, 76, 77
in the home 7, 9, 28, 29, 44
personalised 43
pupil drop-out 40, 156-7, 159, 196
teachers' low expectation 30, 33
see also educational failure
family 7, 27, 31, 32, 55, 95, 97-134
fathers 46, 60, 105-108, 114-116, 135-139
fathers and daughters 59-62, 90, 109-114, 129-132
femininity 73-76
feminist
educational discourse 2, 13, 79-83
research 2, 68, 78-79
friends xvi, 88-90,156-58

gaze 47, 47-48, 62
gender
differences xv, 16, 26, 78, 79, 101
divisions 78, 80, 81
good provider 105-107, 129
grammar schools ix, 15, 16, 21, 22, 23, 37, 43, 161, 163, 165, 167, 173, 174-175
grant-maintained schools 24, 25, 35

health 4, 12, 14, 16, 27, 32, 44, 102-3, 130, 198
higher education 14, 17, 37-43, 58, 70, 74, 80, 86 *see also university access*
housing 27, 32, 88, 98, 102
identity, working-class ix, x, xiii, xvi, 29, 54, 65, 84, 87, 88, 130, 165, 187, 193, 195, 197
inferiority ix, x, xiv, 2, 5, 6, 10, 16, 20, 35, 46, 48, 51, 52, 62, 73, 93, 132, 152, 164, 167, 187

labour
cheap 4, 118, 131, 132
division 4, 11, 16, 105, 107
Labour Government 23, 36, 37
language
academic xiv, 73, 148
linguisitic deficit 19, 27, 28, 43, 91, 167, 168

manual worker ix, 77, 99, 102, 130, 131
masculinity 71, 131, 153
marriage 74, 117 , 124-126, 133, 190-1
mother's 118-119
mothers
education 1, 14, 16, 117-118
hard lives 119-120, 124-126
mother-child relationships 10, 27, 31
positional power 2, 3, 77, 118-124
mothers and daughters 5, 6, 51-59, 127-128
educational support 139-141
role models 132-134

negative labeling 19, 21-24, 29, 31, 32, 41

occupational categories 14, 67, 69, 70, 99, 100, 187
oppression 3, 17
class xi, xiv, 29, 44, 46, 58, 61, 62, 74, 78, 80, 81, 89, 95, 133, 193, 194
ordinariness 31, 41, 47, 47-48, 62
Other 20, 47, 47, 48, 50, 62, 65, 74, 85, 168, 169, 170, 194
parental support 129-149
pathology in child rearing 19, 27, 43, 56, 58, 62, 89
patriarchy 73, 78, 79, 80, 83
peer group ix, 149-153
poverty 14, 32, 39, 44, 51, 54, 99, 100, 120, 129, 133, 162, 167, 197
primary school 31, 32, 33
teacher attitudes 136, 140, 176, 178-180, 182, 183-185
privilege xi, 86
academic viii, xiii, 22, 43, 60, 61, 66, 67, 163, 164, 169, 171, 193, 194
psychoanalysis 45, 46, 49-51, 56, 62, 63
psychological simplicity 45, 48-49, 62

qualifications xi, xii, xiii, 8, 16, 23, 25, 26, 39, 95, 132, 133

race vii, 49, 52, 54, 60, 62, 66, 67, 68, 69, 80, 82, 83, 86, 194
racial discrimination 35, 36, 69
racism 51, 54, 63, 82, 86
researcher's approach 85-94
  see also autobiography
  cultural analysis 71
  other approaches – conflict theory 71
  post-moderinsm and post-structuralism 83
  youth culture studies 71-73
resistance 8, 12, 17, 74, 200
  to school 174-176

secondary schools 3, 4, 12, 15, 22, 23, 24, 32 *see also comprehensive, grammar, grant-maintained, secondary modern schools*
secondary-modern schools 15, 16, 22, 167, 171, 172, 173, 180, 181
segregation xiii, 3, 5, 43, 158, 171, 172, 194
self xvi, 87, 88, 91
  self-esteem 23, 46-47, 51, 95, 130, 131
  self identity 43, 86, 87, 95
  self-worth vii, xv, xvi, 1, 19, 41, 47, 86, 94, 179, 180, 182, 197
selection 14, 15, 23, 24, 35, 170-174
  streams and sets 23, 29
sexuality 77, 80, 112-114, 152
shame viii, ix, 30, 140, 157, 163-165, 182, 194
siblings and cousins 153-154
social mobility 18, 71, 98-101
standards
  improving 36, 37, 43
  low 32, 34
  universal 35
struggle xii, 42, 59, 74, 75, 78, 87, 89, 134, 143, 179, 194
subordination 1, 4, 5, 10, 71, 73, 75, 77, 81, 122, 147, 163

teachers 9, 10, 28, 30-34, 176-180
  see also failure; primary schools, teachers' attitudes
teenage pregnancy vii, 112, 118

underachievement vii, 32, 33, 44, 73, 80, 196
unemployment 27, 32, 39, 44, 130
uniform 143-144, 151-158
university access 37, 38, 39, 41-42, 76, 155, 156, 170, 188, 189
  see also higher education

work
  education and work 117-118,129-132
  role modelled 3, 4, 9, 10, 11, 12, 14, 74, 77, 78